Duncan Minty
29 December 86

THE GREAT
CAVING
ADVENTURE

Martyn Farr

Best wishes,

Martyn Farr.

The Oxford Illustrated Press

© Martyn Farr, 1984
Printed in England by J.H.Haynes & Co Ltd,
Sparkford, Yeovil, Somerset

ISBN 0 946609 10 1

The Oxford Illustrated Press Limited,
Sparkford, Yeovil, Somerset BA22 7JJ

To

Thomas Patrick

Acknowledgements

I am indebted to a number of people for their help in the production of this book. In particular my long suffering wife deserves a special mention together with Chris Howes. The latter made constructive suggestions throughout and was a constant source of encouragement at every stage. It is impossible not to mention Rodney 'Bomber' Beaumont, who, toiling away behind the scenes, has for many years kept my equipment operational and designed radical new equipment when the need has arisen. Likewise to my caving friends who regularly and selflessly provided both physical and moral support on the various undertakings, please accept my sincere gratitude. To all who feature in the following pages — who make caving what it is — thank you.

Martyn Farr
Llangynidr
January 1984

Contents

Introduction

Few people can comprehend the motivation for caving. It appears totally illogical to them that a group of people can want to drag themselves off underground into cold, wet, confined passages on a glorious summer's day. It seems equally as crazy during the depths of winter, when to watch a party changing into semi frozen wet suits, shivering and moaning on some bleak mountainside, is enough to confirm the suspicions of any dubious spectator: cavers are quite unique.

In this book I do not intend to delve into the reasons why certain people take to caving, rather to describe the ingredients of the pastime and some of my more memorable caving experiences. Not all have been pleasant, indeed many have involved frustration, exhaustion and sadness. However for me the lure of caving, with all its many facets, is something that transcends the physical and mental barriers; it has become a way of life.

My father first took me caving at the age of ten. The early trips were boyish adventures, the spirit of which I have never really outgrown. By the age of sixteen thoughts of original discovery were uppermost and increasing efforts were made in this direction. Attempts were made to lengthen certain caves in the home area by digging, but gradually the idea of finding something completely new asserted itself. Searching the moors for draughts — a sure indicator of a major cave — came next, and roaming Llangynidr mountain in winter yielded the key to success. One particular day will remain with me always. The ground was carpeted with a heavy hoar-frost and I had been walking for hours. It was dusk; I was cold and slowly making my way back to the road. But suddenly I was confronted by a trench-like depression where the roof of some shallow cave network had collapsed long ago. And there, on the facing side, was a patch of green grass. Warm air was rising. I tore away at the turf while directly beneath small stones tumbled away as though into a sizeable cavity. Within five minutes I had a hole large enough to enter and throwing pebbles into the blackness beyond echoed something big and open. This was incredible. But it was late and I had a long way to walk. For a week my imagination ran riot. There were no known caves within a mile of the new site. How far would it go? How deep? Was it blocked around the next corner? So many uncertainties. In the event, Ogof Cynnes proved itself to be one of the largest caves in the area — over 1,200 metres long — and it was explored with the aid of a couple of school mates.

The discovery heightened my aspirations; caving was the sport of the future. At the time interest was inevitably gravitating towards caves further west, in particular to the Swansea Valley, where in 1966 and 1967 a spate of major discoveries was made: Ogof Ffynnon Ddu, Dan yr Ogof and Little Neath River Cave. These were probably the finest and most exciting explorations ever made in the British Isles and it was highly likely that many, many more remained to be found.

To get in on the act, I joined South Wales Caving Club, who possessed an ideal base for cave explorations, an isolated row of terrace houses, at Penwyllt. Choice of university was likewise dictated by this interest and a period of intense activity in the Swansea Valley followed.

Within a short while my old school mate Mike Ware and I had found our feet; squeezes, boulder chokes and vertical avens were all under pressure. Virtually every weekend we chalked up a hundred metres or more in the two main systems. But sadly however, almost from the moment we joined the club, the dynamic atmosphere, the overwhelming vigour of Penwyllt, seemed to drain away. For some reason the momentum set by the tremendous discoveries earlier in the decade could not be maintained. The people who had put so much into the club retired from the scene; others rested on their laurels. In retrospect I suppose that this was to be expected. After all how could anyone ever hope to equal the scale of the discoveries, never mind better them? Slowly I became disenchanted with tacking on extra bits of cave to Ogof Ffynnon Ddu; it was time to get my teeth into a big project. More impetus was given to the idea the day Mike and I discovered a kilometre of passage near the Smithy in O.F.D.2. Back in the club hut hardly an eyebrow was raised and to my knowledge no one even visited the extension for a year or more.

South Wales Caving Club needed revitalising. Perhaps another big breakthrough, something really substantial, would do the trick and where better to look than Dan yr Ogof. The explorations of the '60s had barely scratched the surface. There was so much still to find, not only in Dan yr Ogof but also in the Neath Valley, the Twrch Valley, indeed everywhere that there was limestone. And with a broadening perspective came the lure of caves abroad; radically different environments to those of Britain but with a common denominator — tremendous scope for exploration.

The cave quest had begun.

1

A Near Disaster

DAN YR OGOF

I was dragged from the water to the sandy beach. Purple, coughing and gasping I had all but passed out. Were it not for the prompt action of Mike Ware I would have been unconscious within a few more seconds, and then dead. My first cave dive in Dan yr Ogof, August 1971, was undoubtedly a complete disaster.

Some would say that I was a reckless caver but the risks I took were always calculated. At Swansea university the opportunity to train as a diver was too good to miss. A few of my college friends joined the local branch of the British Sub-Aqua Club who used the pool on Monday nights and I followed suit.

Training B.S.A.C.-style was heavy going. If I thought that the swimming tests would be easy I was wrong. But I stuck it out and after a frustratingly long period of time eventually graduated on to the bottles. The pool might only have been 2.5 metres deep but getting to grips with a flooded twin-hose valve was difficult. I guess I was a slow learner, and because I was not an attractive female seemed to miss out on the instructor's attention.

The tests were long, the lectures laborious, but above all I failed to be impressed by the inflexible attitude of the trainers. I had no motivation whatsoever to become a sea diver, a viewpoint that was reinforced after a harrowing snorkelling test across a storm-lashed Caswell Bay. From the start my sights were set on those submerged sections of cave where extensions were postulated. Even if I was not instrumental in the discovery itself I would certainly be there in the role of supporter. Ogof Ffynnon Ddu and Little Neath River Cave had been opened by divers and it appeared as though Dan yr Ogof would be next.

On a chance visit to Porth yr Ogof one cold and damp day in February 1971 I met a group of experienced divers including the legendary John Parker. To an aspiring cave diver the name was

4

to be revered, as he was widely regarded as the leading contemporary diver in the country. This squat, dark-haired Welshman with a pronounced Pontypool accent could not fail to impress anyone on first sight, but all I can remember thinking is 'Just look at the size of those hands — like bloody shovels!'

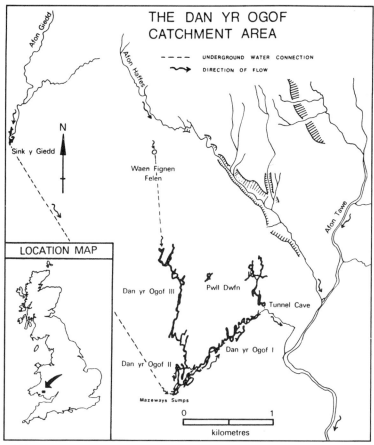

THE DAN YR OGOF CATCHMENT AREA

- - - - UNDERGROUND WATER CONNECTION
~~> DIRECTION OF FLOW

Afon Giedd

Afon Haffes

N

Sink y Giedd

Waen Fignen Felen

Afon Tawe

LOCATION MAP

Dan yr Ogof III

Pwll Dwfn

Tunnel Cave

Dan yr Ogof I

Dan yr Ogof II

Mazeways Sumps

0   1

kilometres

The group were not engaged in any routine programme, rather the retrieval of equipment left in the upstream network, following the death and attempted rescue of Paul Esser. This was probably not the best of times to broach the matter but after quietly ascertaining the feelings of the group I came to the point.

'I fancy doing some diving. How would I go about joining the Cave Diving Group?' The reception was mixed. Eyes turned upon the figure who I knew to be Dr Oliver Lloyd, a trainer and the senior member of the group.

'Not at the moment,' he muttered and stalked off alone to his vehicle.

'That's blown it,' I thought and stood there feeling quite embarassed.

'Don't worry about Lloyd,' said Jeff Phillips. 'He's like that.'

'We could do with a few more keen people in the Group,' said John.

The ice was broken and we chatted away. They were just a normal set of cavers.

Back at the hut I got to talking with Mike Ware. He was a diver in the Royal Navy and experienced in open water techniques. We had undertaken a great deal of caving together both during and since our school days and had already discussed cave diving at some length. The decision was made.

The question of what equipment to buy was now a pressing issue. Knowing the desperate nature of some of the sites that Parker had dived and acknowledging he was still around to recount the explorations, I judged that what was good enough for him was good enough for me and sought his advice. The college grant was then channelled towards a specific breathing regulator: a U.S. Diver's 'Deepstar'. Another member of South Wales Caving Club, Mike Coburn, presented me with a 'tadpole', a 26-cu/ft cylinder pressurised to 1800 pounds per square inch. These dumpy little bottles were not recommended for use as diving cylinders, and very few people could be persuaded to fill them. Originally, they had been designed for use in fighter planes, during the Second World War, when they contained pure oxygen at 3000 p.s.i. Now their use was frowned upon, especially by the B.S.A.C. How they were obtained, I never knew, but it was reputed that some individuals had obtained theirs from a crashed plane whose remains still litter an isolated area of the Black Mountains, west of the Swansea Valley. My bottle was old and rusty, conceivably of the same batch, but I had it cleaned, painted and tested — and it passed (within a few years there was to be a complete ban on their filling and testing). A word of warning accompanied the gift: 'Tads have to be treated with care,' said Mike. 'Just remember Rod's.' Rod Stewart's tad, or rather the remains of his tad, is nailed to the wall in our club hut. It had exploded upon testing, wrecking the test rig and the room he had used for the test; fortunately no-one had been in it at the time.

This then was my basic equipment. I never displayed a natural aptitude for diving and as far as I was concerned, my interest in diving and associated equipment was merely to get me through the sump. Having achieved a certain level of proficiency in the pool and river, Mike and I quickly persuaded other more experienced divers to take us through Dip Sump, in Ogof Ffynnon Ddu, for our first cave dive.

The big day was to be Saturday 3 July 1971. It was a day never to be forgotten. Several times I had helped porter diving equipment to Dip Sump for other divers, and had observed their wary preparations before disappearing into the flooded tunnel beneath our feet. On each occasion there was something totally absorbing in the spectacle: watching as the glow from the divers' lights died in the pale blue water; watching as the glugging and plop-plopping gradually ceased, and I was left looking into a tranquil pool of muddied water and with a nagging uncertainty regarding goings on below.

Now it was our turn. Five of us were to dive. Mike Ware and myself were complete novices, Bob Radcliffe had been through before, while Frank and Penny Salt were old hands. Conditions were cramped in the approach passage to the sump and as the moment of immersion drew close feelings were mixed. For me it was something I wanted to do yet something it would have been so easy to have opted out of. Bob's nervousness welled up in chatter, Mike seemed quite confident, I just kept quiet. This was to be a dive of 55 metres, reaching a maximum depth of 6 metres, through to Niphargus Niche in the Dip Sump Series of O.F.D.2.

Now we had begun there was no escape, I had to go through with it. The order of diving was Bob first, then me, followed by Mike, Penny and Frank. The minutes passed and it was my turn to go. Water closed over my helmet, I switched to survival mode and tried to keep calm. Feet first I slid down into the hole, clearing every metre or so. Bubbles rumbled from my exhaust and suddenly the water was clear and I could see the passage I had to follow. With a tight grip on the line, I moved on into the silent, grey world of the sump. I had no idea of how far I had travelled when I chanced upon a weight belt, Bob's weight belt, lying on the sand. Picking it up, I had no thoughts of how it came to be there, merely that I would give it back to him. I struggled on for the last couple of metres to reach the welcome landing place — air at last. Clear rational thoughts returned. One by one the others arrived, complaining about the visibility, or rather the lack of it.

This was no place for a lengthy social chit-chat, especially as some of us were cold, so as soon as we had satisfied ourselves that no-one had any serious problems, we dived out, slowly groping our way along the line, with visibility less than a metre.

Following the immediate elation, Mike and I made a more sober assessment of our dive. It wasn't that bad we thought, and down the pub that night we started planning ahead. The following week, I dived the sump from Bridge Cave to Little Neath River Cave; there was nothing to it! Our confidence bolstered, the next objective was that of the Turkey Sump Extensions at the upstream end of Agen Allwedd. With hindsight this was a most ambitious progression, but at the time we felt up to it. We knew beforehand that this isolated network, 615 metres in length, terminated at Sump 5; secretly we held hopes that we might extend the cave by diving it. A couple of friends were recruited to help with the porterage and only two weeks after our first cave dive, a sixteen-hour reconnaissance trip was successfully achieved to the furthest known reaches. Our enthusiasm was running high.

Shortly afterwards we met John Parker and friends at our club hut.

'I hear you've been up the Turkey Extensions,' said Jeff Phillips.

'Yes,' I replied.

'Well, that's our sump,' said John, 'keep off.'

There wasn't much to say; clearly he too held designs upon the terminal sump. The air was tense and we were left in no doubt that we had broken some unwritten rule of caving. In a none too friendly manner, we were told not to try any poaching again — or else there would be trouble. John might not have been a big lad but I'd noticed that no one argued too forcefully against him. John's word was law; you accepted it or shut up.

We were learning fast. John was possessive about his sumps and we were in the wrong for not having taken the trouble to find out if anyone else was intending to dive there. It wouldn't happen again. After this incident John and I went our separate ways, and I looked more carefully at sites in the Swansea Valley. Mike and I were no longer 'followers' but cave divers in our own right.

The greatest potential in the Swansea Valley lay at Dan yr Ogof and the lure was many miles of cave passage. The reasoning behind this was simple. There are several points on the mountain, well above and beyond the furthest parts of the cave, where substantial streams disappear into the limestone. By the use of dye, Sink y Giedd had been found to be the principal feeder for Dan yr Ogof and this lay several miles to the north-west. At this time explorations in the cave had progressed but a short distance towards the stream sink and it seemed logical to conclude that by far the largest part of the cave had yet to be found. The Giedd Series, or Dan yr Ogof 4 could modestly be estimated at a good 10 miles.

Previous explorers had established the fact that the main flow of water entered the cave in a complicated sector of the Lower Series known as Mazeways. This area terminated in a network of sumps which had been dived in 1968. Terry Moon, Dick Arculus and Colin Fairbairn had made considerable progress underwater and it was generally believed that diving would eventually prove the key to the mysteries of the Black Mountain.

From lengthy chats with Terry, we learned that the Left-Hand Sump was the most promising place to dive. Previous dives had all taken place from the Right-Hand Sump and had concentrated upon following passages trending west and north. This was based quite logically, upon the fact that Sink y Giedd, by far the largest feeder to the system, lay to the north-west. Now it was apparent that there could well be something substantial to the south-west, and following the left wall out of the Left-Hand Sump was the best way of reaching it.

The date of our push was to be 21 August 1971 and we were quite surprised by the enthusiastic support given by fellow members of the South Wales Caving Club. Equipment was carried in, several days in advance: two cylinders and two valves per person. Bob Radcliffe opted to join us and on the Saturday morning, a small mountain of gear lay strewn around the approach passage and beach. In party atmosphere, the cameras clicked.

I kitted up slowly and carefully, adopting a new high-pressure 'Draeger 45' as my main bottle. Never before having worn a spare set of equipment, I was quite concerned, indeed apprehensive of the bulky appendages. Rather than risk an entanglement and perfectly confident of my valve, I threw the spare set aside.

All three of us stood ready about the same time. I was to dive first and take the line reel as far as possible. Agreement was reached about the signals I would use, if I should get through, and perfectly confident I dived away. The water held a deep orange gloom and there was nothing whatsoever to relish along the muddy walls. A slight negative buoyancy was no problem and with a fine glide a steeply sloping section led down into a more pleasant passage. The floor was now free of sand and mud, clearly defined scallops indicating that I was on the right trail and heading upstream.

Back at base Bob had taken the position of line holder while Mike, as standby diver, sat down at the water's edge. By the 'feel' of the line Bob could tell that I was making good progress.

The line had indeed gone out steadily and after 25 metres I emerged, very much to my surprise, into clear water. It was as though I had stepped out from thick fog to a fine sunny day. I stopped to look around — ahead the visibility was excellent while directly to my right the undisturbed water lay as dense as a cloudy pint of beer.

I moved on. Suddenly I breathed out and my heart nearly stopped. The valve had jammed shut. I was in no position to consider its 'fail-safe' qualities or the ironic 'lifetime guarantee' which it possessed. All I knew was that there was no burst of life-giving air — either I got out fast or I was dead. With a numbed brain, I grappled with the mouthpiece before panic finally took over.

Bob, meanwhile, was oblivious of the crisis that had developed. By the feel of the line he could tell that I had stopped and alerted the others. It was then that they felt my desperate tugs on the line: one, two, three, four. They knew it wasn't one of our agreed signals...

In the sump the deathly silence was impossible to forget. I had discarded the reel as soon as I'd got into difficulties and in a blind

10

panic I was finning and pulling hard back along the line. Small silvery bubbles of air were escaping from the rubber valve in the face plate of my mask, but these made no noise. I had no conception of distance, no thoughts of those at base; panic was master of all. Vivid and horrifying were the thoughts of the end, as the line I was following led me into a tight bedding plane. In no state of mind to consider how it was that the line had taken this position, the craving for air became too much. I pulled out the mouthpiece and breathed water. Everything I had learned was forgotten in the utter desperation of the situation; I was resigned to my fate; I was convinced that I was dying.

Back at base trouble had rightly been diagnosed, and on the count of six it was time for action. 'I think you'd better go in Mike,' Bob had told him.

In a matter of seconds Mike had made his final checks and waded out across the pool and dived; uncertain of the nature of the emergency, or what was expected of him. A minute or so later he surfaced telling the others I was alright and coming up. Half a minute later when I had still failed to appear, he went in again.

Only then did I see his light, the image of a diver silhouetted in the passage. The survival instinct was still strong and leaving the crack, I made straight for him. In his turn Mike assumed that all was now well and swung around, finning for base. Pathetically I followed the last few metres to safety. After a 28-metre dive from 7 metres depth, without air, I was still alive — just. Once at the surface I was dragged from the water, groaning feebly, and turned onto my back. Sparing the others the kiss-of-life I gradually came around, and after about five minutes I was able to talk about it.

What a change of atmosphere now existed; the party was over! Anyone would think we were all assembled for a funeral — mine. There were long faces, searching questions and an air of total, absolute defeat. I felt a fool.

By the look on their faces, neither Mike nor Bob now wanted to dive. I recalled one of our elder member's comments on cave diving back in the hut. 'Statistically there's a 7 per cent chance of snuffing it, on any single dive.' Tonight the doom-mongers would be confirmed in their views.

We persuaded Mike to make a quick dive to retrieve the reel

and then disheartened, ferried all the equipment out of the cave. For my two friends, the incident acted as a sort of portent; it destroyed any future aspirations that they may have had. Neither Mike nor Bob made an exploratory dive again.

The lessons to be learned were very simple. Training had been woefully inadequate and confidence somewhat the inverse. The valve with its 'Lifetime Guarantee' should have been 'fail-safe' that is, if it failed at all, it ought to fail giving air; too much air. Here it had failed giving none. It was all rather demoralising. Had the purge button been depressed the valve would almost certainly have given air. It was working normally when Bob tried it at the sump base. The solution was plain; all the inconsistencies lay on the human side. Keeping cool was everything and in this I had failed totally. I had been far too impetuous; rational thinking had been lacking. With it all logically worked out, a new programme commenced in earnest. Based on a far greater awareness of the realities, I was richer for the experience, and extremely determined not to give up.

In the weeks to follow, I slowly rebuilt my confidence. Proficiency in the use of a reserve system was my number one priority, and in open water I practised swapping valves under all manner of adverse conditions. During September, October and November dives were made at other sites in Dan yr Ogof, but I knew all along that the reality lay at Mazeways; a reality and a personal challenge.

At the end of December I went back, supported by Bob (Soz) Saunders, one of the lads that I had portered for a couple of years before. Access to Mazeways is via an awkward duck which for the majority of the year is sumped. On this occasion the water level was in its high position but I knew that there was a small airbell less than 2 metres through. Wearing a single set of diving gear I proceeded to this while Soz felt confident to free dive. But it was almost as though the place was warning us off again, for as I stood neck deep in water, ready to guide him up to the airspace, he pulled the line out of my grasp and dived straight past me, missing the airbell completely. Beyond me the line pulled in to an undercut in the left hand wall and within 3 metres Soz realised that he was in trouble. With lungs about to burst he

managed to turn around and thrashed back the way he'd come —
until I grabbed him. There wasn't a lot of room in the bell and
with Soz coughing and spluttering there was even less. 'You drag
me in to some places Farr,' he said, followed by a host of unmen-
tionable abuse.

Soz wasn't the sort to give up just like that and with a bit of
coaxing we continued warily to our destination.

'Remember to purge, remember to purge,' he gesticulated and
shouted as I went down. Yes, Soz was shrewd. He realised that
he needed me to guide him out!

The previous limit was passed and at 30 metres I entered a
large chamber; the psychological barrier had been passed.

In January, with Terry Moon's help and a reserve set I
proceeded well beyond, into an area which, had water levels been
lower, would have yielded an airbell. A few inches of silvery air
were noted at 80 metres but at 92 metres it was time to tie off and
exit. Yet again I'd lost my knife but clasping a stone more primitive methods achieved the desired effect.

I seemed to get through a lot of diving knives in this period but
fortunately no expense was involved. Never having seen any
point in wearing the unwieldy contraptions that sea divers used
to fight off sharks or whatever, and knowing that any knife
would probably get lost anyway I resorted to an endless stock of
ordinary cutlery from the college cafeteria. These were quickly
sharpened on the steps outside and using two or three per dive I
could usually count on one being there when I needed it.

In the early summer of 1972 I met Roger Solari, a person who
was to have a significant influence on my future activities. His
reputation and reports concerning his exploits had long preceed-
ed him and I had been looking forward to the meeting for some
time. Physically Roger was tall and lean, with a ragged, mousey
beard and glasses. He looked like an academic: serious, precise
and certainly not one to waste words. These may not have been
the qualities that I had come to associate with my normal caving
friends but Roger exuded an unparalleled enthusiasm which I
found infectious. A partnership was soon forged.

I learned a lot from Roger in a short while. Our diving experience was similar, but for the fact that Roger had never had

anything go wrong. As a surveyor he was extremely talented, and of his dedication and determination there was no question. In the caving world he was also widely travelled, possessing a great knowledge of the Yorkshire Dales and experience in Derbyshire, Mendip, Sutherland, Ireland and the Pyrenees. Whilst at university in Birmingham he had initiated the Cave Projects Group a club 'designed to further interest in speleology'! In the quest of virgin exploration, for example Roger obtained an explosives license. In fact there was no facet of speleology that he could not discuss in depth. Apart from being a highly talented individual, he was without question one of the hardest cavers that I have ever known.

Roger became a frequent visitor to South Wales. The summer was pleasantly dry and water levels dropped. The challenge at Dan yr Ogof now assumed a greater priority and in mid July Roger helped carry in for a further dive at the Left-Hand Sump. The conditions were ideal and we felt there had to be air at the furthest point reached in January. On diving this proved to be the case and after taking one false turning, the way on was found. From a 40-cm high bedding at the start, the route became gradually larger and then deeper. The line was tied off 108 metres from base.

The following week was perfect for a further attempt, the plan being for Roger to dive as far as a tad would allow, drop the line reel, and return. I could then push on using a 45-cubic-foot cylinder. Three of us went in to the cave, Mike Coburn, Roger and I. The carry was hard and after setting Roger on his way we were glad of a rest. Twenty minutes went by and Mike raised his eyebrows. After thirty minutes we were both concerned. Roger only had 26 minutes of air in his bottle. I kitted up.

We had to be optimistic but underneath it all we were worried. Anxiety was forcibly suppressed and I left Mike with the parting shot: 'If I'm not back in an hour we're on to something.'

While Mike went for a wander to try and warm up, I slid cautiously in to the water and finned away. Passing the previous week's limit the line went on and there was still no sign of him. A wall of boulders passed on the right and the passage increased to 3 metres in diameter.

'He's doing well on a tad,' I thought, trying to stop the ugly question 'Supposing something's happened to him?' nagging at

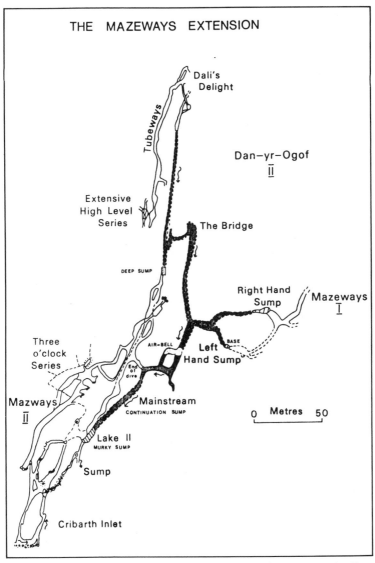

THE MAZEWAYS EXTENSION

Dali's Delight

Tubeways

Dan-yr-Ogof
$\underline{\text{II}}$

Extensive High Level Series

The Bridge

DEEP SUMP

Right Hand Sump

Mazeways
$\underline{\text{I}}$

Three o'clock Series

AIR-BELL

BASE

Left Hand Sump

Mazways
$\underline{\text{II}}$

End of dive

Mainstream

CONTINUATION SUMP

0   Metres   50

Lake II
MURKY SUMP

Sump

Cribarth Inlet

me. A few metres further on, and 118 metres from base, the line surfaced abruptly to air on a fault plane. There in front of me was a set of kit, safely stowed on a narrow ledge and just above a small passage that led off into the distance. There was no sign of Roger though. This had to be good. I quickly dropped my gear

15

and set off. Visions of endless galleries began to flit excitedly through my mind. Just what had we found? I discovered Roger 60 metres away groping along a dismal canal passage which was three quarters full of water. In his hand he was clutching the reel and in the process of winding in the line.

'You jammy sod!' I said. 'Well done.'

'It wouldn't be so bad if I could actually see what's here. You haven't brought my glasses have you?'

'Sorry.'

Having left his glasses with Mike, Roger was all but blind and was relying on the line to lead him back to his kit.

'We're on to something here all right.'

'I reckon I've covered 120 to 180 metres and there's holes all over the place.'

It really was quite laughable. He'd found what could well be Dan yr Ogof 4 but wouldn't be able to tell anyone what he'd seen!

About 245 metres of dry passages was quickly explored and another four sumps located. The most promising lead was a large, high-level passage set tantalisingly above an impossible 4-metre climb. Being able to peer up and hypothesise was downright annoying as we were both reasonable climbers, but without any gear there was nothing we could do. Having exhausted every passage above water level we dragged my diving gear over and began tentative examinations of the main sumps. At the northern end of the extension lay a very enticing pool of crystal clear water. On diving the route became deep and complex, with several junctions running off. When the main passage reached the top of a second deep shaft the exploration was curtailed. At the southern end of the extension Lake II possessed a good flow of water but in atrocious visibility little headway could be made.

Amid the excitement we were totally oblivious of the time and since neither of us possessed a diving watch there was no way of knowing how long we had been away. When at last we made our way out Mike was greatly relieved; he'd been on his own for over four hours. He was so cold it was all he could do to raise a smile. 'This'll cost you a pint.'

In mid August we returned well equipped with boots and climbing gear. Despite a long dive we soon warmed up, and with the prospect of big discoveries ahead, morale was high. At the climb a small projection was lassooed, and I heaved myself up with no problems. A decent belay was found and in minutes we were standing there together, beaming with smiles, raring to go.

This was it! A 3-metre diameter, clean-washed tubeway led off; evidently some form of flood overflow passage. We almost broke in to a run. A large junction was passed and following the main route left and south, a tremendous roar of water could be heard away in the distance.

'Can you hear that?'

'Bloody hell!'

We raced forward. It had to be the long lost main stream. I was in the lead but Roger was pushing the pace.

'Blast, it's choked.'

'It can't be.'

'It is, it is, I tell you.'

We split up to conduct separate explorations; Roger taking to some high level rifts in the hope of finding a high level by-pass, while I set to on a dig which looked as though it would be short. Only a metre or so of debris separated us from from open passage. Demonically, rubble and stones were hurled aside. This was exploration fever. A quarter of an hour later I wriggled through.

'I'm there, come on! — hurry up!'

Roger appeared from nowhere and in seconds we scrambled forward through a three-dimensional maze to reach our goal.

Our faces fell. One glance at the volume of this stream told us that it was not the main river; it was a large inlet. The sound that had been so alluring only minutes before was generated by the water cascading over a 1.3-metre waterfall in to a sump below. How deceptive. But there was no way we could remain disappointed for long: the foam-strewn passage confronting us was sizeable and promising in itself. We carried on. Once through a low crawl the route again became spacious but 60 metres from the waterfall a major choke was found, the Cribarth Inlet Choke.

Returning towards the original climb, above Lake II, a very complicated series of several different levels was entered. The main passage was highly reminiscent of Hanger Passage in Dan yr Ogof 2, about 10 metres high and the best part of 6 metres wide, which led for over 90 metres to another formidable boulder choke. We eventually packed up after spending nearly six hours beyond the sump.

On the following weekend the objective was to begin the survey. In a week the water levels had fallen appreciably. Before we began the dive in we agreed that, where practical, we would wait for each other at convenient intervals. On this occasion I made my first stop waist deep at the 80-metre airbell. The line began to twitch and shortly after Roger surfaced. 'Goggle-eyed' and looking a little discoloured he dropped his gag, simultaneously gasping for air.

'That wasn't very nice! Talk about being sparing with the air; hardly got a breath anywhere.' He was extremely grateful to reach the bell.

We quickly isolated the problem, which lay surprisingly in the bottle itself. Something seemed to be blocking the pillar valve. Fortunately I had a spare bottle with me and he changed on to that. On examination later we found that the valve had been partially obstructed by rust flakes. Presumably moisture had got in to the tad at some time and having been left in the cave for nine months corrosion had taken place.

The survey of the principal routes was a long job and about 500 metres of additional passage was found within the previous boundaries. The total extension amounted to over one mile but the frustrating thing was that there was no obvious way on. Several promising climbs remained to be achieved and the anticipation of Dan yr Ogof 4 on the next trip was still very real.

A couple of days later I received an interesting letter from Roger, supplying the details of the survey and an account of a pub conversation. It appeared that he and John Elliot had met John Parker while dropping in for a pint at the Brittania at Crickhowell. Having discussed the major dive that Parker had just achieved 'downstream' in Agen Allwedd (according to Parker a total of 615 metres had been explored involving a dive of over 308 metres from the last bell) Elliot had asked him what his plans were for the future.

'Chiefly Hepste Valley, Tuck's Rift is going to go and Dan yr Ogof.' Parker had told him.

'You're too late kid.' Elliot had replied.

'No I'm not.'

'You are, Mazeways has gone.'

'No it hasn't.'

'It has; he (pointing to Roger) has been through it.'

'It can't have; you haven't got to the stream anyway.' Parker satisfied himself that we had gone wrong. Roger continued:

'He didn't want to know otherwise — a very odd attitude. I don't think he knows enough about Dan yr Ogof — except that Sink y Giedd lies vaguely north-west — and that anything south to south-west could be ignored as going downstream. He hasn't been beyond the Entrance Pool and is under the impression that Mazeways is a long canal. He is probably diving there the weekend after next but unless he's shown the Left-Hand Sump I don't think he'll find it; not only that — I don't think he really wanted to know. He wants his weights back, which you borrowed, — it's all he has, apart from the ones he's left in certain caves. It might be worth letting him go his own way for a bit — he might find something useful — he's dead keen to get up the long sump in Mazeways.' (The one Terry Moon had dived for 154 metres in 1968.)

For Parker, the conversation must have been food for thought, and for whatever reason he let his plans for Dan yr Ogof fall by the way. By October all the easily accessible passages had been pushed and it was becoming all too clear that the trail to Dan yr Ogof 4 was becoming cold.

Resumption of diving operations was a logical step and this cleared up many loose ends. The 'Deep Sump' for example was linked with Terry Moon's long sump and later connected with the downstream sump in Dali's Delight, Dan yr Ogof 2. By the time we had completed this programme over 430 metres of submerged passage had been accounted for but disappointingly there was no apparent way on below water.

It had been noted from the beginning that Mazeways 2 possessed a good draught, a positive encouragement to any caver. In June 1973 we started work on several chokes at either end of the extension. Roger was particularly adept at this facet of exploration; indeed most Wednesday nights he was out digging somewhere or other with his mates from 'The Forest' and his explosives license was invaluable in protracted excavations. I'd received a fair amount of tuition in this art with my clubmates but under Roger's guidance I got to use the stuff for myself.

The key to good digging is experience and being selective. Where to put the explosive is the first consideration but equally as important is the amount to be used. Too much can often bring down boulders needlessly — making more work and quite possibly rendering the whole place more unstable than before the dig was begun. Firing the explosive must obviously be done at a discreet distance, normally by means of an electrical detonator set off by a standard caver's battery pack. However electrical detonators are not among the cheapest pieces of equipment and being hard up, most of the time, some people will occasionally use the infinitely more exciting method known as the 'Slow Fuse'. As the name suggests, a match is applied to a slow burning fuse which, after reaching the detonator, sets off the charge. But the fuse is often difficult to set alight, especially in damp conditions underground, and despite the fact that it burns at only 0.3 metres per minute the big temptation is to 'run like hell'. It always reminds me of childhood days and fireworks; seeing who would dare to hold the banger longest before throwing it. Seeing grown men bolting down a passage tripping and sprawling, then cowering in some alcove waiting for the bang — which always seems to take an eternity — is always good entertainment; provided of course you weren't the one who had to strike the match!

Whilst our digging was underway we also assessed the possibility of scaling some avens in the roof. Maypoles were out of the question as we couldn't get them through the Long Crawl. The most promising climb lay in the main passage, where a combination of ingenious acrobatics seemed necessary.

With typical brilliance Colin Fairbairn, who had already joined us on several trips, came up with the idea of attaching a rope to a suitable stone and trying to lodge this in a crack about 9 metres above the floor. In such a way we hoped to be able to prussik up the rope instead of having to bolt and peg our way through the overhanging section. And with a couple of throws we were successful — the rope hung free. The stone was precariously lodged but on testing it held the weight of two people.

In July the rope was climbed and after 15 metres the first high level passage was gained. The Three O'Clock Series gave 215 metres of passages but all were blocked by chokes. A few weeks later another climb was tackled. A further 60 metres of passages were found and at the last minute a connection was made with the Three O'Clock Series. Virtually all the high level openings were now accounted for.

In 1971 and 1972 well in excess of a mile of dry passages were discovered in Mazeways 2; just enough to whet the appetite. Further intensive digging and diving took place over the next six years but it was not until 1978 that the endeavours met with any success. Another ¼ mile, 450 metres, was found on that occasion and it is still abundantly clear that by far the largest portion of the system still remains to be found. The Mazeways area holds many secrets and in all probability the key to Dan yr Ogof 4.

The quest for the missing miles at Dan yr Ogof had been one of the main reasons for taking up cave diving but the disastrous first exploration there had nearly proved the last. On reflection it had been a very cocky start to a hazardous pursuit — a start which I was lucky to survive. The lesson was costly and embarassing but there is little doubt that it was timely. Had it not come when and where it did — when I was fortunate to have another diver to get me out of trouble — then surely there would have been no second chance.

2

The Luck of The Irish

TULLYHONA, ARCH-NOONS

It was Easter 1972 when Pete Ogden and I accepted Paddy O'Reilly's invitation to visit some Irish caves. Few British clubs ever frequented the place and Paddy was overflowing with enthusiasm.

'And Martyn you can bring a couple of diving bottles.'

That was it.

We looked around for some relevant literature but other than that on County Clare there was hardly anything. The U.B.S.S. had worked the Burren for many years but it was Jack Coleman's book *The Caves of Ireland* that set the scene. There were caves in virtually every county and by comparison with mainland Britain the place was virtually untouched.

In the pale grey light of early morning we were met by Paddy in Dun Laohaire and our excursion was under way. First on the agenda was County Clare. Trips were made in to Pol-an-Onian and Pollnagollum but my lasting impression of those first few days was the endless rain. Everything was in flood and for the main part we had to content ourselves with a guided tour on the surface, drying out in front of the pungent peat fire at McCarthy's Cottage.

Mrs McCarthy was an old friend of Paddy's and upon his advice she had turned an old outhouse in to something of a hostel. It certainly wasn't the Ritz or even a patch on our club H.Q. back in South Wales, but anything with a sound roof was a welcome refuge from the elements outside. In fact it turned out to have an interesting history of its own. On our arrival our hostess had shown us around and was about to leave when Paddy made an enquiry about the wall near the fireplace. The plasterwork was shattered and scored in a peculiarly oval pattern.

'What happened there?'

22

'Ah, don't worry yourselves; 'twas our neighbour from up the road. He smashed the window over by there and blasted the room with his shotgun.' This tale was accompanied by an indifferent shrug of the shoulders which seemed to intimate that such incidents were not rare.

'Don't be alarmed; the Guarda have their eye on the man — but watch out for dem terrible children of his.' And with this she left us. We found out later that he had no less than twelve children all as wayward as himself and with a fine reputation for stealing, breaking and entering.

Late one afternoon we left for Co. Fermanagh, the south-western province of Northern Ireland. Perhaps we would get some decent caving at last. As we bumped and jolted north the daylight began to fade and Paddy put his foot down. With the accelerator pedal flat out on the floor the ancient Morris 1000 lurched around the corners, bottoming on its suspension with almost every dip in the road. The Irish drivers were cursed and cursed again for poor driving, hogging the road and failing to dip their lights.

I was petrified. It was just like being in an R.A.C. Rally except that here a crash wouldn't just put us out of the race; it would be the end — my diving bottles were on the roof rack! But nothing seemed to worry Paddy; it must have been his faith in the life hereafter.

After one of the most horrific journeys I have ever made we reached our destination; McGovern's Bush Bar in Blacklion. The Bush we learned was the focus for any cavers coming to the area and we were quickly introduced to Billy Shiels, Blacklion's resident caver.

Next day we made a tour of the main sites. The streams were still in spate and considering all the rain which we had experienced over the past few days thoughts of tackling our prime objective, Reyfad Pot, fell by the way; thoughts hastened by the virtually non existent rescue organisation. Reyfad is the longest and deepest system in Ireland, possessing 3.7 km of passage and an overall depth of 90 metres.

Alternative trips were considered, and with plenty of air I was keen to have a dive. Shannon Pot, the rising of the River Shannon proved disappointing but later the same day we were taken to Tullyhona, near Florence Court. There was reputedly an undived sump about 150 metres in to this resurgence system and plenty of potential for further dry passage beyond.

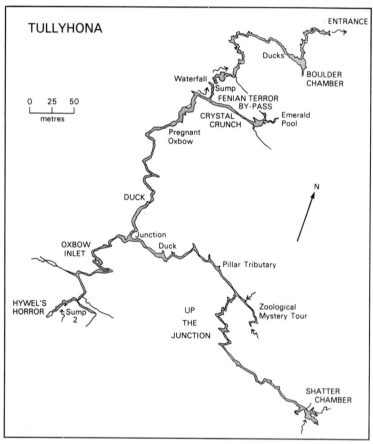

TULLYHONA

The trip had already begun badly when, just inside the awkward little entrance, the fibron surveying tape was lost down an impenetrable water-filled fissure. But spirits rose as we progressed and the proportions of the cave increased substantially. Amid a torrent of water the last squeeze was negotiated up through a section of loose boulders and we arrived in a spacious chamber occupied by the sump.

I kitted up with Pete in attendance, while Paddy set off to survey out, now using a tagged length of rope instead of a tape. Diving off I was quite amazed to surface within a metre or two into a low canal. Ahead the place was 'going' so I free dived back to Pete to persuade him to follow through. In minutes we were on our way, striding along an increasingly impressive and sporting streamway. It was really becoming exciting when suddenly we rounded a corner to be confronted by a five-metre waterfall, and directly at the top were faced with an insurmountable obstacle, another sump.

'Well, of all the places to find a sump!'

'Just what happened at the head of the O.F.D. 2 streamway,' said Pete.

'And look at this.'

I held up a length of old detonator wire attached to a flake of rock. Someone had been here before! We couldn't even congratulate each other on a reasonable extension. Our predecessors had attempted to lower the water level by blasting the lip of the fall. They were obviously unsuccessful; this perched sump marked the end of the cave.

To any serious caver the prospects spoke for themselves; the place looked extremely promising. We left, planning to tackle the sump the following day.

Twenty-four hours later water levels were down and where we had dived the previous day there was now a good 20 centimetre's airspace. I felt optimistic and with plenty of support the carry was easy. The sequence of events was to be much the same as the day before with Paddy surveying the area upstream from the duck.

Underwater the passage was completely clean washed and after 7 metres a squeeze was reached. This was easily overcome but despite the larger proportions beyond I had begun to worry. Instinct was trying to tell me that I was too inexperienced for this sort of stuff. There wasn't another cave diver within hundreds of miles. Then I noticed that the roof had disappeared. I started up and almost immediately surfaced into a totally enclosed airbell. Enthusiasm was all but extinguished. Ducking down once more a black space appeared to the left and again of an instant I reached another surface; but this time it was a deep froth-ridden pool with the sound of a flowing streamway. With no conscious thought, the worry and stress was banned. The kit was quickly dropped, the line tied off, and I set off to explore.

A few corners later the narrow rift opened out and a roof tube appeared above my head. Elementary knowledge of cave formation suggested a high level route, possibly heading back downstream, thereby by-passing the sump. There had been no evidence of a high level passage beforehand and I climbed up eager to see if it also went in the downstream direction. It did. An 'old' abandoned passage superbly encrusted with crystals and flowstone on the floor, Crystal Crunch Passage, led to a fair sized chamber. But from this point there were no obvious ways on. I retraced my steps and continued upstream.

By comparison with the cave downstream from the sump, the extension was well decorated and plenty big enough to move along at a fast pace. The floor comprised nicely rounded stones and areas of sand and gravel, which was fortunate as I had no boots. A low canal and a couple of awkward ducks posed the only minor obstacles.

Eventually I reached an area of avens and chokes. Debris here took the form of large brownish-black, slimy boulders and cobbles. A small stream issued from a minute sump but it was clear that the main route lay upwards and that in all probability I had reached a point below the surface sink known as Whisky Holes.

En route I'd noticed a fair-sized passage off to the left and returning downstream this in its turn was followed. After 300 to 400 metres a similar setting was found again. Water poured from a cleft in the roof and flood debris suggested the proximity of a surface connection.

With a mental note of distance and direction I made my way out. My wet-socks were torn through in several places and my feet were beginning to feel the worse for wear. Still, a little discomfort was nothing compared to the excitement of the find. By the time I returned to the others I had been away for an hour and over 1200 metres of cave had been explored.

In 1974 a sump by pass was discovered, giving non divers access to the extension. The location of the Fenian Terror Passage is far from obvious but it is significant to note that it was 'wide open'. An awkward traverse and squeeze lead to the chamber at the end of Crystal Crunch Passage. Today therefore Tullyhona constitutes a fine day's caving for any visitor to the area.

Shortly after the Irish visit I met Roger Solari, who was also intensely interested in the prospects offered by the caves in Fermanagh. Over the previous two years he'd made several visits to the province and had acquired a far greater knowledge of the area than I. Along with John Elliot, Roger had made significant explorations in two of the area's major systems, namely Arch Cave and Prods Pot, and at both the way on was wide open. Ironically the 'Forest' lads had had Tullyhona on their 'short list' of objectives in 1971 but on the allocated day their porters had mutinied in favour of the pub. I had pipped him to the post. He was naturally rather envious of such an easy find but there was no animosity; in fact the find drew us together, and very soon we opted to spend a couple of weeks in Fermanagh over the summer.

Student life at this time was a frugal experience, necessarily so if I was to save any money at all for caving. But it did mean that the course work was kept under control. When the year finished at university and I went home to raise some cash for Ireland, the standard of living underwent an improvement. Square meals in particular were a welcome change after the vegetable stews to which I had become accustomed. Weekends were mostly spent in the Swansea Valley and in July the big break was made at Dan yr Ogof (see Chapter one).

That September, 1972, Roger and I piled all the cylinders we could borrow, together with an incredible selection of other gear into Roger's van and set off. The weather was superb.

Prods Pot, just off the Marlbank Scenic Loop, was our first big objective. Anyone familiar with the system will tell you that the trip down the cave is one of the finest in Northern Ireland. The difficulty is minimal and the place well decorated. However the Entrance Series, three small pitches and a total descent of 50 metres is irritating, especially if you are carrying equipment. The route here comprises a succession of rifts which are rather too narrow to negotiate at floor level. This results in a series of traverses between the pitches where you must be mindful not to let anything slip. Bottoming the last 13-metre pitch you join a fine free flowing streamway which leads for 600 metres to the terminal downstream sump. Further sumps are encountered upstream. In both directions the potential was excellent.

We tackled the downstream sump first. It was over a mile in a direct line to the boulder-choked rising, at the head of Cladagh Gorge, and over this distance the stream apparently fell by at least 22 metres. Roger and John had dived it the year before but could make no headway in a maze of blind rifts. Exactly the same thing happened again! It was almost as though the large stream filtered through the sandy floor.

The next day we dived the upstream Cascade Passage sumps. Roger and John had passed a constricted Sump One the previous year to discover a canal which led up to a second sump. Again it appeared that we were destined for failure, for having passed the first sump, Roger's valve developed an incurable leak. We were diving with only a single bottle and valve apiece, and the escaping air gave rise for serious concern.

Having stripped the valve down and isolated the fault, we were powerless to do anything about it. There were two alternatives: abandon the dive, or try and ignore the problem. As it was Roger's valve, the choice was his. The leak didn't affect his breathing and he wasn't feeling in a submissive mood. We pushed on.

When least expecting a breakthrough, it happened; Sump Two was 6 metres long and Sump Three about 3 metres. Ahead lay good open passage, finely decorated. However we were in for a shock. The further we progressed, the worse the passage became. At 250 metres we reached a junction and as the flow clearly originated from the right branch we continued along that. A further 80 metres of tight rift led to Sump Four, by which time our wets suits were rather the worse for wear. There was little respite from hardship at the other lead. By the time we had pushed everything to its limit, Prods was 600 metres longer but the life of our suits was appreciably shorter.

Our Mars bars and sole porter had been left at the first sump. On return a few hours later, the place was deserted and our Mars bars gone. It required no detective to solve this crime. We had a few choice words to say when we got out.

Next on our programme was Arch Cave, known to the local inhabitants by the sinister sounding name of Ooghboraghan. Here a major stream resurged from a cavernous entrance, draining the extensive upland area of Tullybrack Mountain. This was

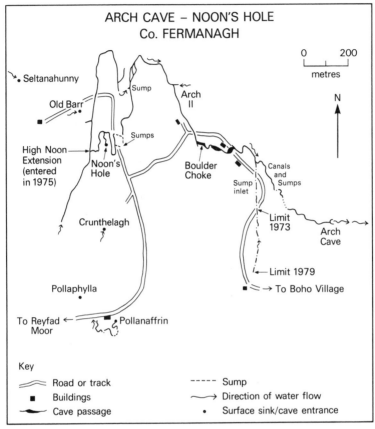

ARCH CAVE – NOON'S HOLE
Co. FERMANAGH

0   200
metres

N

Seltanahunny

Old Barr

Sump

Arch
II

Sumps

High Noon
Extension
(entered
in 1975)

Noon's
Hole

Boulder
Choke

Canals
and
Sumps

Sump
inlet

Limit
1973

Arch
Cave

Crunthelagh

Pollaphylla

←— Limit 1979

→ To Boho Village

To Reyfad ←
Moor

Pollanaffrin

Key

〰️ Road or track

▪ Buildings

〰️ Cave passage

----- Sump

⌒→ Direction of water flow

• Surface sink/cave entrance

one of the big Irish question marks and a site of great potential. The famous French speleologist Martel, had visited the short cave as early as 1895, but it was not until 1959 that the local explorer, Duncan Millar, passed the duck near the entrance to discover 300 metres of fine stream passage leading up to Sump One. In 1961 divers using oxygen rebreathing equipment had probed the sump, found it to be shallow and located an airbell after 40 metres. Somewhat amazingly it was to be ten years before a further attempt was made, this time by Roger and John Elliot. After a 28-metre dive, they had located another large airbell, which they believed contained 'bad air' (a high proportion of carbon dioxide).

With a single set of apparatus apiece the 300-metre carry to the sump was easy. Roger dived off first carrying an 80-metre reel of line. In what seemed to be a very short space of time he was back, having laid out all the line and belayed to a flake in a fair-sized airbell. In fact the whole dive had been shallow and had incorporated several bells after the 30-metre mark.

Transferring further line from a rather poor reel to the one that Roger had used, I set off to continue the exploration. As I finned through the gloomy blackness I couldn't help wondering how on earth Roger had managed to route-find so quickly in such a large passage. Rarely could I see the walls. At the airbell it was clear that ahead lay a section of deep water with an increasing amount of air-space. Rather than waste line by laying it along this passage, I opted to make a quick recce ahead to assess the lie of the land.

Hurriedly I left the bottle and valve on a convenient sand bank and started swimming up the canal, still wearing my lead weights and fins. Almost immediately the chamber degenerated into a jagged rift approximately 2.5 metres wide. The walls were undercut and everywhere the bottom was out of depth. After about 25 metres, a sharp turn to the left led out of the tall wide rift which I had been following, until it narrowed at water level almost forming a sump. Luckily I was able to pass this and with relief I emerged not only into another large chamber but also into shallow, knee-deep water. Relief was short lived however as another 30-metre swim and a similar duck led to a sump proper; clearly I would have to collect the diving equipment.

By this stage I was convinced that the sump would be short. A pattern seemed to have developed which with reflection applied through a fair proportion of the cave. Very simply this concerned the parallel nature of the joints and the way the water took advantage of this structural weakness in the rock. Where the flow followed a joint the route was easily negotiable along a rift. Where the route altered direction by crossing to a parallel joint then the passage was smaller, and here beyond Sump One these sections closed to the water. Optimistically the theory indicated that Sump Two would be short, probably only an off-set rift similar to the low sections that I had just passed.

Beginning the swim back I wasn't aware of just how cold I really was. On the second canal I learned. A sudden bout of cramp in both legs nearly proved disastrous and inwardly I cursed my stupidity in not removing all of my lead before undertaking the swim. A mouthful of water, panic, and a spate of gasping followed until my hand caught hold of a minute flake protruding from the right wall. In a minute the crisis passed and with great relief I carried on the last few metres to shallow water, safety and the kit. 'Must invest in a decent suit one of these days' I thought, as I jumped around attempting to get the circulation moving. Then again I had spent virtually every penny I had on this trip, so it was unlikely I would be able to do anything about it in the short term when I got back. Inevitably I would be lured into spending money on doing things, rather than improving my equipment. When I could feel my fingers again, and my body had stopped shivering, I kitted up.

With abundant air reserves in my bottle I wasn't too worried about trouble on the next sump. However with a limited amount of line, about 45 metres, I certainly did not have any to spare on the swim up to Sump Two. This was cut and tied off to a large flake.

Fully kitted once more, I set off up the canals taking the occasional breath from the bottle. With little difficulty a belay point was located less than 7 metres before the sump, and I dived on.

The visibility had not improved; a dull orange glow emanated from my head-piece, and featureless black shadows accompanied me once more. After about 9 metres, the floor was clearly seen to be rising and shortly I surfaced in a deep canal similar to the one I'd left a couple of minutes before. There was one difference however that was immediately apparent, namely the foam floating upon the surface of the water. This dirty, creamy-coloured substance can be seen on any mountain stream, or beneath a weir, but one thing is necessary in its formation — turbulence. This meant one thing; upstream there was either an open streamway or a cascading waterfall.

Swimming on, eagerly anticipating shallow water, the line ran out and had to be left, belayed only to the line reel in about one to two metres of water. Continuing upstream into deeper water I was lucky to find a narrow ledge on the left-hand side where the depth was less than one metre. Now I dropped the bottle and valve (carefully noting the position in case they should float away), and swam on desperately in search of dry land. Rounding another corner I was shivering with the cold again and feeling particularly isolated. The tension was mounting.

About 60 metres from the sump, the sound that I had been waiting for, for so long, assailed my ears; the distinct echo of running water. A few metres further, and shaking uncontrollably with relief, I stepped out of the water onto a nicely cobbled area of streamway.

My feet had only just felt the discomfort of dry land when other needs suddenly became pressing. I had been drained of nervous energy and an immediate call of nature was demanded. There was no question of feeling embarassed — just annoyed: at the very moment I should be trying to conserve body heat, rather than lose it, I was forced to undress. Wearing a long-john trouser suit with fixed shoulder straps the sense of urgency was almost overpowering. Everything was now directed towards this one objective. It was ridiculous but I had no choice.

Contortions over and the call satisfied, I realised that the stream water felt warm upon my bare legs. My mind seemed lucid and I knew enough of physiology to interpret these symptoms; I was verging upon exposure. I became aware of how far out on a limb I was, far more so than ever before. There was no question of diving straight back out as I was much too cold; I was totally committed to this exploration.

Wandering on upstream my spirits rose as the magnitude of the discovery became apparent. Another short swim or two and I reached a large scree slope leading up into a starless void. The significance of this was not lost and carefully I scrambled to the top.

My one and only light was far from brilliant: the head-piece was at least half full of water and I dare not unscr⸱⸱ ⸱⸱ the bezelled front-piece to drain it off for fear of damaging ⸱⸱⸱ bulb or the fragile reflector contact. Still, the illumination it presented was sufficient to tell me that this was no ordinary chamber. It was vast. I stepped lightly from boulder to boulder eventually making my way to the far side. Dropping down over a couple of large boulder slabs another scree slope led temporarily back to the stream. Shortly afterwards and almost incredulously I emerged into an even larger chamber.

By now I was almost warm and able to remove my wet-suit hood. Wandering carefully around (again minus boots) trying to conceive its true proportions, I soon realised that a major choke lay ahead. From wall to wall and from floor to roof, huge blocks of limestone were stacked in a haphazard manner. But unlike so many chokes that one encounters underground, there was a noticeable absence of small debris, such as mud, sand and gravel. Having located a possible entry to this obstacle, common sense came to the fore. If my light went out here I realised that I'd be in for quite a stay. Roger did not have enough air to come to my aid and a rescue due to light failure would be most embarrassing. Today, ten years on, a light failure is not critical as everyone carries at least one reserve light unit. Looking back, it's surprising that until the mid 1970s when the use of a spare became common, more incidents of light failure did not occur.

Returning downstream, a superbly decorated oxbow was explored at leisure and in what seemed to have been quite a short while I was swimming back downstream in search of my discarded kit. Luckily it was still there. It hadn't moved or been obscured by the foam.

Several hours after I'd left Roger I emerged; the solution to the Arch Cave mystery was within our grasp.

Two days later we returned and taking additional line the first thing to be done was to establish a decent belay point beyond Sump Two. Equipped this time with boots, we covered our old ground quickly and pressed on up the extension. The choke was relatively solid, but even so we moved cautiously between the house-like cavities.

It soon became obvious that the ruckle was equally as vast as the chamber which preceded it. Moving forward, we created small cairns and arrows to direct us on our return. Normally we would be disdainful of such practice, but in this instance the action was simply common sense. Innumerable routes developed and we split up, keeping in verbal contact. Roger chose his passage near stream level, a good eight to ten metres below me; I just kept moving forward whenever possible. The cavities continued and the place remained fairly stable. Eventually my route was terminated and rather than turn downwards I looked up. There through a narrow chink in the boulders was the tell-tale blackness of an open cave. Clearly it was something big.

I quickly retraced my steps for a few metres, squeezed past a couple of slabs, and in a matter of minutes was standing in a chamber. The way ahead looked clear. I shouted back to Roger, who was goodness knows where below. By the time he joined me I had erected another cairn and we moved off directly up the passage. Via another fine chamber, adorned with a two metre flowstone pillar, we regained the stream. Magnificent proportions continued and we were in little doubt that we were now going places.

Dwarfing Tullyhona, Arch Cave was like Dan yr Ogof all over again. Following the trunk passage we moved swiftly, occasionally clambering over large boulders or wading the odd deep pool. After 900 metres, side passages were noted on the right and left, but these were inconsequential compared to the mainstream. Ahead an oxbow loomed up, which for about 100 metres was probably 13 metres wide and 3 to 4 metres high. Regaining the stream it dawned on us that the passage dimensions had dwindled considerably.

The main route must have been lost at the head of the oxbow. Next we lost the main flow and less than 100 metres later arrived in an area of rifts. Refuse now appeared on the floor, an old kettle, rusty tins, etc, and we realised that we must be approaching the surface sink.

Out of a small container Roger produced an old compass which we had borrowed from a friend. Perhaps this would help. Yes, we had a north-south axis alright, but which end of the needle pointed north? Both were of the same colour! This was a farcical situation. We didn't have a clue as to which bit of mountain we were under and discussing the issue we arrived at a sump. This was an isolated spot but one that appeared tantalising promising. The way that the roof plunged sharply suggested that the sump might just be free-diveable. We agreed that it had to be worth a try. In fact an airbell was reached after a metre or so, but it was clear that the main continuation lay at greater depth, necessitating the use of a bottle.

Searching for a by-pass we located a promising passage a hundred or so metres downstream. This unfortunately terminated at a series of high avens, one of which was climbed for about 16 metres. Coated with a slimy kind of flowstone, this and the adjoining shafts were just too treacherous to attempt without the protection of climbing aids. We couldn't risk an accident here so retracing our steps we set off back down the cave to examine other possibilities.

At the upper end of the oxbow there was indeed a major choke. The significance of this was now clear. We had followed the trunk route for nearly 1½ miles to this point, to be confronted with a dead end. This choke with its firmly cemented boulders and drapery of flowstone was it. A detailed examination showed that extensive flows of calcite had sealed off any hope of a dry route on. Beyond this barrier lay something big but for the moment it was not for us.

Further downstream none of the other passages led for more than 100 metres and it was a very weary pair who eventually surfaced at 11.00 pm. All in all it hadn't been a bad day — over one mile of new passages had been explored.

The following day, Paddy and friends from the 'South' arrived. Enthused by our find they entertained the idea of taking a look down Noon's Hole, situated roughly between Reyfad Pot and Arch Cave. No-one had been down this system since 1970 when U.L.S.A. had discovered over 300 metres of passages known as the Afternoon Series. It had to be worth a visit. Tired, but none the less keen, Roger and I decided to accompany them and to make a dive at the sump in the Afternoon Series.

It was a long drive from our hut south of the border and on the way, Paddy related the legend of the hole. Its name derived from a certain Dominic Noon, who being a traitor to the Irish cause, had been thrown the 35 metres down the entrance shaft. We passed the farm at which we had parked for the Arch Cave trips and a few minutes later reached the brow of a hill. Here the metalled surface ended and the road degenerated into two rough tracks. Paddy pointed to an insignificant hollow overgrown by stunted trees.

'There's Noons.'

To this depression a sluggish little stream wound its way from boggy and reed infested fields. Enthusiasm was now at a low ebb, but we dragged out all the ladders that were necessary to rig the shafts and Paddy strode off to get things sorted. Our suits were wet but having moaned and groaned our way into them we were committed.

The 35-metre entrance shaft was superb. 'The finest in Ireland', bellowed one of the Southerners, Gareth Jones, in response to my shrieks of ecstasy. 'Just like a giant bottle of

Hennessy Whisky.' The rest was lost amid the echoes of the cascading stream.

Pot after pot, all went smoothly. At the bottom we left the surveyors to their task and I assisted Roger to dive the sump. The approach passage and base area were dismal and depressing. A fresh scum and dark brown mud clung to the walls. Assorted flood debris such as leaves and the odd tin were scattered in every direction. The place was far from promising.

Over the course of a 40-metre penetration, Roger had passed five airbells, attaining a maximum depth of about five metres at the furthest point. In the poor visibility his impression was that the sump was one big phreatic maze. A further dive at a neighbouring passage substantiated these ideas. We carried out.

I ascended the 35-metre ladder on the Entrance Pitch first to haul the tackle. Load after load appeared smoothly until the time came to pull up the box, containing Roger's valve, mask and compass. It came to within three metres of the top before it caught on a projection. A tentative lowering achieved nothing, so more forceful methods were applied. Next the lid handle appeared, but no box. Simultaneously a crash and an irate shout echoed from the depths. The box had shattered just one metre from Paddy. Luckily no-one had been hit and Roger managed to salvage bits of his valve. The rest was a write-off.

Thereafter all loads ascending or descending pitches were thoroughly checked; we had been sobered by the thought that had one of the bits of equipment been a full cylinder then the subsequent massive explosion in such a confined space would have been disastrous. This incident quite effectively marked the conclusion of our first joint venture to Ireland. We had run out of time and air, and now Roger was without a valve.

The following year, 1973, we returned in August; our prime objective being the Arch Cave terminal sump (3). I was still carless and Roger's organisation was virtually flawless. There had only been one setback — missing the ferry — but apart from that everything was fine.

The plan was to dive through to the extension with two bottles apiece, leave the depleted ones at the bottom end of Arch II and then each carry a full one up to the terminal sump. Despite assistance with the porterage down to the cave, things were not running smoothly. Just inside the entrance one of the plastic cylinder bands shattered and the bottle fell out. We had not made a particularly early start and by the time we had reached the sump, it was decided to postpone our push until the morrow. Somehow we had become 'psyched up' by the prospect of the long trip.

We were underground by 11.00 am the next day and everything went like clockwork. The sumps were passed without incident and we waded out on to the dry cobbled area beyond.

The used bottles were quickly deposited and in silence, the long trek up the cave commenced. Roger carried his Sea Lion 40 cu/ft cylinder, while I toiled with my Draeger 45 cu/ft bottle. At the choke, progress was slowed. Laboriously we passed the gear from one to the other, moved on and repeated the exercise — time after time. At the streamway we got into our stride once more.

With a decent compass Roger soon had our approximate course charted. A connection with Pollanaffrin now seemed most unlikely; in all probability we were heading straight for Noons. Neither of us possessed a watch reliable enough to be taken underground on such a trip as this so we had no idea of the time taken from the entrance. This did not seem to matter anyway; our thoughts were preoccupied with what lay ahead. Fatigue and the prospect of the slog out were dismissed.

At Sump Three the water was dark and gloomy. Roger made the first exploration but was back within ten minutes convinced that he had gone the wrong way.

'Been up a twisting rift in clear water for 55 metres; you lose the peaty stuff after about 10 metres. I reckon the way on is to the right just a short distance in.'

Now it was my turn. Following the advice I hugged the right-hand wall and after approximately 8 metres turned a distinct corner, to ascend into a small enclosed airbell. Continuing several more bells were passed and I emerged after 45 metres at a familiar sight — the Noons Hole sump! Instant disappointment, even depression, descended on me. We might after all have established this connection last year and saved ourselves one hell of a lot of trouble. Roger must have been within a metre or two of Arch II but it was my luck to make the link.

The place was just as dismal as it had been the previous year, but I was not going back until I had at least seen a flicker of daylight from the entrance shaft. Who knows, someone might have rigged the pitches. Our friends had been talking about doing so either today or tomorrow.

Transporting all the boots, Roger eventually turned up to find me shouting plaintively up the shaft.

'Hello... Anybody up there?... Hello... Hello, mutter, mutter, — bastards!'

There wasn't a lot to say, but it was very frustrating. Instead of a swift half an hour spent climbing the five pitches back to the surface we had the prospect of another three to four hours travelling back through Arch Cave. Roger wasn't impressed and left me to it. Shortly I set off, following him downstream, back through the mountain.

By the time we had kitted up, our thoughts had cleared and we discussed the significance of our discovery. This 45-metre sump was certainly a far easier route into Arch II than that from the resurgence. A through trip was a must and for his part Roger was keen to do an accurate survey. Consequently we deposited our bottles just downstream from the sump with a view to bringing these out, via Noons, in a couple of day's time.

Arriving back at the bottom of Arch II we were about to start on the first of the swims, when Roger noticed an inlet. This issued a substantial stream, probably accounting for about one third of the total flow just downstream of this point. It was almost completely concealed on a corner, easy to miss. Feeling keen we entered the narrow rift to find the passage heading south. Eagerly following it we were disappointed to arrive at a sump within 25 metres. The obvious answer was Pollanaffrin, lying the best part of a mile away! The jig-saw was fitting together very well.

Feeling fresh and full of plans, we emerged 8½ hours after entry to a fine warm evening. Over the following days we discussed how best to undertake the exchange trip while at the same time conducting the survey. I must admit that having established the connection I had no great desire to survey it all; reading tapes and instruments held no interest for me. But Roger thrived on it, and when I saw the end product, I had to admit that he was very skilled in the art.

Following the discovery of the major inlet at the bottom of

Arch II Pollanaffrin now assumed greater significance. On our initial reconnaissance we found it pure hell. The entrance lay a few yards downstream from a farm. Here an 11-metre ladder pitch led to a sizeable chamber, festooned with household rubbish and animal carcasses. The fetid smell almost made us retch, particularly as we were required to climb over the remains.

An awkward climb then gave access to a boulder squeeze, which in turn led to the terminal constriction. We knew that this had been passed to yield a pool and a desperately awkward canal-cum-duck; this had yet to be tackled. The preceding constriction was certainly tight and while Roger divested himself of his wet suit jacket to try and get through, I thrutched on to examine the duck. Roger's hood was quickly requisitioned and cautiously I edged forward into the flooded rift. The passage was tight and I could feel no floor.

Utilising the minute air-space was very difficult and I wished I had a snorkel or a small set of breathing apparatus to help. Holding the helmet out ahead, every movement had to be but a matter of centimetres. One eye and an ear were completely submerged and it was only with great difficulty that my mouth could be kept clear of the endless ripples. This was certainly the most desperate situation I had put myself in for a long while; claustrophobic to say the least. It was never that bad if you knew you could get your head up at the far side, or indeed if you could retreat quickly to the start. Here a quick retreat was impossible and any sudden movement could have meant disaster. Slowly and steadily I slid forward.

Through the water a dim glow percolated, not that I needed any fantastic illumination. Breaths came in gasps as the cold water lapped across my face. Completely engrossed, I was wondering how much longer I could sustain the tension when suddenly, a mere three metres from the start, the roof raised to give a clearance of a metre. Ahead spacious proportions loomed out of the blackness. I was through.

By now, Roger had passed the squeeze and was donning his wet suit to follow. The fact that I'd used a wet suit hood was no deterrent. If he could pass the squeeze he would certainly follow me through the duck. I passed a few instructions.

'It seems to be wider lower down. Best keep your cell on your side though.'

He took a deep breath and dived through smoothly. We waded on, with everything in our favour — until we were brought up sharply by a complete sump, a mere 20 metres further on.

A few days later I was back with diving equipment. There had been nothing enjoyable about any part of the cave so far, and slowly it became apparent that the passage ahead was just as bad. The sump was awkward but after 40 metres it surfaced. The extension, a tortuous 48 metres long, led to Sump Two. Exploring Pollanaffrin would not be easy.

The climax of our 1973 visit was to be the Noons-Arch exchange trip and the plan was as follows: Roger and Dave Underhill (on his first cave dive), were to enter via Noons and survey down to the bottom of Arch II. I would enter via Arch I and conduct exploration off the main passage, in particular the new Southern Inlet. Leaving my first bottle near the bottom sump, would enable Roger to make his exit via the resurgence. As the survey would occupy by far the greater period of time, I would then ferry Roger's valve and mask down to the bottom sump and make a communal brew in the vicinity of the boulder choke. After Roger had made his exit, Dave and I would surface at Noons, detackling as we went.

Unfortunately, bad weather delayed the execution of the plan. The Noons entrance shaft was in full spate for a couple of days and we could only imagine what was happening to our bottles cached beyond the sump. We made the best of inactivity. Our suits and equipment received some much needed attention, but inevitably our pockets felt the pinch as we frequented the Bush Bar rather earlier in the evening.

When the time came, we were ready and everything felt right. It was a fabulous day. The weather was hot and clear with the odd puff of cumulous drifting hazily across the sky. In preparation Noons had been tackled days ago. Somehow or other we had no volunteers to assist us with the transport of equipment, but this was of no great inconvenience.

It was too hot to wear my wet suit jacket to the cave and having been dropped off by Roger and Dave, I staggered off down the hill — sweating like a pig and increasingly wishing that I had someone to accompany me. The horse-flies had a field day, as it was almost impossible to swat them. Cursing profusely, I fought my way down through the tangle of undergrowth on the last section to that incredible entrance, Oogboraghan.

The cool air of the cavern brought with it peace from the accursed flies and a sense of tranquility. Even so I was definitely nervy. I had never undertaken anything on quite this scale before. The loneliness was very real and I could not help churning over the remote prospects of rescue, should anything nasty occur beyond another longish sump. We were using our last full bottles and it would be days before any help would arrive.

With two journeys up to the first swim, it was clear that the rest of the cave would not be easy. With hands full of gear I started across the first deep pool. This would normally pose no problem at all — just a thorough immersion, a few good strokes and then a stagger out onto the boulder-strewn passage at the far side. However, I hadn't realised just how heavy the 50 cu/ft bottle was and I certainly had not counted on sinking so fast. Pushing off from between the narrow walls I got in at least two strokes with my left arm before I went down. Taking a good lungful of air as I went, I remember feeling very embarrassed.

There were but two courses of action. Either I jettisoned some gear, or I carried on. I couldn't afford the former, so clutching hard on the fins and reel in my right hand, I made a couple more strokes in a predominantly submerged position and very luckily my feet touched down. Gasping with relief I quickly waded to shore.

Two kilos of lead were deposited in an obvious position for Roger to collect on his exit, and I carried on. At the next swim I kitted up completely but with a gag in my mouth, just in case. With the exception of my fins I was ready kitted on arrival at the sump and in a matter of minutes I was away, preferring action to reflection and worry. Under my belt I tucked the snorkel which Maurice Febry had loaned. To my knowledge this would be the first time that anyone had used such a thing for caving here in Britain; it would be perfect for the long sections of canal beyond Sump One. I finned away smoothly.

The next little hiccup occurred beyond the sump; I'd lost the snorkel. 'Damn; that'll cost me a few pints in the Bush.'

But it was no good worrying, especially as I didn't stand much chance of finding it were I to go back and search. The visibility would be reduced and I didn't even know if it would float or sink in the water. I went on without it.

At the junction with the inlet passage I was as cold as ever, but by now fully psyched up for the proposed exploration. Frantically I jumped around to restore the circulation and in a few minutes I was ready.

Sump followed sump, interspersed with canals and a short, fast flowing section. By the time the 200 metres of line ran out, 13 metres in to Sump 7, the air reserves in my single bottle were approaching the safety margin. 280 metres of new cave had been found, all heading in a predominantly southerly direction.

Perhaps I had not made the big break we were expecting but psychologically I was pleased by the way that I had coped with the isolation. Cold but cheerful I returned to the mainstream junction. The reel and the bottle that Roger required to make his exit, were left on a convenient ledge and I moved off up the cave.

Near the Oxbow we met. Dave had undergone his crash course in diving: 'Just breathe normally, squeeze your nose and blow if you feel any pain,' and like a lamb to the slaughter he had followed Roger to each airbell in turn. It had been a perfectly satisfactory first cave dive.

When we parted company I set off for the top sump, collected another bottle and made for the sump near the Oxbow. It was here that the main flow of water was lost, where, therefore, the greatest potential for more cave lay. There was a very large catchment area extending to the north and this sump looked a good bet. The chances were that the big trunk passage would be regained after a short dive.

A degree of improvisation now became necessary owing to the fact that I had no diving reel. All I did was to lay out the line on the gravel floor, attach one end to a large and immovable boulder and the other to me. On diving the line would trail behind; my limit of penetration set at 25 metres. It required two attempts to get the 'self base fed system' to work, but after 20 metres I encountered a new problem — a complete boulder blockage. This was very frustrating. (I felt even more peeved a few years later when it transpired that I had been within a couple of metres of yet another mile-long extension — the High Noon Series, which was discovered by Paddy and Jeff Phillips!)

Leaving my gear on the floor of the main passage I set off downstream with the equipment which the other two were expecting. I caught them up in the choke, passed them and started the brew. In minutes the paraffin stove was purring merrily. Yes, this had been a well planned trip . . . but wait a minute, where was the tin opener for the Irish Stew? A few minutes with a large rock soon solved that problem though it took five minutes more to extract part of the contents from between the pulverised segments of can, and scrape the rest off the wall and floor. The resulting meal looked good and was at least hot, but I can't say the gravel added anything to the flavour.

The survey concluded we said our farewells. Roger set off out to Arch I while Dave and I started on the long trek back up to Noons. Everything was going smoothly. I tested the gear for Dave, made sure that he had more than ample air reserves, then sent him off first to get the better visibility.

It took me quite a while to get my own gear organised as I was doing all the portering. Everything sorted I dived away, but emerged according to Dave, only seconds after him. He had become entangled at several points and almost unbelievably had found none of the air-bells! Like a young child who has broken something valuable he pointed apprehensively to his air contents gauge. It read 'O' and popping the gag back into his mouth the cylinder was sucked empty on a single breath. I didn't say a word; the look on his face told all.

Slowly and laboriously we gathered our possessions and made our way up to the foot of the shafts. Here the real work began. Dead beat we slogged away at the cumulative task of gear hauling. We reached the 35-metre Entrance Pitch and suddenly, miraculously, we were revitalised. At the top flashing lights spelt instant relief; our non-diving friends had turned out to give us a helping hand. A voice of command echoed down.

'Tie on.'

'Up. Up.'

Load after load speedily disappeared into the blackness.

Then it was our turn to climb. With a last reassuring pull from the lifeline I eased myself over the grassy lip and stared straight into the beaming face of Maurice Febry.

'How you doing lad?'

'Bloody great! thanks.'

Roger or someone thrust a can of Guinness forward; it hardly touched the sides. The time was 3.00 am and we had been underground for 18 hours. Aches and pains were forgotten; we were out and into a sort of euphoric dreamland.

The day had been an unquestionable success. Roger and Dave had completed the survey of the whole of the mainstream passage and I had explored several hundred metres of additional passage. We had not solved all the mysteries of the system it was true, and we were resigned to the fact that in time we would be lured back. This was the frustrating part of the sport. There was always something else that needed to be checked; some boulder choke or sump that had not been conclusively explored. But for the moment we were satisfied.

We had achieved the first exchange trip in the Noons-Arch system, a traverse of nearly two miles of cave, involving spectacular shafts, easy sumps and a megalithic choke. From sink to resurgence involved a descent of 120 metres; the finest and most sporting through-trip in the British Isles.

3

Success and Tragedy

AGEN ALLWEDD

In southern Britain, the supreme challenge in the early 1970s was the terminal downstream sump of Agen Allwedd. During 1972 this achieved the status of being the longest cave-dive in the country, and, according to certain authorities, apparently it held the potential for a world record.

It wasn't so much the challenge of the dive that drew me to it, as the thought of what lay beyond. Like Parker I was enticed by the miles of cave to which the sumps appeared the easiest short term access. Pushing such a major site was a daunting prospect, but more of a deterrent was the difficulty of the carry which had to be made to one of the most distant points of one of the longest caves in Britain. Roger Solari and I had contemplated the idea of tackling the terminal sump for some length of time, but hadn't done anything about it for fear of upsetting Parker again.

The relationship with John Parker had deteriorated since the reconnaissance dive that Mike Ware and I had made to the upstream extensions of Agen Allwedd in 1971. Several incidents contributed to this situation. Parker and his partner, Jeff Phillips, had passed Sump Five in the Turkey Series in December 1971 and discovered 600 metres of passages. When a year elapsed and the pair had still not followed up their exploration of this series Roger and I went to view the place for ourselves. On our visit in January 1973 we passed an intimidating canal at the furthest point and found a further 600 metres. Another event was the exploration which Roger and I made at P8 in Derbyshire. Parker and Phillips had made a spectacular advance in this cave in 1972 when, being the first to pass Sump Four, they continued well beyond, into Sump Nine. Knowing this we realised there was potential for further exploration and nine months after their last push, we extended Sump Nine to 169 metres (July

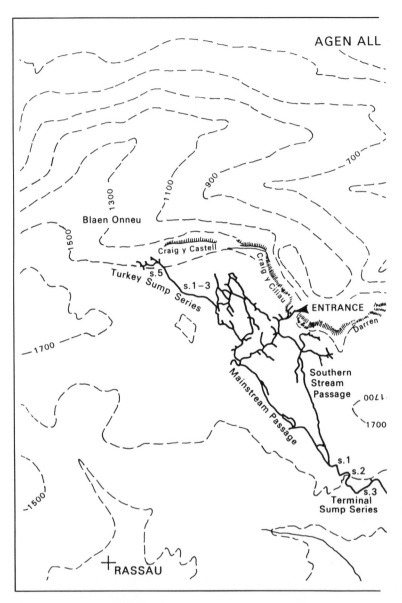

AGEN ALL

Blaen Onneu

Craig y Castell

Turkey Sump Series

s.5

s.1–3

Craig y Ciliau

ENTRANCE

Darren

Southern
Stream
Passage

Mainstream Passage

1700

1700

s.1

s.2

s.3

Terminal
Sump Series

RASSAU

1300
1100
900
700
1500
1700
1500

1973). This was considered by Parker to be poaching.

At this point the cave diving scene was definitely becoming cramped and with some divers claiming 'ownership' of certain

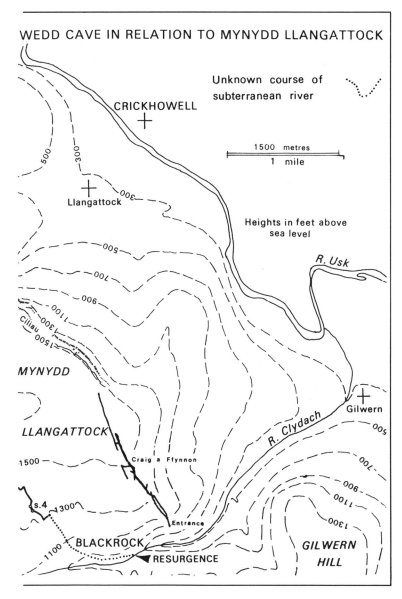

WEDD CAVE IN RELATION TO MYNYDD LLANGATTOCK

CRICKHOWELL

Unknown course of
subterranean river

1500 metres
1 mile

Llangattock

Heights in feet above
sea level

R. Usk

Ciliau

MYNYDD

Gilwern

LLANGATTOCK

R. Clydach

1500

Craig a Ffynnon

s.4

Entrance

BLACKROCK

RESURGENCE

GILWERN
HILL

caves yet not undertaking any new exploration, the situation was getting even more difficult. It was becoming impossible to do anything without treading on someone's toes. It was definitely time to expand, but where to? Expensive expeditions abroad were out of the question and even our trips to Yorkshire were to be controversial. In February 1974 for example we made a breakthrough at Boreham Cave in Littondale, and in the process we inadvertently upset Geoff Yeadon who, unknown to us, was still actively exploring the place.

Inevitably it was our own area, South Wales that interested us most, and in particular places like Agen Allwedd where the 'end' of the cave was wide open. Since the last dive downstream in Agen Allwedd, in mid 1972, John had lost his partner, Jeff Phillips, who had taken a job in Eire. This was a severe blow to John as the two of them had been inextricably associated with all the major southern breakthroughs, and this appeared to affect his enthusiasm for the sport.

Roger and I had established a partnership based on our respect for each other as individuals. Our characters were dissimilar and we didn't particularly regard ourselves as close friends. I was the easy-going opportunist whilst he was the reserved, more analytical one. Roger could be pessimistic, even stubborn on occasions, but if we disagreed on certain issues because of our different temperaments, I also think these characteristics were complementary and probably were the strengh of our partnership. But above all, my respect for him as a caver was total; he was the 'hardest' person I knew, who never grumbled, and possessed unparalleled stamina.

We waited, planned and dived. Our reputation spread along with our sphere of activity, but an aura was lacking. In this respect I was envious of Parker, who, by his daring and exceptional feats, had cultivated a unique charisma. It seemed to attract flourishing support, an indispensible asset on difficult ventures and undoubtedly a great psychological boost. But by the spring of 1974 it became clear that he was now in semi retirement so far as cave diving was concerned and we began to make our plans for the assault on Agen Allwedd terminal sump.

By now we realised that no matter what operations we planned we always seemed to be lacking in equipment. Fortunately the Cave Diving Group had a number of communal cylinders in Bristol, upon which we became increasingly more reliant. The use of these was strictly controlled by Dr Oliver Lloyd, a slightly eccentric, elderly, pathologist. Few other people seemed to be taking advantage of this equipment and Oliver was more than happy to sponsor our explorations provided that the bottles were returned each week for use in pool training and that we submitted regular reports of the dives. After a particularly good night at the pub we took the plunge. Surreptitiously the bottles were ordered and the date for the Agen Allwedd trip was set: Saturday, 4 May 1974.

At Easter that year Roger went to Fermanagh for ten days while I spent a frustrating time at home due to family problems. Even so some trips were achieved, notably to Elm Hole in the Clydach Gorge and to Wookey. Each was to prove surprisingly beneficial in terms of experience and training for the venture in May. At Elm Hole for example a connection was discovered to the main river flowing from Agen Allwedd at a depth of 18 metres. The lesson to be grateful for in this instance was the sheer size of the place which induced a disturbing sensation of agoraphobia. The passage was an immense grey void and engendered feelings of acute loneliness, the intensity of which I had never previously experienced.

Completing my mental preparation was an incident at Wookey Hole where I was forced to exchange mouthpieces underwater while under considerable pressure. The use of two completely independent breathing systems had been accepted for some years but everyone followed the rule that one set was strictly for use in an emergency. It was all very well practising the swap over on to the reserve set in the open water pool situation; it was altogether different in an actual cave diving crisis. Deep in the murky waters of Chamber 14 at Wookey the feeling of panic was real but as logical thoughts fought their way through I realised that I could cope, and on reflection I was grateful for the experience.

Back at the sump base in Chamber 3 there was Oliver waiting to collect the bits and pieces of equipment that I had borrowed. Hardly had I clambered out of the water than he realised that I didn't have the line reel.

'Sorry Oliver, I got in to a lot of trouble in there and it got lost in Chamber 19.'

He never said a word. Oliver just stood there aghast, shaking his head slowly and tut, tutting. Gradually silence settled upon the whole group, who were waiting to hear the judgement passed. Then with all the reverence that years of lecturing instills the regal utterance came.

'You'll *have* to get it back you know.'

Thoughts were racing. The fact that I might have snuffed it was immaterial; the main thing was that Oliver wasn't too upset. We all knew he was quite unique. After all with brothers named Christopher Wren Lloyd and George Washington Lloyd, Oliver Cromwell Lloyd had obviously come from an unusual family. Our 'godfather' was renowned for his little 'ways' but the fact that such a minor loss could assume the proportions of a mortal sin left one dumb-founded. I resigned myself to the fact that I had indeed got off lightly and left the cave in disgrace.

Fortified by the experiences, plans for Agen Allwedd continued — beset as usual with countless little setbacks. Roger returned from Ireland incapacitated with a knee injury; there was no way that he would be fit enough to come. Other support was also questionable. Finding any porters is difficult enough but reliable people capable of reaching the terminal sump are few and far between. Despite putting the word about well in advance most enquiries yielded the same response. 'Sorry, going over to Mendip that weekend' or 'Promised to take the wife out'. Was it any wonder so many supposed cave divers preferred to talk about doing things in the pub rather than getting on with them!

When Friday night, May 3rd finally did come round, things were no better; the night before our trip was unforgettable.

The coach bringing me back from a week-long college trip was late and when I walked in to the flat it was to walk into a scene of absolute chaos. There was caving gear everywhere and Rodney 'Bomber' Beaumont was arguing with our landlady Mrs Solomon, who was apparently upset both about the mess and the fact that our other flat mate, Chris Howes, had been in the bathroom for two hours doing his photographic printing and she wanted to use the toilet.

'Really, those friends of yours Rodney! The airing cupboard smells like a brewery; the beer making will have to stop. ...Those girls about the place... well in my younger days... no shame! The bath...I don't know what's been going on in there but it will never be the same (Chris' chemicals).' I left Bomber to appease her while I tried to get some order into the chaos. There was still little confirmation of help with the portering and we still had no bottles. Hurried arrangements and frantic phone calls didn't appear to help and when we left the flat for the journey to Crickhowell we still had neither. When we arrived it was closing time at the local. Not good. At half past midnight, in desperation, I dragged fellow caver, Colin Edmunds from his bed, collected the C.D.G. cylinders which he had brought from Bristol, and made my way back to the hut and sleep. At this juncture there was myself, Bomber, Pete Robinson (who'd come down specially from Huddersfield) and promised help from some Chelsea Speleological Society members.

Up at 6.45 am Bomber, Pete and I reached White Walls (the C.S.S. headquarters) before 9.00 am. We then made sure of help from Ian Penney, Barry Weaver and John Cooper and set off. We reckoned that we might just be able to do it. Bomber carried a 40 cu/ft cylinder, Pete a large ammo-box and a 185-metre line reel, and I a 45 cu/ft cylinder and fins. The Chelsea party were to follow later equipped with a 40 cu/ft cylinder, additional wet suit jacket and an extra cell.

In the Main Chamber, 45 minutes underground, our pace slowed somewhat as I was on pilot bulb to conserve the life of my battery, and Bomber's cell (borrowed earlier) died. At the Southern Stream junction faulty memory took us down the wrong hole and we wasted half an hour, to everyone's dismay. I had been down to the terminal sump only once, and that had been over eight years previously. My memory was therefore a little hazy, but our little detour certainly gave us the full flavour of what was to follow.

Southern Stream is 1500 metres of stooping, crawling, squeezing — it's hard work and boring and just goes on and on. There are virtually no landmarks, just a two-metre high waterfall about two thirds of the way down. After this the going is rather easier with awkward muddy rifts for a change, but the detail of the passage is best forgotten.

I led, with Pete bringing up the rear and supplying most of the light. Mercifully our Chelsea friends caught us up before the waterfall, thus supplying a much-needed psychological boost. Another friend, Colin Anderson, had joined their party and together we made much better speed towards the sump. There was never a more welcome sight than the large, desolate Mainstream Passage, only a couple of minutes from our destination.

Down at the sump we found a large store of lead, which had

been left by Parker. Shrugging my shoulders I looked over to Bomber apologetically and waited for the broad northern accent.

'Well bloody 'ell; I've 'umped this 10 pounds for nowt!'

You can never stop a Yorkshire man till he's had his full say and we let Bomber ramble on until he'd finished.

Kitting up was as arduous as that for a medieval knight and by the time I waded into the sump pool I could barely move. With the additional wet suit jacket over the top of normal attire all the turmoil of life in a straight jacket was experienced. With a bottle on each side and another hand-held with the line reel, I really wondered what the hell I had let myself in for. Lighting-wise I had planned to wear an extra cell to supplement my normal Nife cell, but it was clear that the additional encumbrance would be too much. In the end it was discarded (spare lighting such as the compact aquaflash was unheard of at this stage).

The spare valve now developed a second-stage leak and only after some hefty clouts did the emission reduce to a tolerable level. The plan was to dive as far as the start of Sump Three where bottle one would be dropped, to be used on the dive out. This would enable me to dive on with two full cylinders.

I dived. Sump One was passed with little difficulty and found to be short, probably 77 metres, instead of the reported 92 metres. Wading down the airbell, Sump Two was reached in less than 45 metres. This was even shorter, probably 25 metres, but on entry to the airbell beyond, confusion developed. Sump Two was reputedly 92 metres in length. I had only dived 25 metres and could see the passage sumping within the next 30 metres. Surely the account had been mis-read and a 'duck' had been forgotten. With slight hesitation the dive proceeded.

After a further 90 metres, at approximately 5-8 metres depth, I realised the error of my judgement. I hadn't allowed for the 'Exaggeration Factor!' Instantly everything was clear, the tension was gone. In my hand was a knot and continuation of line of a different thickness. This I knew was the line that Parker had laid on his second dive here, line that had been added at a point 139 metres into Sump Three. John had a habit of getting carried away by his enthusiasm! The trouble was that one could never be certain which way the 'factor' worked, and there was only one way to find out the truth. Everything depended upon whether John wanted, or didn't want, people to go to particular places.

For example, if a cave was worked out it would be 'easy' regardless of the difficulties. Clearly the opposite applied here.

I dropped my reel and attached it to the line in case it could not be found due to the poor visibility when I pressed on. Then a return was made to the airbell between Sumps Two and Three to deposit my first cylinder. This was quite a homely spot I reflected, the low roof being devoid of mud (the depressing feature of the cave prior to Sump Two), and covered in a glittering array of white crystals. However it wasn't a place to delay as there was no dry ground, just knee-deep water at the shallowest point crouching against the wall. On the last dive Jeff Phillips had stood around here for an hour or so, chilled to the marrow. That was a thought I did not fancy.

The valves were swapped and within a short time I was finning confidently back into the disturbed waters of Sump Three. The reel was collected with no problem and I continued. As to the size of the passage I was completely lost as visibility was generally one metre, the water being extremely peaty and murky. By the depth gauge on my wrist, 8 metres was not exceeded and occasionally an attempt was made to surface, only to find the roof and surprisingly, the strange phenomenon of layered water. I had seen this before but never in such clearly defined layers. Near the roof, but not comprising a continuous layer, was a relatively clear layer of water giving visibility of perhaps 5 metres, while directly below was the normal layer of orange water where visibility was extremely poor, at about one metre.

As I travelled on bend after bend passed and I had few thoughts; this was certainly some dive. Eventually the reel dropped by Parker was reached, with 6 metres showing upon my depth gauge. The distance covered was estimated to be about 230 metres. A look at the pressure gauge confirmed my apprehension and the fact that it would not be feasible to reel out my 185 metres of line after using up the remainder on Parker's reel. John had estimated about 60 metres left and thinking that this would be ample for the air reserves left in my bottle I tied my reel to the existing line and pushed on into virgin territory with John's reel.

Route finding is certainly not easy in a huge passage with visibility at one metre and clearly it had been a fantastic feat, on John's part, to take the line reel as far as he had. I ended up following the right-hand wall with one or two attempts at surfacing. Generally the floor was the guide. I seemed to be bearing left all the while, when to my surprise I emerged into an airspace and continuing canal. It was almost beyond belief, a mere 30 metres beyond J.P.'s limit.

Within a few metres I was able to stand up, the water only knee deep. A large stone was soon found and the line belayed. I was still incredulous about my luck, but there I was, consciously standing beyond the longest sump in Britain; taciturn, but inwardly bursting with joy. In the distance there was a familiar rumble. It sounded like a waterfall. However, the characteristics of the passage beyond gave every indication of sumping once again. There was an estimated 45 metres of line left on the reel, so wading off downstream I let my curiosity take me on. The noise, a quiet rumbling, could mean one of two things: either the passage broke into open streamway and it lost its drab canal characteristics, or, which seemed more probable, an inlet made its entry... tumbling from some unknown height onto almost completely static water, prior to another sump.

Where I stood the passage was 8 metres wide and 3 metres high with deepening water in all directions. Within a few feet the floor ran out of my depth and I made an attempt to swim. Keeping your head above water is a problem when lightly equipped, but with the addition of a line reel it proved too much and I was forced to use bottle air, tactfully from the reserve cylinder. Cramp felt imminent but before it struck, my feet touched down on the floor, and 60 metres from Sump Three I was on a dry gravel bank; the stream tumbling away over a set of low cascades. In seconds the kit was lying against the wall and I set off to explore. The passage dimensions rapidly increased to an average 15 metres high and 8 metres wide, the stream itself (not noticeably larger than above Sump I) frequently occupying a narrow incised trench which I was forced to follow, owing to the extremely slippery nature of the rocks in the locality. Wet suit socks provided little protection for my feet, and progress was slow as I cautiously negotiated areas of brittle and crumbling ledges, before deciding to wade along in the water rather than attempt to stay dry. It might have been slower and cooler, but at least I couldn't fall anywhere.

The place was a gift and named Maytime in accordance with

the names in the rest of the cave. After some distance, later estimated at 180 metres, I came across an inlet on the left-hand side, issuing about the same volume of water as Southern Stream Passage; unfortunately from quite some height above the floor.

Beyond, the passage assumed pleasurable characteristics, often a flat, white limestone floor with shallow water, or mud and sandbanks. On either side innumerable passages were noted at high level and borne in mind for the return. Suddenly, as surely as it had turned from canal to stream-way below Sump Three, the stream rounded a corner and wound its way into the inevitable sump pool. The roof came down at a sharp angle, but the water looked surprisingly clear and inviting. The passage at the sump pool was 8 metres wide and 2 metres high and it looked like a short dive. Kit would be essential but psychologically I didn't feel up to the carry, especially as the gear was some considerable way off.

Feeling quite elated I made my way back, entering one high-level passage on the right-hand side after an airy 10- to 13-metre climb. The passage was in fact an oxbow but well worth the effort. Here I discovered a grotto with one particularly amazing helictite straw, two metres in length.

Other passages would clearly require boots to enter, as my wet socks gave no purchase on the steep mud. I made a brief attempt to gain the one and only active inlet but this was impossible. It emerged over ten metres up and would have to be left for the future.

Back at the kit, the total find was estimated to be somewhere in the neighbourhood of 460 metres plus. It was certainly the dream of every cave diver, but the euphoria was easily suppressed with the prospect of the outward journey.

The initial canal leading to the sump was now found to be less of a worry than hitherto when it proved just possible to tip-toe around the left-hand side. Then it was on into the long sump, the traverse consuming just ten cubic feet of air. A momentary stop was made in the airbell between Sumps Two and Three and the smooth uneventful exit was completed.

People could be heard in the distance and with a call they were at hand, helping the weary traveller from the water. I had brought Parker's reel out, but had left mine where I had tied it.

Everyone was in high spirits, but there was no mention of a further dive to explore beyond. We were all too tired to contemplate another trip and all we wanted was 'out' and a pint. The loads were distributed rather better on the outward journey, but as luck would have it, I still had a bottle to carry.

The time spent underground amounted to 12½ hours... a superb team effort. The whole trip had gone without a hitch and though we missed Saturday night at the pub, everyone felt pleasantly satisfied, in spite of being rather weary. Sunday was spent in the cavers' local hostelry — The Brittania — catching up on the two day's abstention.

It was to be a while before the compelling necessity to mount another trip arose. When it did, it was no snappy decision, but the inevitable outcome of an insatiable curiosity. What, I wanted to know, happened beyond Sump Four?

The earliest date that we could adequately arrange for a return was Saturday 15th June, and much preparation was needed to put the programme into operation. Support had been the greatest problem on the previous dive, but this trip was to be well publicised and we would make use of any volunteer we could possibly persuade to give us a helping hand. On the logistical side, gear was to be taken into the cave one week before, on 9th June, allowing us a 'free carry' in for the actual push. Additional support was to arrive later on in the day to help us out. But again there were problems, ones that were to lead, indirectly, to the final tragedy.

The greatest single setback was the failure to secure C.D.G. bottles from Bristol. This blow had been occasioned by our failure to return the borrowed cylinders, used on Saturday 25th May at Ogof Afon Hepste (Ystradfellte). Here Roger and I had passed a short sump at the end of Eastern Passage to discover 275 metres of passage. However we were late surfacing after the exploration and were subsequently unable to return the bottles to Bristol for filling and use in training the following week. Oliver's ban on our borrowing meant that a valuable source of air was terminated. More grievous as far as we were concerned was the loss of the specific type of bottle: the Draeger cylinder has the advantage of being less buoyant, when empty, than any other medium-pressure bottles. Another advantage lay in the fact that they were ideally suited to long carries possessing a special 'T' shaped cylinder neck valve. The previous dive had been completely dependent on these C.D.G. bottles and their future non-availability was a stunning blow.

However, we were not forced entirely onto our own resources. Roger had the use of a friend's 40 cu/ft cylinder (low pessure and a larger version of the 'tad') to supplement his own 40 cu/ft low-pressure Sealion bottle. I possessed two high-pressure negatively-buoyant 45 cu/ft bottles, but unfortunately could only get one filled for the occasion. I had the option of using a Sealion 40- or a 47-cu/ft bottle. The latter was chosen, despite its disadvantage of being heavy (just over 18 pounds), purely because of its negative characteristics and consequent ease of management when depleted of air. Apart from bottles, our equipment was personal. Roger had at last invested in a new valve, a Typhoon, to supplement and in effect replace his trusty Snark II Silver, which had really done the rounds. The latter must have been fairly robust, for it survived a 43-metre fall, down the entrance shaft of Noon's Hole in Ireland: it did however, require slight repair. My valves consisted of two U.S. Divers Deepstars, an early and late model, both of which were of proven quality, and thoroughly trusted.

The unknown factor in any such preparation, is the porters and of one thing you can be certain — hardly anyone will carry for you twice, especially to a place like Agen Allwedd. Living in a flat with cavers I had a slight advantage. Over a particularly good evening session down the pub, Bomber got so oiled that he agreed to loan me his bottle. I couldn't believe it. He'd only bought it the week before and there wasn't even a scratch on it! The next morning was a totally different matter though and when Bomber discovered that he'd talked himself into a corner, he reluctantly found that he had to join the expedition if only to keep an eye on the bottle. Quite clearly immediate diving friends would not provide the numbers we needed. These were supplemented by writing and persuading other associates.

Sunday 9th June, and our date for carrying in arrived. Parking at the 'tramroad car park' west of White Walls, it was evident that not all the gear could be taken in. Yes, the so called glory of portering had died years ago! I had arrived from Penwyllt, the H.Q. of South Wales Caving Club, accompanied by Bomber and two others while Roger who had recruited Dave Underhill had arrived separately. We split into two parties to facilitate faster movement through the cave and about midday Bomber, Geoff Billington and I set off. Geoff carried the large ammo box, Bomber his new bottle, while I was lumbered with my bottle, fins and a 90-metre line reel. We didn't meet the others inside the cave, and it was clear that our party was making the better time.

At the sump, and some three and a half hours later, we deposited our respective burdens. I also divested myself of an old wet suit jacket to save having to carry it in the following week. One woollen jumper, worn beneath, proved to be ideal for the journey out, which to make the trip more interesting was via Biza Passage and the Fourth Choke (The Grand Circle Route). The gear was checked for damage or loss of air and satisfied with our work, apart from Bomber's reluctance to leave his new bottle to rust, we set off. The whole trip took six hours, emerging to a beautiful, warm evening and the scent of hawthorn blossom carried on the breeze. Reaching the car park and feeling hungry, we located Roger's keys, which were concealed in his bumper, helped ourselves to a few of his biscuits, and left a note before departing. The second party made faster progress via the Fourth Choke and were only an hour behind us on exit.

At this point in time things were looking up. Support increased as throughout the week we received confirmation of help from several groups. The week drifted by, apprehensively split by a dive to Wookey 20 on the Wednesday night. This was to retrieve the C.D.G. line reel that I had lost at Easter, and was performed entirely on borrowed gear.

On Friday night, 14th June, just before closing time, we gathered in The Brittania at Crickhowell. I wouldn't call it a premonition, but there was definitely a feeling of unease beneath the superficial jollity. We learned that Roger had undertaken a solo trip on the Tuesday night, carrying his ammo box, tad and a wet suit overjacket which he had deposited at the Waterfall, three-quarters of the way in. His trip had not been without its share of excitement though, for in the Main Chamber his main bulb had blown and he had had to fumble around in the complete darkness to relocate his pilot bulb in the main bulb socket. What other person could undertake such a task after a days work (in Chepstow) in the knowledge that if he had had an accident there would have been no-one to help him and that he would have been unable to cave on the Saturday? There are few people of his calibre.

Accommodation for the night had been arranged at the Ruin, a cosy little hut some distance from the Chelsea headquarters. It was a superb spot, one of the few places where one could be guaranteed a decent night's sleep. As this was unable to cater for everyone, another group of people found a roof at White Walls, whilst Colin Fairbairn and John Elliot slept beneath the stars.

Saturday morning there was no desperate need to get underground early; the pressure was off. Outside Terry Moon was found asleep, curled up in the back of his car. The day promised to be one of the best that a British summer can offer.

The plans were finalised. John and Colin together with two lads from Harlow were to set off at 10.30 am for the sump, transporting the last few items of equipment to the diving base. They were then to await our arrival.

In our turn Roger and I left the Ruin about 11.15 am, being accompanied up to the tram road by Bomber and Terry. Both were to come in later for the slog out. At White Walls the motley and merriest group of individuals one could meet cheered, or rather hurled abuse, as we approached.

'Late again Farr!... Should have been underground hours ago.'

'Pull your bloody finger out!' and so on.

Old and valued friends chatted beneath a now scorching sun and cloudless sky. It was almost too good to be true. The plans were outlined. Never had so many people turned out to help. I turned to Bomber:

'Be at the sump about 5.00 pm... you may as well go for a pint while you wait.' And with that Bomber was gone.

Terry walked over to the cave with us and with the customary farewells, we were away. The pace was deliberately slowed, to prevent sweating sapping our energy. We saw no-one until we arrived about two hours later at 2.00 pm, at the junction of Southern Stream with the Mainstream. Here Roger, Colin, John and the two Harlow lads sat back as I relieved myself into the streamway a few yards downstream. This is a difficult manoeuvre underground at the best of times, but more-so amid a bombardment of mud and attempted splashing.

'Bloody hell Farr you must pollute every cave you go to,'

somebody shouted, referring to my well-known need to relieve myself before any major dive. By now I was immune to the jibes and the tension relieved, we set off on the last 100 metres for the kit and the sump.

Within half an hour we were gone, each wearing a tad for the first two sumps and allowing two full bottles for Sumps Three and Four. Our friends similarly departed from the sump base, aiming to exit via the Fourth Choke.

On diving visibility was a good three or four metres, at least for myself in the lead. The pot-hole in the floor of Sump One was clearly visible, but not the bottom. With no hesitation, I just cruised straight over the top, but recalling as I did so the problems encountered by another team during first exploration in 1963.

Then they had humped full-weight oxygen sets down the cave, a real feat in itself. The quantity of lead required for bottom walking must have been considerable and apparently one of the divers had stumbled over the edge of the pot, being unable to see it through all the silt which he had kicked up. Such an occurrence was critical in those days for even if the diver or his equipment were undamaged after a fall there were other hazards to be overcome. If the hole or total depth was over 10 metres then oxygen poisoning would ensue. If the hole was particularly precipitous or overhanging then there was the very real problem of how to get out again. One only had a very thin guideline and these were not designed for pulling upon, merely as a route marker. The early pioneers certainly deserve the highest tribute. Here in Sump One the diver had managed to grasp the line before he overbalanced and though shaken made his exit unharmed.

We were now diving separately but met again after a few minutes at the airbell between Sumps Two and Three. Here we deposited our tads on a rock before continuing. Everything was proceeding happily to plan and Roger's only comment concerned the length of Sump Two, maintaining that he would free dive it on the way out.

I dived on with Roger allowing me a lead of several minutes. Progress was deliberately slow and relaxed as we were both carrying reels and boots. In such a manner the least amount of air would be used. Roger surfaced about a minute after me in the canal beyond and we waded to the shore, the start of the flowing streamway.

We had both carried Mars bars through the three sumps, tucked inside our wet suit jackets, and surprisingly enough they were were still recognisable. Placing the squelchy food on the sand bank, we donned our boots and were away. Fully loaded, the carry was far from pleasant, and in no way easier than it had been remembered. A fleeting thought brought John Parker to mind, who only a few weeks previously had returned by himself with the expressed aim of diving Sump Four and exploring whatever he could. In the event he had failed to dive Four but had managed to enter a few more side passages, largely owing to the fact that he had taken boots. Nothing significant had been found.

As all was going smoothly I was optimistic and I could sense Roger thoroughly enjoying the passage, difficult though it was.

'How far did you say it was?' (between Sumps Three and Four).

'460 metres' I replied.

Roger maintained that it was rather more and together we estimated 615 metres to be more realistic. Passing a huge boulder perched in a sand bank we arrived at the final corner, and here the characteristics of the passage changed. The roof came down at an angle of 5°-10° and this trend continued below water. On the previous trip, the pool had been quite clear, that is with visibility of about six metres. Today, it was peaty and ominous.

'How are we going to tackle it then?' I asked. The question had to be put in one form or another.

'I don't know' he replied, followed almost immediately by 'I'll run out this 123 metre reel and you can carry on.' The clear implication was that if we were to dive separately he would set it up for me to make the breakthrough. I did not want this.

'Or we can dive together?' was my alternative.

'O.K.' he replied and an air of quiet satisfaction settled on us.

We changed over our main valves (only the main valve carried a pressure gauge) onto the full bottle, leaving the other which had been used in the 260-metre sump as reserve. A cursory joke was passed about either one of us turning back at whatever point we wished and we thoroughly dealt with the signals to be used underwater. These were based on common-sense and experience.

'Are we taking boots?' he asked.

AGEN ALLWEDD   TERMINAL DOWNSTREAM

Plan View

Key :

A   Sump 4 Explored for 185 metres

Sump continues

Inlet

Cross Section from A to A1 on above plan

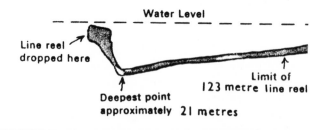

Water Level

Line reel dropped here

Deepest point approximately 21 metres

Limit of 123 metre line reel

It was as though he too felt that it was to be just a dive with no dry extension beyond. Optimistically I replied that it had been done in wet suit socks before and a little further would not hurt. Depositing our boots on the mudbank just before the sump, one of Roger's last comments was that he was underweighted.

Then taking up the 123-metre reel he was gone. I waited

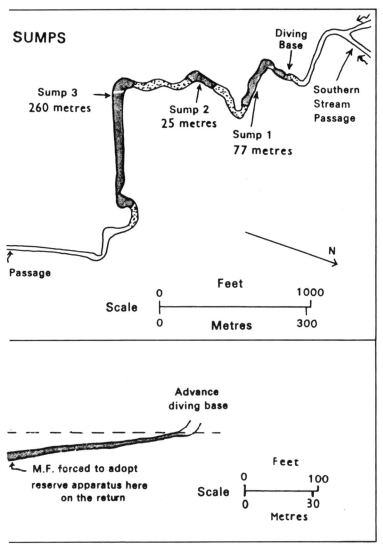

SUMPS

Sump 3
260 metres

Sump 2
25 metres

Sump 1
77 metres

Diving
Base

Southern
Stream
Passage

Passage

N

Scale

Feet	
0	1000
0	300
Metres	

Advance
diving base

M.F. forced to adopt
reserve apparatus here
on the return

Scale

Feet	
0	100
0	30
Metres	

perhaps a minute or two and followed, soon catching him up. Being directly behind him I had visibility of only about a metre, so I took the line diagonally to the left where I was able to see clearly again, and followed at a distance of about two metres. The route was straightforward and spacious (6 metres wide, 3 metres high) and things were going smoothly.

63

Roger stopped several times and complained about clearing his sinuses, which he did each time close to the roof. I indicated that if he was not happy he could turn back and I would go on with my reel. But he went on, always beneath the roof, while I followed hugging the floor. It was clear that we were going deep, though how deep I had no idea. Suddenly he stopped, and when I looked at him he indicated 'end of line!' Instinctively I looked at my pressure gauge which read about 90 atmospheres. Originally it had been over 160. I held it up to his face, as I had not seen him look to his. I indicated that I was going on, and tied my reel onto Roger's line. At this point he cut his reel free of the line and attached it with a simple knot to the now continuing line. It was a wooden reel and as such was disposable, but even so we intended to take it out for future use. Now it floated one metre above the floor like a hydrogen balloon tied down by a cord. I went on unsure if he would follow.

About 30 metres later, I reached a very steeply ascending gravel bank. The passage was greatly reduced in size at this point, but was still over 1.5 metres in height. Knowing full well that my air reserves were very low, I nevertheless felt compelled to take the gamble. I glanced back. There was no sign of Roger. I shot off as fast as possible, the effort of ascending being extremely demanding. That there had to be air up there somewhere was my only thought. The gravel bank ended at a vertical wall which I ascended: 6 metres, 7 metres, 8 metres. I continued up to over 12 metres before I met the roof! There was nothing to say. There was no air; water was everywhere... but at least I was on my own. I looked to the right and gained a few metres, but to no avail. Turning back there was Roger against the roof above me. I looked to my pressure gauge — 50 atmospheres! Hurriedly I swam over to him, indicated that I was going back to base, dropped my reel to one side and sped off down the line.

This was the last that I saw of him.

He looked worried but still had firm hold of the line. At the bottom of the slope the depth was estimated at 15-18 metres. My sinuses were painful, due to the 'crash' clearance. It was a long way to air and any minute I would need to change to my reserve set. I passed the 'joining of lines' one third of the way back (furthest point being 185 metres) and psychologically attuned for the crucial exchange. A little beyond I stopped, took a couple of deep breaths and swapped. The spare breathed easily and one crisis was past.

At this point I had 145 atmospheres in the reserve while I left 25 atmospheres in my first bottle — a meagre reserve for the long dive out. Waiting for two to three minutes I contemplated heading back a short distance but ruled against it. There was no feel of Roger on the line. I carried on out, the visibility being greatly reduced.

As I surfaced I became aware of an incredible head pain and for about five minutes I stood there waist deep in the pool in agony and barely able to see. If Roger had been on the line during this period I had no way of telling. Then, shocked, I came to, realised the seriousness of the situation, and began to wait for his emergence. The most unpleasant possibilities, together with my headache, were pushed to the back of my mind as I thought of what Roger might be doing. My hope was that at the furthest point he had located air . . . perhaps even dry passage and had either gone off to explore or was resting before his return.

Some time later I pulled in one or two metres of slack line and left it floating on the water. As soon as he was on the way back this piece of line would be jerked and I would know in advance of his approach. Still kitted I climbed out of the water onto the small mudbank. There was nothingness.

For us to be apart for any length of time was not unusual for I had frequently been off exploring solo for several hours beyond sumps. On the Arch cave breakthrough (Fermanagh), which Roger had set up, I was away from base for nearly three hours, during which time Roger had insufficient air to make a return dive and search. I was away for over an hour at both Tullyhona (Fermanagh) and Boreham Cave (Yorks.). In Dan yr Ogof Roger had made the breakthrough into Mazeways II and had been exploring for over half an hour before I joined him. We both knew the score and had complete faith in the ability and commonsense of the other. All that I could do now was to wait.

After what seemed like an eternity, but perhaps was only half an hour, I could stand the waiting no longer. The sound of the stream trickling into the sump pool was playing tricks on my hearing and sounded like muffled and distant voices. The overwhelming feeling of helplessness was indescribable. I had to do something and, de-kitting, arrived at a course of action. I would take the empty bottle back to the top sump. Doing this I would be saving time later and at the same time I could pick up the food and bring it back to Roger. If he wasn't back by the time I got back, I would have a look down the line.

The return to Sump Three was just a matter of getting there and I saw little. Dropping the bottle I collected the food and suddenly feeling nervous I virtually ran back to Four. But still there was nothing; had been nothing, for the loop of line still floated limp in the water. I could not bring myself to kit up straightaway so I curled up on the mudbank and tried to rest. I ate, or rather pushed down a Mars bar. Worried as I was, I nearly fell asleep. I felt stiff... walked around... settled down again. There was no feeling of cold but the time lay heavy. Slowly, ever so slowly, I realised what I had to do. I had to go and have a look. I had 100 atmospheres in the bottle, at least 50 of which I needed to pass Sump Three. If I used 20 out of the 50 that I had at my disposal to dive in on, I would get virtually nowhere. However it was an effort that I had to make. Kitting up I waded in. I didn't want to dive.

Now I decided to pull on the line to try and establish if he had belayed it securely beyond, or the possibility that didn't bear contemplating — that is if I was to pull direct upon the line reel. If the latter were the case it could only mean one thing, that he had run out of air on the return. One way or another I would have an indication. I pulled... slack, pulled... slack. It was 30 metres before the only alternative that had not occurred to me presented itself. The line was coming in much too easily. I threw it by the armful onto the mudbank... passed the knot at 123 metres, and 9 metres later reached a perfectly cut end.

I cried. He had become entangled on the return and had cut himself free. There are only two occasions when a caver cuts the line while on a dive. The first is when he reaches the limit of exploration and the line is to be left in place. In this instance it is purposely cut, the loose end being tied to some object and the reel brought out. The second is where he becomes hopelessly entangled and has to cut himself free before the air runs out; this is very rare and only occurs under extreme duress.

In Roger's case the trouble with the line could only have occurred during the five minutes that I was incapacitated, otherwise the slack line that I had pulled in would have been jerked taut. Now I was in a situation whereby I had no reel, as the simple retaining knot on the wooden reel had worked loose, and 132 metres of thin orange line strewn on mud-bank and water. Even though a self 'base-fed' system for laying line would not have been impossible to rig up (simply dragging a length of line after myself) — at least for a few metres — I knew in myself that there was little that I could achieve. I knew too, that in truth I could not face it.

I took my fins off, donned my boots and walked away in a complete daze. Had I known the line to have been cut earlier, what would I have done? It could all have been a dream were it not for the pair of Roger's boots left lying on the mud-bank.

At the head of the extension I kitted up and waded the canal to the sump. There I wished him farewell and dived. Cramp developed in one leg, then in the other, but it left. Reaching the tads I had no clear thoughts but decided to bring them out. Sumps Two and One were not easy being grossly underweight, but my mind was peaceful. There seemed to be no feeling of stress, only calm resignation. My breathing was very relaxed and little air was used.

Tired and mentally exhausted, I crawled out of the water expecting to see someone. Surely not everyone would have gone — but they had. Still calm — a little detached from all that was happening — perhaps in shock I bore no malice. They had probably thought that we had found another extension, and had gone off to explore. The pitiful irony. De-kitting in silence, I packed my valves neatly in their box, cast a sorrowful glance to the rear and set off. For several minutes I stood at Southern Stream Junction, watching the turgid brown discharge from the tributary being engulfed and dispersed by the Mainstream. Then I was away.

The entrance: mechanically I signed out with not a clue as to the time. A few paces further and I noticed a distinct light in the skies. Was it dawn? It had to be. But no, the final touch to the unreality of the events came in the form of sheet lightning. There wasn't even any rain. Confused and dazed I wandered back along the track. How different to past trips. A glow worm! I couldn't remember ever having seen one before, so I stopped. It was a small inconspicuous little caterpillar, only about one centimetre in length and glowing a beautiful luminous green.

There was still a chance. There had to be. I made straight for the Ruin to alert Bomber and Terry, but on arrival found no-one in residence. Dropping everything I realised that they must be waiting up at White Walls, probably drinking. The walk was brief. I pushed in the door and I guess my expression said it all. Only Bomber had arrived back from the pub and he initiated the call-out.

EVENTS SUBSEQUENT TO THE CALL-OUT

At midnight Bill Wilkes, of the Gwent Cave Rescue Team, was alerted at his home in Govilon. He quickly assumed the position of Rescue Co-ordinator and the laborious job of setting wheels in motion began. As usual the police were the first to be informed (due to the need for insurance cover on rescue personnel). Bottles were organised from Bristol and capable divers had to be contacted, not the easiest thing after midnight on a Saturday.

A major call-out was initiated and people descended on White Walls from all points of the compass. Telephones were laid into the cave and when the key personnel had arrived, a decision was made to start a recovery attempt at 8.00 pm on Sunday. By this time it was hoped that all the preparations could be carried out. It would also give the divers John Parker and Colin Edmunds time to rest and psychologically prepare for their task.

From my point of view I felt there should be no delay as every second wasted would reduce Roger's chances of survival. In my opinion John and Colin would do better to go straight in; they were unlikely to sleep, just worry, and by getting straight on with the job they would have no time to ponder. I was hopeful that Roger had found air. There had to be air. Despite the optimism and apparent ability for clear thinking my nerves were shattered. I felt that I just could not bring myself to see him if, as I really felt, he was dead and floating beneath the roof in the murky water.

About 3.30 am Bomber and I left for my home five miles away, to rest and notify our parents. The upsets were great when our respective families were informed, but we both slept for a couple of hours, ate and arrived back on the scene about 9.30 am.

During the night Roger's parents had arrived but left shortly afterwards, on hearing of the state of affairs. It was no place for them. Another event colouring the incident was the fact that a party from Swansea University (who had come to help us) were long overdue and a secondary rescue had to be organised on their behalf. They finally emerged just before 7.30 am extremely fatigued but under their own steam. On failing to route find in the Third Choke they had been forced to return, through the Fourth and back up Southern Stream... their way of entry.

During the night bottles had been carried into the cave, but deposited in various caches down Southern Stream, and plans had been officially formulated for the day. These involved establishing a food dump at the sump, portering the rest of the diving gear to the site, and arranging personnel for the various jobs. At 8.00 pm it would all start.

Inside White Walls the 'commanders' reigned supreme. A blackboard exhibited the plan of campaign. Outside, police radios were constantly in use and a landrover or squad car was ever present. A further addition to the gathering was the one element I deeply resented: the reporters. Without even a basic understanding of the whole affair they asked the wrong questions; misinterpreted the answers and later wrote the greatest trash a person could have the misfortune to read. They had their job to do and they did it. Such was the atmosphere that pervaded the Llangattock escarpment that day.

All through the day people arrived and left, while key personnel took their rest. Bomber and I had been to the pub at lunchtime. It all felt like some horrible dream, from which escape was impossible. Returning to the tramroad later we had strolled over to the cave and back to meet some close friends. The air still felt tense and sporadic electric storms were hindering communications. At one point the telephonists actually received a shock when lightning struck a cable.

19.35 hours and the diving party, John and Colin, left for the cave. Five cavers went along in support. After their departure Bomber and I left, returning in the early hours of Monday to inquire after the outcome. About 3.30 am it was learned that the dive was a complete failure, owing to bad visibility in Sump One. It was now clear that diving would have to be abandoned for the time being. Shortly after 6.00 am there was a general stand-down from the rescue, following the exit of all personnel from the cave.

This was tragic. All hope was now ruled out. The only two divers in the country who, it was generally agreed, were completely capable of reaching Sump 4 had turned back. Why? The answer was not flooding, as several papers were later to print, but simple human miscalculation. Southern Stream had been churned into a mud-bath through the passage of so many cavers. This in turn had muddied the Mainstream leading to the inevitable lack of visibility in the sump. Colin had dived for about 15 metres experiencing zero visibility and had returned. As leader, John had then called off the dive on the assumption that a search would be pointless under the conditions, and an unnecessary risk.

Both divers would clearly need a few days rest before another attempt and in this period it was hoped that the water would clear. Any further attempt would now be of the nature of a recovery.

Plans were laid for Thursday to locate the body and if possible remove the bottles for the coroner's inspection. Bringing the body out was probably beyond the bounds of possibility and it was hoped that a burial could be made in a sandbank between Sumps Three and Four. The whole affair was escalating into a living nightmare. I wanted it over, behind me. One of the worse moments I remember was actually returning to Cardiff and my flat. The sun was shining and it all seemed so peaceful — yet I was leaving one of my best friends behind. Was he in an airbell?

On Tuesday Bomber, Geoff Billington and I went down to the sump and collected most of our gear. We had heard that one bottle at least had been severely treated on a partial carry out. It had been dropped and left somewhere just upstream of the Waterfall. We brought out the more valuable items leaving the two tads in the cave which might be of some use later.

On Thursday, June 20th, the whole procedure began again. Communications were re-established between White Walls and the cave, food dumps were manned and John and Colin, in the absence of alternative capable volunteers were ready to try once more. At 2.45 pm the divers and their support party left White Walls. On arrival at the sump, conditions had indeed improved and both dived without problem to Sump Three. Here they encountered mud. The possibility of the turgid waters not having been swept from the sumps had not been entertained. Surely the rain earlier in the week would have flushed the system? Clearly this was not the case.

Colin was feeling uneasy and returned to base. John pressed on alone. Knowing that Sump Four would also be muddy this was a truly selfless and praiseworthy action; a typical expression of his phlegmatic nature. He searched over 120 metres into Sump Four, but in the poor visibility could find no trace of the body. He confirmed the findings with the cut line and brought the last metre out with him (for the coroner). Everyone in the diving party reached White Walls by 1.25 am on 21st June and after discussion, it was decided that no further attempts would be made. A total of 2,760 man hours were taken on the rescue.

A memorial service was held at Holy Trinity Church, Drybrook, on Sunday, 30 June 1974, with a massive attendance by friends and comrades from all over Britain.

It was six years before I could find the courage to go back to Agen Allwedd. In August 1980 I, accompanied by Mark Campbell, ferried a full set of climbing equipment through the sumps to the dry passages in the Maytime Extension. All the high-level openings were thoroughly explored as it was considered that there might be a connection with the recently discovered system Craig ar Ffynnon situated close to the Agen Allwedd Resurgence. Unfortunately the total length of passage in the extension was not appreciably increased and the active side inlet became impassably tight within a very short distance of the main streamway.

A marathon 17-hour assault was made on the cave in October 1980 when, assisted by Rob Palmer as far as the last sump, Dave Morris and I attempted to continue the exploration. The dive was thwarted by bad visibility, an entanglement 30 metres into Sump Four and fatigue incurred by the carry.

In July 1981, again assisted by Rob Palmer, I made another solo exploration of Sump Four. The deepest point in the sump was found to be 22 metres while a short distance beyond, at the 1974 limit, the depth registered one metre. I encountered a few disturbing remains at this point, but moving on in the direction in which it was presumed there could well be an air surface, I found that the trend was once more downward. Here difficulties were presented by route finding, bad visibility and the old line which as predicted had been swept downstream. I abandoned the dive about 30 metres beyond the limit set in 1974.

4

The American Odyssey

CAVING IN THE ROCKIES AND MEXICO

From school I had progressed to university, and from there to work and teaching. Having come full circle as it were I yearned to do something unusual, certainly away from a mundane or academic point of view. While at university in Cardiff my sights had levelled on those elusive places such as Castleguard, El Sotano and Golondrinas; magical names conjuring up images of classic systems and offering a wholly different experience to that of Britain or Europe.

At this time, the early 1970s, it seemed as though virtually everything was happening in North America. The Mammoth-Flint Ridge Connection was made in 1972, some deep and exciting new systems were being discovered in Mexico, some exceptionally hard caving was getting underway in the Rockies and the cave diving in Florida was breathtaking. Equally as significant was the fact that the Americans had developed the S.R.T. (Single Rope Technique) system to a level unequalled anywhere in the world. However there was no way in which I could even hope to go directly after graduation as I had no funds. I had to get some cash together.

Having landed a teaching post, doubt followed doubt as I pondered the idea of taking a year or so off. My parents' eyebrows rose at the thought; I had no support there. By comparison with other jobs school holidays were generous and I could usually manage to confine expeditions to them, but the caves that I wanted to visit now would have to be visited in the winter and I would need a few months to do them in. Situated in the high Rockies of Alberta, Castleguard, for example was flood prone during the summer owing to melting snow and ice, and could only be visited in winter. Then too, both El Sotano and Golondrinas lay in north eastern Mexico (south of the tropic of

Cancer), many miles from civilisation or even roads, and so intense was the heat in summer that it virtually precluded any access to the caves. Talking to Pete Lord who had already undertaken a grand tour of North America and who possessed a long list of caving contacts, finally decided me: as soon as I was fully qualified I was off to 'do it while I could'.

My first experience of a large comprehensive in Cardiff was a nightmare. It was only four years since I had left school myself, a small grammar school of 360 boys, and the baptism to the system which I now joined was definitely by fire. Discipline and respect were at a very low ebb; the role of teacher was clearly that of entertainer. My sanity was retained only by thumping the odd lout and leaving the job behind at 4.00 pm.

In retrospect, evening routine at this stage was amusing, especially to Bomber. I'd get into the flat first, face like thunder; the cat quickly learning to not get in the way. Breaking out a bottle of home brew I'd stagger over the six diving cylinders rolling about at the head of the stairs, slump into an easy chair and proceed to drink the lot — sediment and all. By the time Chris arrived I would be in a slightly better frame of mind, we would swap tales and then I would watch Chris hit the bottle. The landlady was convinced we were a bunch of debauched alcoholics; it was nothing to see 20 empty bottles, littering the floor.

Much to my relief I gained my probationary qualification, — and shortly afterwards I applied for three months 'leave of absence' to undertake the American venture. The authorities had different ideas though: they called my proposals irresponsible and the county advisor made it clear, in no uncertain terms, that if I went I'd never get a job in the area again! Had I been a rugby player no doubt there wouldn't have been any problem. Unfortunately I was just a caver. Disillusioned, I threw in my job. I justified the venture to myself with ease; I was a geographer and the experience and first-hand information I would gain would be invaluable for future posts.

With stomach churning I left Heathrow on 13th October 1975.

There was no way out now. I must have looked a real greenhorn as I boarded the plane tidily dressed with brand new duvet, gleaming boots and jeans; but not an inch of space was wasted, the relative merit of everything carried being carefully scrutinised countless times beforehand.

On arrival in New York I experienced that cold off-hand behaviour that everyone in the States seems to associate with people from the north east. Difficulty was found getting to the city itself and I was eventually befriended by this 'arty-type' chap off my flight who invited me to stay at his place. I should have known better; he was queer.

The next morning I felt even more apprehensive and it was almost with relief that I boarded the Greyhound Bus at the Port Authority Building. With the two-month pass which I had purchased back home the plan was to travel as far as I could first, then reach the Mexican border in mid December, when it expired.

My first contact was Bill Boman in West Virginia. Here I was introduced to the best of American hospitality and after a weekend caving, or 'pit-dropping', as they called it, I moved on to Calgary, Alberta, in the hope of doing a trip or two in the high Rockies — including Castleguard — before the weather closed in for the winter. Bill's wife Donna very kindly furnished me with a food parcel, and, attempting to live on one dollar a day I set off on the three-day, 1500-mile, journey. By now I'd picked up additional caving clothes and boots which added appreciably to my load. The Greyhound system was superb in that I could freight any unnecessary items on ahead free of charge, and these would then be stored safely to await collection in a few days or weeks time.

Once in Calgary I planned to call up my contact Mike Shawcross. I was also hoping to meet up with the Australian Neil Montgomery who'd left Britain after a whirlwind tour of our classic caves. Neil had earned enough in eight month's working as a refuse collector to fund a year's caving around the globe. If anyone could fix up a trip to Castleguard it was Neil.

Journey's end, and I was glad to get on my feet again. After sleeping two consecutive nights on the bus and suffering all the contortions this required, my body was stiff though slowly becoming attuned to roughing it. I found Mike's number and dialled. Someone answered.

'Boon speaking'. Completely unknown to me the famed Mike Boon was staying at the Shawcross flat.

'No wheels, you'll have to get around as best you can,' he said.

75

It was only about two miles to walk but the air was crisp and the temperature down to freezing point. How different the weather was from New York where autumn had barely taken a hold. Weary muscles needed the exercise while the mind was still trying to grasp the scale of things; still juggling with British comparisons.

An hour later I had tracked down the basement flat and was firmly ensconsed. I'd met Boon once before at a B.C.R.A. conference in Manchester. At the time he'd not been overly sociable due to a surfeit of ale. Here he was totally different: friendly and accommodating.

Dishevelled and unshaven he gestured to the stove where a saucepan of soup was quietly simmering.

'It was a stew, but I finished off the good bits yesterday, help yourself.'

A quick glance around confirmed suspicions; times were hard.

I guess Boon was something of a hero to me. Single-handed he had tackled probably the hardest cave in North America and pushed it by climbing an aven miles underground, a point that the then leading Canadian cavers had only managed to reach after several major expeditions. I remember vividly listening to Tony Waltham relating an anecdote concerning the 'crazy exploit'. Boon supposedly had set out with three carbide lights; one was accidentally dropped down an impenetrable fissure near the entrance, and when the other wouldn't work instead of giving up he made the three-day trip using just one light! It made a good story even if it wasn't strictly true. Boon was also the character who had pioneered the use of open-circuit, aqualung equipment for cave diving in Britain, had made several intrepid breakthroughs in Swildons and who had subsequently turned his attentions overseas, latterly Mexico — and all on a shoestring!

I'd missed Montgomery by a couple of days and there were no immediate plans for a trip. But Boon was nothing if not resourceful. Nakimu Caves, in the Glacier National Park, possessed an unexplored streamway which he was keen to survey. Weatherwise, conditions were ideal for such a project as the flow of water through the system would be minimal during the winter. Situated over 100 miles away, the Rogers Pass was one of the 'local' caving areas. The sheer distance involved in reaching American caves is a feature that quickly impresses itself upon any visitor.

Boon had no car so Wesley Davies was recruited. Late one night we arrived at a forestry cabin in the Park, a welcome haven after the blizzard we had just battled through. Inside it was spartan but none the less a superb refuge for anyone marooned by the elements. The three of us crashed out on wooden tressles, and despite the cold, were quickly asleep. Breakfast was cooked by courtesy of a hill-billy-type cast-iron log-burning stove, and even a good stack of logs was provided. I couldn't help thinking that the park wardens wouldn't be impressed by the thought of scrounging, dossing cavers taking up residence (most caving huts back in Britain were in a far worse state).

Outside, more snow had fallen and it was a very eerie feeling peering through rare gaps in the depressingly low cloud on the silent pine slopes. Renting the hillsides at every angle were gashes inflicted by the annual avalanches. A blue jay cheekily hopped to and fro near our door eagerly devouring anything that was thrown its way. But apart from its squark and fluttering wings the silence was complete; I found it oppressive.

A mile or so down the road lay the parking spot from where we were to make the long trek up the steep forest path to Nakimu Cave. When we got there however, it was to find a couple of ranger's wagons parked and Boon cursing. Unknown to me the cave was officially closed and we would have to return to the hut and bide our time until they left. The day was passed taking coffee, looking at a potential diving site and sleeping on the horribly uncomfortable park benches in the hut. Boon obviously had a great affinity for sleeping — he was totally indifferent to his surroundings and clearly in his element snugly wrapped up in his tattered bag.

Only with the approach of dusk did we venture forth again. The snow was knee deep on the slope and we had been trudging along in silence for probably half an hour when Boon casually let it drop that only recently bears had killed a couple of rangers in the area. Wesley passed some comment; I looked over my shoulder. Until that moment my thoughts had been wholly absorbed by the cave and the physical difficulty of getting there. Now I felt queasy; the dark forest and hidden recesses made an ideal trap for the unwary. Once again I felt green and discreetly I manoeuvred from last place to the middle of the group. The flickering light from our carbides danced mystically across the precipitous slope;

to the left lay a valley of unfathomable blackness; the route was hard and the doubts were mounting.

We reached the entrance, slid in over a drift and changed. While trying to put on a brave face I was really beginning to wonder what the hell I'd let myself in for. The cave was extremely cold and as one might expect, the stream was barely above freezing. It was easy to see why this section of passage had not been traversed before. Very steeply-inclined small pitches were interspersed with raging, swirling and thundering cataracts. Aesthetically it was beautiful: the rock itself comprised innumerable bands of varying colours; heavily metamorphosed limestone glistened like marble in the flickering light of our lamps.

Eventually we succeeded in making a survey of the section, by which time Wesley and I were shaking with the cold. Boon, although wearing an ill-fitting and borrowed wet suit appeared quite comfortable. We regained the entrance chamber to change at 5.00 am, and not a moment too soon.

Scampering under a boulder near my clothes I noticed a squirrel-like creature with a beautiful bush tail.

'What's that?' I asked.

'A bloody pack rat,' shouted Boon. 'Check your things.' And sure enough my socks and balaclava had been ravaged to furnish the little sod with his winter nest. I was learning fast!

Boon then told us about his Castleguard trip, when having carried in relays, three rucksacks over the difficult terrain to the cave entrance, he had woken the next morning to find a pack rat had eaten the tongue and substantial part of his boot; his one and only pair. Enraged, Boon forgot the cave and set to hunting down the pest. All morning was spent checking out every crack and alcove. But by the time he'd tracked the rat down and had it at his mercy all enmity had dissipated; in a highly philosophical frame of mind he let it go — on the grounds that it too had to survive.

Only later did I learn a few other details concerning the venture. It transpired that having walked down to civilisation Boon was totally broke, without even sufficient money to get him back to Calgary. Ever resourceful he marched into one of the large newspapers in Edmonton and sold the story for the price of a bus ticket to the flat. Once described as a 'latter-day Oliver Twist' Boon certainly has a knack for survival, though apparently no aspirations towards customary worldly possessions.

In worsening weather however our trip to Castleguard was out of the question. I wasn't going to risk falling into a crevasse on the Sasketchewan Glacier and I was really feeling the cold. Back in Calgary, Boon came up with the suggestion that I travel up to the Yukon, several hundred miles further north, to take a look at a promising virgin area. But with the maps spread out on the floor enthusiasm for the project rapidly cooled. The area was extremely remote; I'd have to talk nicely to the bus driver, make arrangements to be picked up two days later at an isolated point on the trans-American highway, battle over rough terrain to the cave area and sit up all night with a blazing fire to ward off the bears, wolves and wolverines. As we were talking a mate just happened to drop by for a chat and the next thing I knew they were trying to fix me up with snow shoes. If Boon had been able to go then I might have gone for the idea; as it stood he was broke and I had visions of providing an easy meal for the first hungry wolf that happened to come my way. In short I declined the offer.

The best idea seemed to be to head in the opposite direction — south — before I ended up prey to another of Boon's ambitious projects.

Down in Montana I fell in with Jim Chester. He struck me immediately as a sort of cheery airforce squadron leader: he sported a superb moustache and exuded an air of knowledge and efficiency. The warm atmosphere and the very best home cooking made Jim's house a memorable landmark of the trip.

An isolated cave site, Crystal Cave, was on the agenda for the weekend and as this was a few days away I had some time to pass. Meanwhile Yellowstone National Park was on the doorstep; an opportunity too good to pass up. Sleeping rough for three days I probably saw the area at its best and almost completely devoid of tourists. The rangers were in the process of closing the place for the winter, and deep snow was already preventing access to side roads. Apart from the normal attractions like 'Old Faithful' and the travertine terraces of Mammouth, just keeping my eyes open rewarded me with some incredible sights: herds of buffalo and elk grazing peaceably on small patches of ground (which due to thermal heating were free of snow) and more rarely, the occasional sighting of a coyote and a pair of Trumpeter Swans.

After my solitary pilgrimage I was more than glad to meet up with the cavers. Again I was introduced to a typical 'walk in' — this time one that was over six miles long, in snow, and gaining 460 metres in altitude.

Crystal Cave lay at a height of approximately 2,100 metres and in view of my previous experience of the cold I was feeling wary. I wasn't quite sure what to expect, and my overall impression of the cave was slightly disappointing. It appeared to be a particularly youthful system, with immature passage development and a virtual absence of formations. There was nothing grand or exceptionally exciting about the place.

But it was there to be explored and eight hours were spent underground. During this time the cave was extended by a further 300 metres and we attained a total length of about 1,500 metres. As expected it was very cold and I wished that I'd constructed my suit of rather thicker neoprene than the 4 mm which seemed to be inadequate for such conditions. By comparison the local lads were largely oblivious to the low temperatures and the dedication which they applied to tasks like surveying certainly left me impressed.

A week later the next trip was to Neffs Canyon Cave, at that time the deepest in the United States at 360 metres. In the land of 'bigger and better' the caves were unquestionably long but they were not that deep, Neffs Canyon being only slightly deeper than the British Ogof Ffynnon Ddu. The cave itself, which was virtually in the suburbs of Salt Lake City (Utah) was nothing special; there were only five pitches, the longest drop being 49 metres; the rest comprising climbs and steeply descending rifts. Other than the sense of achievement that any caver feels after visiting a 'record classic' Neffs Canyon was most disappointing. I guess the lure of exploration and the inner satisfaction that comes from participating on a discovery was too well ingrained. The company of seasoned cavers was first class, but Neffs Canyon could only ever be a good tourist trip.

Neil Montgomery had joined us for the Neffs Canyon trip, and afterwards we decided to go off together by bus and hiking, to the Arches National Park. This was to be my first real experience of desert terrain. Via the small town of Moab we hitched into the wilderness. All around were the incredible sandstone towers, etched and pitted by the relentless attack of dust and ages. It didn't take much imagination to conjure up a tribe of renegade indians thundering from behind a distant butte, and like so much of America the landscape was totally devoid of human influence for as far as the eye could see.

This was a land where existence was hard; a land of juniper and sage brush, bayonette grass and the occasional stunted spruce. Disappearing into the shrubs small and agile antelope squirrels could regularly be seen, but never photographed owing to their speed. A young porcupine however proved more obliging and apart from this and a few deer we were left very much to ourselves. It was uncomfortably cold, and even though strictly prohibited, we lit a fire to warm ourselves and cook meals; water we begged from other passing sightseers. The like of the actual arches I had never seen before, the most vivid and memorable being that of the Delicate Arch which, outlined against the distant and snow-capped La Sal Mountains, provided one of the most majestically beautiful scenes imaginable.

We were both working to a tight schedule. Following the descent into the Grand Canyon and a visit to Cave of the Winding Stair (where incidentally Neil met the girl who was subsequently to become his wife, Donna Mroczkowski), we split up. As his bus pass was about to expire, Neil had to move on to Texas to meet up with John Parker. John's sister lived in Corpus Christi fairly near the Mexican border and on a previous visit John had discovered the enchantment of Mexican caving, namely miles of unexplored caves. While in the Berger the pair had decided to team up for a lightweight expedition before the main body of cavers descended on Mexico for the traditional Christmas break.

I still had some weeks of bussing to go, and being a glutton for punishment, had accepted Jim Chester's invitation to join a long pushing trip on Thanksgiving Weekend, the last weekend in November, to the Scapegoat area of Montana. Several articles had appeared concerning the potential of this far flung location which seemed to be the area with the most promise in the state. The main site was Green Fork Falls Cave, yet another of those systems which can only be explored safely during the winter. Several attempts had been made on the cave under summer conditions but the volume of water resurging rendered progress extremely difficult. It was a challenging site even under optimum

81

conditions, involving a 16-mile walk in, many climbs, pitches and zones of deep water; most important it was still going, deep into Scapegoat Mountain.

The journey north was programmed to take in Carlsbad Caverns, the world famous show cave in New Mexico. The self-guided tour here was really quite amazing, lasting for 2½ hours. Visitors were equipped with an earphone which supplied full details of every part of the cave in a variety of different languages. Rangers patrolled the route providing help if required. The so called 'Big Room' has to be seen to be believed — over 400 metres long, 60 metres high and littered with a profusion of stalagmites and stalactites. The actual formation although mega-lithic in size was disappointingly lifeless. Because a desert regime now exists in the area no water is to be seen at any point; like a petrified forest the stal is completely fossilised. The tour was quite a walk, involving a long and winding descent of over 246 metres, and like the other visitors I was glad to enter the cafeteria at the bottom. The scale of the enterprise now became evident. Hundreds of tourists could be accommodated comfortably with a full range of facilities. But where the toilets flushed to was anyone's guess. In the depths below one could envisage some poor caver wriggling along a tight tube and suddenly being confronted by a surge of water and a mass of sewerage. Visions of cavers fleeing, climbing up stals, being plastered in shreds of soggy, multicoloured toilet paper appeared before my eyes. Imagine drowning in the stuff; your mates standing there helplessly; mouth to mouth would be out of the question.

By this stage elderly grannies were starting to quiver and swoon; the thought of that climb back out would make the most stout hearted worry. But never fear; American technology reaches deep underground even in New Mexico. Like the entrance to some huge rocket silo, your exit is made in a large smooth-riding lift that takes you directly back to the surface, and within but a short stroll from the parking area. Amid mutterings of 'Gee, aint that cute', and 'waal this heer speelunkin's raat easeh' I left to start thumbing.

Bussing the 1,000 miles north along the western side of the High Plains it was noticeable how rapidly winter had taken a hold; as we entered Montana the conditions could only be described as arctic. The Greyhound bus service just kept going, and barely falling behind schedule we moved on through the most ferocious blizzard I had ever seen. In Britain everything would long since have ground to a halt but here severe winters were part and parcel of life. My stomach turned over. We were planning three full days of heavy packing and a hard caving trip at one of the most isolated spots in the United States; I was sceptical as to whether the trip would even get underway. Arriving at Jim's house in Bozeman, Montana, I learned that the state highway had in fact been closed behind us, but here the snowfall had been surprisingly light. Jim was completely unperturbed by it all and with road conditions further north 'acceptable' the trip was on.

Back home no one would even consider such a crazy project; in the event of an accident the media and rescue organisations would tear the persons involved to pieces. This was a fundamental difference in attitude and approach. The American cavers operating in isolated areas like the Rockies possess something very much akin to the early pioneering spirit; they are skilled mountain men, highly competent all-rounders; hardy individuals; survivors.

At 7.30 am the next morning we were away. It was a couple of hours' drive and as we neared the end of the road the final 20 miles were made by using chains on the wheels. Fresh snow continually fouled the distributor and when we ground to a halt someone had to dry things out. I began to worry about potential blizzards in the mountains and what would happen to us if we got cut off. The sky looked leaden. What about the walk in and my low tolerance of the cold? There seemed to be so many uncertainties; I was totally amazed at the indifference to the conditions displayed by the others. Mustering what faith I could, I just told myself that the lads must know what they were doing — well, I hoped so! — and kept quiet. The gullible, green feeling developed again.

At the 'Benchmark', the end of the road, there was the faintest glimmer of sun. I received my snow shoes from the back of the wagon and clumsily attached them to my feet. Trying to walk in fins was bad enough; this was worse. With legs splayed apart, rather like some bow-legged cowboy, the technique, I was told, was to shuffle my steps, carefully avoiding any lifting movement with the feet. I guess I'm a slow learner at everything and I seemed to be using a trudging motion, definitely not to be recommended. But with snow over one foot deep and a pack of at least 60 pounds, perseverance was essential. The language deteriorated as my incompetence became more obvious. After one and a half miles my knees were hurting badly and I had to admit failure. Off came the shoes, and I strung them to the back of my unwieldy pack.

The others were sceptical of my ability to walk, but not to be beaten we continued. There was a cabin eleven miles ahead where we were to meet up with Pete Thompson and his crew from Canada. As the evening progressed so did weariness. At no point in the day did the temperature better freezing point, and at nightfall it was bitter. Well after dark the broken trail led to our haven where we met Pete, Linda Hastie and Chris Smart from Edmonton, and Chuck Pease, Eugene and Mike from Great Falls. They had set out at midday and it had taken them eight hours to walk and trailbreak the eleven miles.

Just after midday the next day the trek west was resumed. I loaned my snow shoes to one of the others and set out last, thereby experiencing the most broken trail. But as we neared the great 'continental divide' it was evident that the snow was much deeper; this section was far more demanding. After two miles the location of the cave was visible — three miles in the distance — supplying a great psychological boost. I needed that as much of my time was spent floundering in snow between knee and waist deep. Quite literally crawling from one gulley to the next I was on the verge of abandoning the trip when suddenly I surmounted a rise to find Mike just ahead. He was giving up owing to blisters. Offering me his snow shoes I immediately accepted. Either I took the shoes or I gave up; there was no choice.

Crossing the treacherous valley floor the final slope up to the entrance was terrible; it was covered in snow over waist deep, and it was too steep even for shoes or skis. It was a case of sheer dogged determination and brute strength. Like some Christmas card scene the valley led away from the entrance toward the heart of America, but this was no time for studying the view or even having a rest. It had taken two days to reach this iced up hole in the ground and now the game was only just beginning. Changing 90 metres into the cave amidst a profusion of ice stals was absolutely hell. Soon however I had my two wet suit jackets on, together with a hood, and slowly a sweaty, itchy warmth began to circulate. At this stage our numbers were down by three, Mike, Linda and lastly Eugene having opted out.

It was very good to get moving. Green Fork Falls Cave was an impressive mature system, and in the early stages at least, seemingly long abandoned by any active stream. Exploration had been going on here for several years prior to 1975 but due to its isolation and the nature of the passage, progress was understandably slow and erratic. As the trip was to show, the cave was an unrelenting obstacle course from start to finish.

The last of the ice was left behind about 150 metres from the entrance, and misguidedly I expected that the temperature might now rise a little, but no; it remained about 3-4°C. Pacemaker Aven was the first hold up — a 10-metre climb which was rigged with a permanently installed rope. Chuck ascended on jumars, then the rest of us climbed up on a ladder. This set the scene, a succession of climbs and descents leading eventually to an underground river.

We headed upstream along a large and extremely impressive river passage. If I thought the temperature outside the cave was cold inside Green Fork Falls the crystal blue water was excruciating, and this was made abundantly clear at the first of the swims, Howie Lake. About 150 metres later the route sumped but obligingly an 8-metre rope ascent, the Williams Sump By-Pass, led to a high level passage. A rope traverse over deep water led to a pitch and another swim — and so it went on.

The previous limit was reached after 2½ hours, a climb made above a sump and another pitch discovered. A 20-metre section of deep blue water lay beyond for which, fortunately, the Canadians had come prepared. An inflatable dinghy transported us in turns to dry ground and a fine oval tubeway. About 300 metres of passage was quickly covered and led predictably to another sump. This again presented a by-pass, an 11-metre climb to a large high level passage above. But for us, without the necessary climbing aids, further progress was at an end. Luxuries too, were over. As the discovery was surveyed and we slowly started out it was found that the dinghy was badly punctured and unusable!

It was 9½ hours after entry and 3.30 am when we reached our clothes — hung safely well above the floor beyond the claws of any ravaging pack rats. Pete and Chris had come prepared and quickly crashed out in sleeping bags while the rest of us — Jim, Chuck, Dennis and myself — equally as quickly fumbled with carbides and snow shoes and made for the cabin, five miles distant.

Each person now trekked at his own pace; it was a time for reflection. Off on some hilltop a solitary howling wolf made his eerie presence felt. I had mastered the snow shoeing technique and at last a quiet confidence grew, as though I had completed my apprenticeship. Gulley after gulley passed with increasing monotony and we arrived back, completely exhausted, shortly after dawn. Nestling in the deep valley, blending in perfectly with the environment, what a haven that little hut was. In a land seemingly devoid of colour in a world of misty grey, it reminded me of some trapper's cabin, small, cosy, functional. Water had to be carried from a stream about 100-200 metres away; there were animal tracks in the soft snow; no matter how tired, one stayed alert.

We snatched a couple of hours sleep and made our way out at about one o'clock in the afternoon. The cold was now crippling; on our return to Bozeman we learned that the temperature had fallen to −31°C. There was no doubt in my mind that the caving undertaken under such extreme conditions was by far the most severe that I had experienced. Even the long treks in the mountains of Mexico were to pale in comparison. Caving in the high Rockies is the supreme test of an individual's fitness, stamina and dogged determination.

The following day the Chinnook thaw set in. Time was pressing on and I intended sorting out my SRT before heading for Mexico. At this stage SRT was in its infancy back in Britain; a technique predominantly for the expeditionary caver or for those inclined towards a touch of showmanship. Gaping Gill was the classic spot for those hell bent on creating an image, and shortly before I'd left a student from my old college had immortalised himself in the main shaft when he had used a low-melting-point rope and promptly burnt his way through it, in the process establishing the fastest descent time ever. As this incident showed, comparatively little was known about rope characteristics or indeed about any other facets of SRT. At home I'd learned a lot from Pete Lord who had returned from the States in 1974 complete with a wealth of information and some weird bits of ironmongery. Probably the strangest item that Pete had proudly demonstrated to us, was a thing called a 'rack'.

We had all stood by amazed, hanging on every word, as Pete had expounded its merits while descending from a 30-metre viaduct. Even John Parker was spell bound. But a few minutes later, for some reason which we couldn't quite fathom Pete was upside down and the smooth patter had ceased. Then the comments started.

'Looks interesting, must be some sort of escape mechanism.'

'When do you use that underground Pete?'

Apparently it was a 'technical hitch', but despite the embarrassment he sorted himself out quickly and gave us some expert tuition. We were left in no doubt that the Americans had really mastered all aspects of SRT and the place to go for first hand information was 'TAG Country': Tennessee, Alabama and Georgia.

Another long bus journey took me south east.

In Chattanooga Buddy Lane and Rick Bridges acted as hosts. Both were about my age but veterans so far as SRT was concerned. They looked my gear over and the jokes started.

'Gee Maarten that rack must have been made by an Irishman.'

They had heard of the Irish from Pete Lord; fortunately he hadn't taught them about the Welsh. In any case my home-made rack quickly became obsolete after I borrowed one from Buddy. As I was to learn, a lot more emphasis seemed to go on 'dropping pits', than on the actual cave exploration at the bottom. New shafts were continually being discovered on the heavily wooded upland areas and the cave potential was quite astounding.

In the process of brushing up on the SRT I visited some classic pits — including Never Hole — a tremendous 49-metre shaft at the bottom of which the prominent TAG caver Marion Smith had actually been married. Marion seemed to be a perfectly normal guy, but getting married — a complete service — at the bottom of a deep shaft? That had to be something only an American would do. British cavers are thought to be quite odd by the public, but the Americans really excel in this, taking their individuality to amazing lengths. At a caving club meeting, a 'grotto meet' as they would refer to it, it was nothing to see an array of four-wheel drive vehicles sporting personalised 'CAVER' registration plates. The attitude to alcohol was strange however. At the Greyhound depots I'd seen the police come around violently ejecting drunks; a rather disturbing experience, but again something that one might expect. Somehow I guess that I expected to find American cavers a similarly boozy lot to those back home. How wrong I was.

One of the most memorable occasions of this interlude was the Christmas Party at Cumberland Caverns. The party was to be held several hundred yards underground, a good opportunity or so I thought, for a good session on the ale. Seasonal nostalgia crept upon me: just imagine the 'do' we'd have back home; the barrels all lined up, cavers clutching saucepans, milk bottles, any receptacle at all so long as it held a pint or more; the old hands religiously guarding the barrels to stop the drunks from shaking up the sediment; party games like squeezing through the backs of chairs, getting stuck and being left there for hours on end; people throwing up; people falling down; people being carted off to bed or hospital. If only there was a cave like this back home! On Mendip for certain there would be all sorts of interesting things going on. At one venerable establishment where 'after the pub' parties were held fairly regularly they had devised the most incredible party game of all — sofa rugby. A full length sofa would be used in the same way as a rugby ball — or battering ram — and the two teams, usually from different clubs, would battle away to see who could score the most points. There were comparatively few rules and the entertainment value of a sofa hurtling across the interior of a club hut was tremendous. Yes, there was nothing to beat a good British caving party.

But Cumberland Caverns lay in a 'dry' county, worse still the owner, Roy Davies, was not only a caver he was also a preacher! Things were becoming a trifle confused. The outcome of it all was that it was a festive but sober night. People had come from all parts of the east for the banquet; over 100 people seated around huge trestles, singing carols and watching movies. Outside the weather was miserable but secreted inside the odd four-wheel drive would be a bottle of gin, or such like, which was gradually emptied as the evening wore on. Clearly in this sector of 'land of the free' a new Prohibition Era held sway; all very strange indeed.

I learned a lot in a short period in the south east and soon it was time to head back across the continent, towards Mexico. On

13th December I arrived in Corpus Christi to meet up with John Parker and his sister. Immediately I could sense that John wasn't his usual irrepressible self. Evidently the Mexican trip had not gone too well: the conditions had been atrocious, he and Neil Montgomery had found no new caves, and the pair had just not hit it off. The outcome of this was that John had come back prematurely leaving Neil in Valles, the principal town in the main caving area. On top of everything else he was having visa problems, and was unable to re-enter Mexico; there was now no hope of his doing the big pits when the main groups came down for Christmas.

Next day, the last of my two-month bus pass, I set off for the border. The weeks ahead were undoubtedly the climax of the visit. As previously arranged, Neil was awaiting my arrival at the border (back in Georgia I'd bought him a 150-metre length of Bluewater Rope and he had come to collect it) with his little book of instant Spanish. After half an hour of head shaking it was clear that we were getting nowhere with the customs officials. The main bone of contention was the new rope which they presumably feared we were going to resell in Mexico. A senior official breezed by and when we tried to explain the situation the corner of his mouth turned down and he too shook his head. Neil began to quietly fume as he skipped frantically through the pages. It was like some game of cat and mouse. Then he began rummaging around in his pockets, brought out his wallet and came out with something that sounded like, 'Look, we are very poor cavers.'

Up till now our greasy, overweight official was unmoved by any of our protestations, but suddenly there was a transformation. A sparkle came to his eyes and his fingers began to strum on the surface of the big table. Neil knew the signs, he'd seen them before. But like all good Aussies he wouldn't admit defeat, and more important wouldn't part with money, till he absolutely had to. Out came a couple of dollars, which quickly disappeared into the Mexican's back pocket, and we both walked off. From the tales we heard later it appeared that we had got off lightly: bribery and corruption was rife on the borders.

We crossed the Rio Grande into Mexico proper. It was hardly the impressive river I had expected, in fact nothing more than a sluggish little sewer, barely 10 metres wide. However it must be one of the greatest cultural divides on earth. To the north lay the get-ahead affluence of Texas, to the south the instant squalor and poverty of Latin America.

Travelling on Mexican public transport was a complete contrast to that of the States. At frequent intervals the bus would grind to a halt while outside a group of poor people gathered together their baggage. As a rule things like goats and chickens would be trussed up and stowed in the luggage compartment but occasionally one would have to share a seat with a crate of smelly livestock. With everyone on board the distinctive roar built to a crescendo (something like a thousand tin cans being dragged along), and the bus would hurtle off. The hooting of horns could be heard for miles so villagers always had ample warning to get ready.

From our point of view the big advantage was that it was dirt cheap. Just imagine it: you're so dogged tired that you doze off, the clatter of the bus fades into the distance and not even the magical quality of the endless limestone scenery can hold your attention. Suddenly a sharp stabbing pain almost lifts you out of your seat as some chicken sinks its beak through the hole in your trousers. You clip the thing gently with your hand and smile at the owner; the chicken scowls back evilly. If only you could get your fingers around its neck!

We were heading for Valles, more specifically the Condesa restaurant, which was the normal meeting point for cavers passing through. Here Julia James, Neil's friend and fellow traveller on the year's speleological sojourn, was to join us. Julia is one of the world's leading cave scientists from Sydney. What is not generally known is that despite advancing middle age she is probably, and certainly has been, one of the hardest cavers around. Together with Neil and two other Australians she had bottomed the Berger on our trip earlier that year; now she was about to start cave hunting in Mexico.

No sooner had we reached Valles than we were on our way yet again to meet Marion Smith, Jim Smith and their crew for our first trip. South of the Tropic of Cancer one would imagine that the weather would be fine; I had been looking forward to some sun and heat after the cold and wet conditions experienced in the States. But for two nights in a row it rained. This really was dismal, especially when two or three of us had to cram under one inadequate poly sheet to keep dry. Back home a smelly sleeping bag usually guarantees a decent night's kip: no one will go near you, but here everyone's gear was in roughly the same condition and we all slept together.

Our introduction to Mexican caving came with the system Sotano de Tlamaya, near Xilitla. This area of karst had been the first to be studied in the country and the three-kilometre-long cave had set a Western Hemisphere depth record back in 1965 when it bottomed out, at a sump, after 454 metres.

This was a classic trip but as it involved eight people it was also time consuming. There were about eight pitches, several swims and the water temperature was about 18°C. Despite having left my wet suit in the States the aqueous sections were no problem, in fact after my experiences in the Rockies the water felt almost luke warm.

It was the early hours of the morning when we retraced our weary steps towards the surface, Jim Smith leading. I was third and just about to clip on to the rope at the bottom of the 86-metre entrance pitch when suddenly pandemonium broke out some way above my head. Jim had just crawled on to a narrow ledge, over half way up, to find himself sharing it with a deadly coral snake. Whether it had been there on our descent or whether it had fallen there while we were down the cave was immaterial. Like someone possessed Jim set on it and pounded the unsuspecting creature to pulp. I couldn't help wondering whether the excessive level of violence was actually necessary; one look at Jim, and the blood curdling shrieks which he emitted, ought to have frightened the thing to death.

We made our exit at 4.00 am crashing out anywhere we could away from the incessant rain. Lying on rubble beneath Marion's wagon, my bag, already damp from the previous nights out, became thoroughly wet from the drizzle and smeared in oil from rubbing against the transmission. Sleep lasted for a mere two hours. When I awoke, my face was within centimetres of the wheels of passing trucks; a night best forgotten. Aching, cold and hungry the best thing we could have done would have been to drive to the nearest restaurant, but this was out of the question. On detackling, the rope had jammed somewhere near the bottom of the entrance pitch, and someone had to go down to retrieve it.

It was still raining and enthusiasm was spent. Everyone was racking their brains for the perfect excuse not to have to go down.

'I'm driver,' said Marion.

'I risked my life for you lot down there,' said Jim.

Fortunately someone suggested the time honoured tradition of tossing coins, and I had my let out on the first round.

No sooner had the rope been retrieved and the gear stowed than we set off for what was at that time the third deepest pit in the Americas, Sotanito de Ahacatlan. It was as well that Marion had been there before, as the entrance to this hole is only one metre in diameter set back in an area of clints. The 323-metre deep system comprises just two pitches, the first of 22 metres leading to a large sloping chamber full of scree, which in turn leads directly to pitch number two; the latter 291 metres deep, free hanging with some very unusual characteristics indeed.

Despite being a 'free hang' for the entire drop neither light nor sound contact appeared possible from the top to the bottom. Even more peculiar was the fact that at the bottom there was no way on, other than a minute sump, and according to Marion the quality of the air was not all that it might be; a build up of carbon dioxide was the most probably cause.

Marion and Jim were in charge and strongly advised against anyone moving about on the scree slope above the big pitch. The pattern of activity was dictated by the risk of stonefall and a limited space at the bottom; the trip to the bottom and out was to be undertaken in pairs.

Sotanito de Ahacatlan was certainly an exciting prospect and even the weather now decided to perk up. Things were looking unusually good when our American hosts sprung the news that we had no single length of rope to rig the drop. My stomach began to churn and I felt like creeping off quietly into the bushes — the same sort of feeling that I had prior to pushing a longish sump. However this was suppressed as someone suggested that we do a practice knot-crossing session on the first pitch. Nonchalantly Marion and Jim grabbed their tackle and simply set off.

You'd have to be an odd sort of individual or desperately hard up, to consider crossing a knot in Britain, even today; it just isn't necessary. But in the south-east of the United States and more especially in Mexico, deep shafts were continually being discovered, very often necessitating the use of every bit of tackle the discoverers could lay their hands on. Judging by Marion and Jim's attitude as they left they might have been going to do Sump One in Swildons Hole.

It was about two hours later that our rigging pair returned. The knot was situated about 123 metres off the floor and provided that one moved carefully over the scree slope there was little to worry about. The descents continued smoothly until, late in the afternoon, we found that Neil and Julia were an hour overdue. For such an experienced pair the concern was justified. It was the turn of Alan Johnson and myself to go next and a few items of basic first aid and some equipment spares were taken — just in case. At the head of the big shaft the weight of the rope seemingly indicated that it had not severed, at least not within 154 metres or so of the top. Our only clue as to the non appearance of the missing pair was the fact that the top rope protector was found to be displaced. Could one of them have forgotten to replace it? By heaving up a short length of rope and taking the weight of the near 308 metres hanging below, Alan gave me assistance to rig into my rack. Cautiously I set off.

Minute after minute sped by unnoticed. Watching for the knot, feeling for any slight difference in the weight of the rope and turning over the possibilities awaiting me below I was totally absorbed. Reaching the obstacle everything seemed to click into place; in a couple more minutes I was on the final leg and still there was no indication of what to expect. Only when I was 15 metres or so off the floor could a light be noticed and Julia's broad Aussie accent piped:

'We're all right Martyn, it's just that I forgot to put the top rope protector in place. We thought we'd better wait for someone to come down first rather than risk it.'

This was unquestionably a wise choice. An error had been made and they were prepared to risk personal embarrassment when perhaps one of them might conceivably have gambled upon an unprotected assent. This was a perfect example of the mature, safety-conscious approach the pair adopted to all their underground activities. But it was none the less good to see that even the redoubtable Julia James could make a mistake.

Neil and Julia had spent over two hours huddled in a tiny

alcove and they were more than glad to get moving, and to leave the stifling air of the enclosed pit bottom. We said our farewells and they slowly tandemmed off up the rope. Now it was my turn to wait. In two minutes flat I'd seen all there was to see; all I could do then was just sit, tight in to the wall, as small chippings and stones whistled to the floor like tracer bullets. Cowering in that tiny alcove waiting for the others to exit and for my climbing partner to arrive, there was ample time for reflection. I was immobile yet every few breaths I found myself taking a deep gasp. This was my first experience of carbon dioxide in a cave, other than in a small enclosed airbell of a sump, and it was definitely disturbing. I began to wonder how long such a place could sustain life. In a small airbell this could be counted in minutes, here it was impossible to say. As with diving it became a psychological battle to relax and conserve air. The whole time the mind pondered over the gruesome possibilities; imagine being stranded for some reason, the air becoming thinner and thinner, one's candle or whatever being extinguished, sitting there panting with no hope of rescue. How would the mind cope? It was impossible to say.

Two and a half hours later I was on the move, but even on ascent it seemed to be a struggle to get a full breath for over 154 metres. Back on the surface Julia estimated the proportion of carbon dioxide at 1.5 per cent. Feelings of anxiety mellowed in the warming rays of the sun, hastened even faster when she announced that she was going to treat us all to a free meal in Ahacatlan Village.

As the first full meal I'd had since arrival in Mexico I made sure that bodily reserves were thoroughly topped up. Hamster-like twenty tortillas were neatly tucked away and everyone was in good spirits. Neil and Julia now set off to join Bill Stone and friends exploring for new pits, while my plans were to continue with Marion and Jim and visit El Sotano. Driving to the Utla Bridge we stripped off and washed our mud-caked clothes. This was to be the rendezvous point for other groups from the east and by early evening we had washed, dried, eaten and were swapping anecdotes over a homely driftwood fire.

The next morning eighteen people slowly made their way on the long trek, a round trip of about 29 miles, towards Rancho El Barro and the great pit. We 'first timers' could hardly believe it when, late in the afternoon Bill Boman pointed out the black shadow on the facing mountain; El Sotano was visible from a distance of five miles! Camp was made next to the river at the foot of the last climb. Here a native villager plied us with endless sugar cane, a welcome gift, which we reciprocated with sweets. The following day in Rancho El Barro, the last settlement en route, we bought coke and biscuits and took advantage of the last supply of water to fill up our containers.

It never ceased to amaze us: no matter how isolated the huts, people always had a supply of bottled coke ready to sell. At about four pence per bottle it was just too good to pass over. For a couple of minutes you could dump your weighty sack, just lie back and relax. Phosphoric acid, rotting teeth and general aches and pains were forgotten; until later that is when a crunching sensation in the mouth would indicate that yet another filling had fallen out. I had three appointments with the dentist when I got home and never quite forgot Boon's ideas in this respect. He came back to Britain fairly regularly to visit his mother and in the process remedied minor ailments on the National Health Service.

A mention must be made of the rope which we used. Bluewater 2 and 460 metres in length, it posed several problems with regard to transport. For the walk in to El Sotano the rope was carried in turns as a single load on a pack frame, over 100 pounds in weight. Unfortunately over such rough terrain only five or six people were capable of carrying it. For the return journey Buddy Lane formed it into six coils, each separated by a 6-metre length of tether. In such a way most people took a share. But with someone like Marion or Jim in front it was a forced march; the pace was merciless. To watch, it must have resembled a convict chain gang; people stumbling along, huffing and puffing, some sadistically amused, others cursing the leader or choice of route. To fall somewhere in the middle was to risk being trampled, probably the most dangerous part of the trip.

El Sotano comprised an incredible gash in the slopes of the mountain. Standing on the actual edge of the drop it looked like a totally enclosed canyon, about 430 metres long by about 215 metres wide, a most impressive sight. We rigged a drop of about 370 metres, the maximum possible being 414 metres. Because of the weight, assistance was necessary to clip into the rope and then you were on your own, for the twenty-minute descent to the floor.

'This'll really freak you out Martyn,' said Buddy.

Such was the aura about this hole that one almost felt compelled to reverential ecstasy. My attitude was that with no knots to cross and after the experience at Sotanito de Ahacatlan it was a real treat. It seemed somehow odd that this, the deepest cave shaft in the world, required no light. Daylight penetrated to virtually every corner of the pit and the main concern at the bottom was that of treading upon a poisonous snake. High sided boots were clearly advantageous in this sort of country.

Another familiar face now slid down the rope; that of Pete Lord. Pete had been so struck by the cave potential in Mexico that on his return to Britain he'd taken up Spanish lessons and started looking for a job over there. Here he was, with a couple of days to spare, before starting on a teaching post in Mexico City. A short length of cave led to the remains of a Mexican flag and a log book. Some 80 people had made the pilgrimage before us since the cave's discovery in 1972 and now Pete's name was there twice. Having signed the visitors' book there was little else to do other than wait our turn to leave. After a considerable delay Pete set off first, moved up about 50 cycles and waited for me to clip on. I'd catch up and the tandemming process would be repeated, for all of one hour and ten minutes back to the top.

The walk out to Puerto Utla was made in one day, and we travelled back to Valles under cover of darkness. Another facet of Mexican life now made itself felt, namely Mexican fuel. Marion's wagon broke down three times with a blocked filter.

Everything was falling into place perfectly and next to materialise was a trip to Joya de Guaguas (pronounced Wahwass). There was a three-hour walk in but it was worth every minute to view this particular pit; undoubtedly the most beautiful of any I saw. The jungle was dense but the location of the hole was evident from a distance by the cacaphony of bird noise. As the Joya gaped before us it might have been a sunken aviary as swarms of green parakeets wheeled to and from the depths nattering continuously among themselves. It was as though the roof of a vast underground chamber had collapsed allowing the sun to stream in, a perfect sanctuary for the birds and a fabulous playground for SRT. A huge passage dipped away beneath the high side providing a 215-metre, entirely free hanging drop to the jungle-covered slopes below. From the top one had to strain one's eyes to pick out the specks of human colour; from the bottom climbers presented a perfect photographic setting.

After a day off we completed our tour of the great pits with a visit to Golondrinas. This was a day's walk into the mountains from Aquismon. As with Tlamaya the entrance is situated in a coffee plantation and to the uninitiated there is little to differentiate such an area from ordinary jungle; at first glance it appears equally as dense with no obvious organisation or signs of cultivation. To the Mexican natives however the coffee tree is of great value, a source of rare income, something to be treated with care. It so happened that a couple of the lads came from rural Tennessee, a land where trees were only ever used for fuel, building or pit props. Somehow the old hands had forgotten to enlighten them as to the mysteries of the Mexican economy. At dusk a band of irate natives turned up looking most unhappy and threatening an international incident. From our interpreters it appeared that someone had lopped a few branches off a tree on the edge of the plantation and to placate them a fair sum was offered as compensation. Evidently the natives were satisfied and departed. The Tennessee lads were not so happy; they had to do the paying. In other areas of Mexico relations between the natives and American cavers are strained to the extreme and only by exceptionally good fortune have some cavers narrowly avoided death.

With a vertical drop of over 338 metres Golondrinas might have possessed a lesser depth but it certainly provided a significant contrast to its big brother. Whereas El Sotano was a vast open pit, Golondrinas had a comparatively small entrance, probably less than 60 metres in diameter. However as with Joya de Guaguas, after a few feet one hung completely free and the deeper you went the more distant the walls became. It was as though you were suspended beneath the roof of some immense dome, the walls cold and sinister, everything a dull greyish green. El Sotano had been a colourful setting; this was a complete contrast, a world of eternal twilight; oppressive.

At the bottom, the chamber must have measured over 300 metres by almost 200 metres and very little light penetrated. Looking up seemed strange. Viewing the distant patch of daylight was like peering through a spy glass from the wrong end. Trees at the top were dwarfed to blades of grass and it was only after people had abseiled for about a hundred metres that they could be picked out against the sky. All the while incessant, sometimes deafening bird noises assailed our ears. With such a low light intensity at the bottom the only vegetation comprised mosses and very small shrubs. Wandering around, the Indiana Crack was located, the entrance to a further descent of 185 metres. Exploring this and other parts of the pit required a light and as one entered the darker recesses hundreds and thousands of cave swifts, the Golondrinas, screamed and clawed their way out. Further back under the walls of the big shaft the nauseating warmth and smell of droppings was most unpleasant. Only the swifts dared these lower regions of the pit, all the beautiful but clumsy little parakeets having taken refuge on the ledges much higher up.

At dawn and at dusk it was a most exhilarating experience standing outside on the lip of the shaft watching the comings and goings of these inhabitants. Circling once or twice high above the entrance the swifts, with no hesitation, and like a volley of arrows, instantly disappeared into the depths. By comparison the poor parakeets made heavy work of their diurnal journey; they were forced to circle innumerable times before they came or went, jabbering all the while among themselves. In this process of gradually gaining or losing height one might occasionally collide with the rope and lose a few of its feathers and sadly I could well imagine the day when an aged or sickly bird might plummet to its doom.

Following the overdue arrival of my Welsh friend and long-standing caving companion, Gareth Davies, a brief visit was made to Mexico City before it was time to head back to the States. Most of the American groups were now dispersing and we were intending taking a lift north from Valles with Wil Howie. We hadn't been waiting in the Condesa Restaurant long when Bill Stone and Tracy Johnson arrived, accompanied by Tracy's wife Sheila; the latter looking very much the worse for wear. Apparently Sheila had fallen on a pitch about 246 metres underground in a new system called Joya de las Conchas. It had been a major effort to evacuate her and they had been ably assisted by Neil and Julia. Fortunately Sheila had no broken bones but judging from the bruising and lacerations she had been extremely lucky. All their tackle had of course been left in the cave. This had to come out and they were looking for help. As the conversation continued it was clear that the way on was wide open and if possible they wanted to push on down.

Wil arrived a little late. The lure of some original exploration was too strong and I was hooked. Gareth however wasn't feeling 100 per cent and he left with Wil.

It was a fair drive and walk to reach their camp near La Purisima. The following day we were up before dawn and on the trail by 7.30 am. It was a 40-minute walk to the entrance. The opening was unimpressive, a small dirty hole at the end of a shallow, dry stream course. We were just about ready to go down when it was pointed out that a few days earlier a rattlesnake over 1.5 metres in length had been found just inside. I'd encountered tarantulas and a deadly black widow spider a week or so before but I think a good sized rattlesnake would really be frightening, and since snakes never live alone and this one's mate had just been killed, it was a very wary trio who entered the hole.

We reached the previous limit of exploration at the top of the tenth pitch with little trouble. From 60 metres down, in a huge chamber with a maze of breakdown underfoot, Tracy soon shouted up that there was no apparent way on. Bill and I followed just in case, equipped with an additional rope. The chamber was over 21 metres in diameter and nine times out of ten the choke would have been hopeless. However there were cavities between the blocks and in a matter of seconds Bill was worming his way downward. It went.

Another pitch of 13 metres followed while Tracy remained in the chamber above the choke. When further leads developed it was clear that we needed more rope. Tracy volunteered to collect some which had been left several pitches back up the cave, and jummared back up the 60-metre rope. Four more lengths were soon lowered and Bill and I quickly pressed on. Fortunately belay points presented themselves and there was very little delay. Inevitably the ropes ran out but here we were lucky enough to reach a sinuous section of steeply descending rift where it was possible to free climb. Apart from the isolation and total lack of rescue facilities the place was just like some Yorkshire pot; clean washed with plenty of friction. Eventually we reached a 9-metre pitch which was particularly exposed. This, when Bill later made his calculations, lay at a depth of just over 462 metres. I was thoroughly enjoying every minute, but there was no sign of Tracy who was intending to follow us with yet more rope.

We stood and just looked on for a while; then an idea formed. I still had my SRT bag around my neck and there was a chance that by stringing the bits together I could gain a sort of bridge, cum ledge, on the far wall about 3 metres down. From there the rest of the descent looked feasible. Bill was dubious, but it had to be worth an attempt. Having established a belay and with every bit of tape and sling that I could muster stretched out, I had two to three metres to play with. The drop was undercut with no footholds and very gingerly I lowered myself over the edge. My arms were feeling surprisingly strong and after a metre or so I was able to stretch a leg across to gain the bridge. In a few more moments I was on the bottom.

I shouted back that I'd take a look at what lay ahead and disappeared. Bill stayed put. A small passage now led on to a 6-metre drop which was easily descended. Almost immediately a 21-metre drop appeared, a trifle damp and equally as exposed as the pitch where I'd left Bill. Bridging carefully this too was bottomed. Ahead a 5-metre drop led to a boulder choke. Several blocks were quickly pulled aside to reveal yet another drop of about 9-12 metres. It would have taken 10 minutes or so to dig a way through with safety, so I headed back — first taking the precautionary measure of lighting my spare carbide light, just in case my main light was extinguished on the climbs. The spare was held in my teeth and an uneventful return to Bill was made.

Then came the dreaded task of detackling. Slowly we collected all the ropes, humped them back up the cave and found Tracy. Weariness was now very real and by the time we reached the scene of the earlier accident, at a depth of 246 metres, I was at a low ebb. Travelling light I had next to no food, certainly none that was any good for taking underground. Luckily Tracy seemed to have an endless supply, especially instant-energy giving stuff like sweetened condensed milk. In fact I never ceased to be amazed at what they did manage to carry in their small day-packs; they seemed to be prepared for any eventuality.

With a short rest we continued. I did not feel the cold at any point but by the time we reached the entrance we were all very,

very tired and carrying 154 metres of assorted ropes apiece. Yet more of Tracy's cave food was consumed outside and I'm convinced there were several days' more of it left even then. Despite the exhaustion the comparison with the British caver was impossible to ignore. How often do parties carry spare food back home where even a Mars bar is regarded as something of an expeditionary luxury. Needless to say I was very impressed.

It was about 1.15 am when we set off on the trail back to camp. I felt like a zombie but the body was still going well.

'Won't be long now,' said Bill.

'Not that way,' said Tracy.

A protracted discussion ensued and for a while we were most definitely lost. The plateau was featureless but we trudged on. If I'd learned anything after 15 years caving it was that one only gets lost on or after the good, memorable trips.

Camp was reached about 2.30 am and despite being on the go for 19 hours I really felt as though I was floating on a cloud. The most enjoyable and worthwhile trip of my visit to Mexico was over. Crashing out next to the fire I fell into an instant contented sleep.

Daybreak, the last that I could afford to spend in Mexico came accompanied with a grinning toothless native staring into my face. Ever since Sheila's accident people from the little settlement of San Juan had showered the cavers with tortillas, eggs and the like; a touching gesture of goodwill from people who themselves were desperately poor, who could afford no luxuries like hobbies or holidays. This ragged individual had brought a little more food to camp and shortly my stomach began to ache with the weight of tortillas, which seemed acutely difficult to digest.

We totalled up the depth which we had reached and it came to approximately 505 metres, at that time the fourth deepest in the country. San Augustine was then 618 metres and it appeared that Joya de las Conchas certainly had the potential to go one better. How I envied these Americans. Mountain after mountain still remained untouched and there was always the chance of discovering another pit like Golondrinas. This really was a new frontier and I had little doubt that these were the people who were going to pioneer it.

Bill was already planning an Easter trip but for me it was time to pack up and walk down for a bus.

In the 10 days or so that followed I slowly made my way back through the States to New York. The whole trip had lasted nearly four months. It had been a period of intense activity in places that ranged from the arctic wastes of the high Rockies to the tropical depths of Mexico. I had met up with some of the leading cavers in North America and tackled some of their classic systems. Living on a meagre personal budget I must express my sincere gratitude for the overwhelming hospitality that only Americans know how to lavish. People such as Bill and Donna Boman, Jim and Mary-Ellis Chester, Buddy Lane and family, Donna Mroczkowski, Bob and Jean Weikel and many, many more ensured the venture was enjoyable, and a complete success. With their guidance, patience and understanding I was able to do so much more than would otherwise have been the case. California, the Grand Canyon, Niagara Falls and various national parks were a memorable interlude in the caving itinerary, but to visit places such as Green Fork Falls Cave, the Mexican pits, Carlsbad Caverns, Ellisons and Mammoth Cave was an insight to American caves, cavers and caving that will remain with me always.

I staggered back through the reception area at Heathrow to meet Chris Howes, my sister and my girlfriend. Unshaven and rather grubby, my 'Michelin Man' appearance and the state of my gear spoke for itself. I had a new perspective on the world. From the affluent life of the United States to the dire poverty of rural Mexico — where to now?

5

A Free Trip to Iran

AN INSIGHT
INTO THE WORLD OF TELEVISION

In the development of world caving the British public house has
played an immeasurable role. How many trips that you can recall
were conceived in the pub, planned, started, or concluded in the
pub? Think of places like the Hunters Lodge on Mendip, the
Brittania and the Ancient Briton in South Wales, the Craven
Heifer, Helwith Bridge, Marten Arms and Golden Lion in Yorkshire, the Bush Bar in Fermanagh and O'Connors in Co. Clare.
If you are going to meet somewhere the pub is as good a place as
any. The British caver enjoys his pint and having arranged the
venue it doesn't matter if one or other of you are an hour or so
late.

In February 1976 we were standing, shoulder to shoulder in
the Hunters, swilling back the watery southern ale, when quite
predictably the conversation got around to the Gouffre Berger in
France. The summer before a large group of us had bottomed it,
supping many gallons of French wine in the process. It had been
a typical 'holiday-type' expedition; not too much organisation,
harmonious and successful with eighteen people reaching the
sump. Thereafter whenever any of us met up someone would
inevitably come out with 'Why don't we go somewhere else?' and
this occasion was no exception. But there's a very big step between the 'beer talk' and the actual doing of whatever is suggested; that step is the dreaded word 'organisation'.

'How about the Pierre-Saint-Martin?' someone said.

'They've got some beautiful wines down there' said someone
from the Bristol Exploration Club.

'That's all you bloody Mendip cavers think about, your bloody
booze!' threw in one of my mates. The nearest tables erupted in
jeers and hisses but as the noise subsided Pete Francis followed it
up:

'That's no good anyway; the bloody Yorkshire lot have been there and done it all.'

Things really started now. A few northerners moved in, shoulders back, flexing their muscles. That's one thing I'd learned about the Yorkshire caving scene; they lived a lot closer to nature than we southerners and they were always ready for a scrap on a Saturday night. Mendip people were never short of a word or two, especially on their own territory, and a slanging match developed.

'You bloody Welsh are all the same; you don't know what's going on outside the Valleys boyo; first time over the Bridge boyo?'

Things were heating up. I went for a leak. By the time I got back the landlord had put the dampers on and things were back to normal; well, almost.

'Iran' Richard Stevenson muttered. 'How about going to Iran?'

And so the idea was born.

The two Ghar Parau expeditions of the early 1970s had shown clearly that Iran was one of the last major frontiers of future caving potential. Not only were the extensive Zagros Mountains unexplored but they also rose well above the 3,000-metre level, an essential prerequisite for anyone contemplating a world depth record. But Ghar Parau had been frustrating. On a mountain offering 2,000 metres of vertical-depth potential the cave could only be followed down to the 740-metre level. At the time this had constituted an Asiatic depth record but to all those involved on the expeditions it was an extreme disappointment; so easily might it have blitzed the world league.

By March 1976 we had a provisional team list of over a dozen with Richard as leader, and a date set for the summer of 1977. In the best British tradition of caving politics the southerners, from Wales and Mendip, buried the hatchet, but discreetly gave the northerners the cold shoulder. The caving world was extremely cliqueish; in the past there was no way that anyone south of Manchester ever got on a northern-based expedition, so we didn't see why we should include them in ours. However this indiscretion back fired on us later. Because the Iran team were southerners and the expeditionary purse strings were controlled by northerners we got very little cash! A friend of mine just happened to be in the Craven Heifer not long after the Sports Council awards were made and recounted a conversation something like this.

'Well, they're not cavers anyway.'

'There's some real 'ead bangers goin yar know... there's that secretary of their's, what's 'is name... yar know... the bloke we saw t'other week... wi' a towel wrapped around 'is 'ead, like some arab, an' two black rubber 'and torches for 'is cavin light.'

Laughter.

''ow the 'ell does 'e manage on pitches?'

'Well, we 'ad t' laff... 'e stock one doon 'is wet suit an' t'other 'e 'eld in 'is teeth. Serious chap though; 'e couldn't see funny side. Lads were really ribbin' 'im like.'

'Oo else is going?'

'There's that Welsh bugger Farr, 'im as pirated Boreham off our Geoff; 'e's photographer ar think.'

'Well 'e certainly won't get much diving over there.'

'Good bloody riddance ar say.' (It might have been a little stronger!)

'Oo aye, there's that doctor bloke from Devon; yar know that bloke oo never stopped witterin' at last conference.'

'Yar mean Dr Peter Glanvill; the chap oo spent 'alf hour trying t' get slide projector t' work and eventually gave up?'

'Aye, 'im... never stopped witterin' 'ole time.'

'They say 'e's a first class chap underground though.'

''e don't 'arf get excited though. Bloody 'ell, do yar know what they're goin' over in?'

'No.'

'A bloody great 43- or 50-seater bus! Can yar imagine it? t' mountains of Iran in bloody great bus! Bloody thing's useless off t' road. Ar reckon as they're goin' for 'oliday tour round Med.'

Yes, the lads up north probably had many amusing hours at our expense. But in one respect they had a valid point. As the final team crystalised it was evident that it lacked somewhat in proven hard, experienced cavers. But this was no particular problem as there were a good half a dozen of us who would be capable of doing whatever came our way and being mercenary we needed the others to spread the cost.

The preparations were going ahead well when Richard rang me up one day from work.

'How do you fancy going over to Iran at Easter? B.B.C. 'World About Us' are doing a documentary on some blind cave fish and they need a couple of divers. This journalist, Anthony Smith's been in to see me today.'

Well things like that don't happen to ordinary people everyday so obviously I played along; at the same time taking it all with a large pinch of salt. If we got to go it would at least be virgin exploration and it would be good preparation for the group's main expedition later. We would also be gaining first-hand information of the Zagros, its people, any restrictions and so forth. Who knows, we might even be able to recce our chosen mountain, Kuh-e-Shahu.

It appeared that Anthony Smith, a keen traveller-cum-natural history expert, had been out to Iran in 1976, and entirely on his own, had chased up a reference on some blind white cave fish in one of the most isolated parts of the country. After a lot of trouble he eventually found the site and caught two small specimens to bring back for a formal identification. Miraculously these were transported to the Natural History Museum in London alive. Significantly one of the pair was to prove unique to science; *Neomacheilus smithi*, as it was named, was a member of the loach family whereas all previous species of truly blind cave fish had belonged to the carp family. On this basis Smith had persuaded 'World About Us' to produce a documentary. They in turn soon realised that a study of the habitat would be essential and that they would need some cave divers. A casual conversation led to Richard being contacted and so myself. It was an amazing coincidence that we happened to be going to Iran anyway and an extraordinary piece of good luck. Judging by Smith's photographs there was every possibility of some superb diving in warm, clear water.

In March, Richard gathered together all the necessary diving equipment, hired a compressor, and the B.B.C. freighted it all away. We weren't actually going to get paid for our endeavours, but the expenses would certainly make it a decent holiday. Came the day of departure and producer Alan Bell picked us up from Bristol and whisked us off to the Holiday Inn at Heathrow. For cavers used to roughing it, it was almost like stepping aboard a magic carpet for that 3,000-mile journey; it was reality with a first-class stamp.

106

Above left: Dan yr Ogof: Lake Chamber in the Mazeways Extension.

Above right: A diver negotiates a low section in the Mazeways Left-Hand Sump.

Far left: Dave Morris abseils into the thirty-five metre Entrance Shaft of Noons Hole, Northern Ireland.

Left: Dave Morris stops to admire a flowstone drapery in the Arch 2 extensions.

Below: Julian Walford passes through a beautiful section at the upper end of Arch 2.

Above: A large passage is regained beyond Turkey Sump 2, Agen Allwedd.
Below left: The upstream Turkey Sump 1, Agen Allwedd, and Rodney 'Bomber' Beaumont is about to submerge in the constricted underwater passage.
Below right: A fine section of passage precedes Sump 4 in the downstream Maytime Series of Agen Allwedd.

Above left: Golondrinas in North America is the second deepest free-fall shaft (335 metres) in the world. From the bottom, the abseiling caver appears as a speck of dust against the sky.
Above right: Bill Boman ascends the 49-metre entrance shaft of Hell Hole in West Virginia.
Below left: Starting out on the 16-mile walk to Green Fork Falls Cave, Montana.
Bottom left: Dave Morris views the desolate expanse of the Main Plateau from Antenna Ridge, Iran.
Below right: Our first camp on Antenna Ridge, the morning after the trip down Cyrus Le Grand.

Dr. Peter Glanvill abseils down the funnel of snow and ice in the second shaft of Crystal Pot, Iran.

pacious tubeways like this one at Peak Cavern, Derbyshire, provide a welcome interlude to the
ual difficulties.

Above left: The mysterious Main Rising at the head of the streamway in Speedwell Cavern, Derbyshire.

Above right: Kevin Drakely examines historical graffiti on the walls of Speedwell Cavern.

Left: Robert Palmer floats in the clear water above the entrance to Rat Cay Blue Hole in the Bahamas.

Below left: A typical inland blue hole on Andros Island, viewed from the air.

Below right: Dr. Tony Boycott floats suspended at a depth of 25 metres amongst the huge stalactites of Stalactite Blue Hole.

Above left: The heavily-kitted Rob Palmer passes through the Stal chambers of Conch Blue Hole.
Above right: Rob Palmer fins through a large passage (450 metres) into Conch Blue Hole.
Left: Rob Palmer in a chamber 300 metres from the entrance in Conch Blue Hole.
Below left: The ill-fated hydroid set upon a small stalagmite 300 metres into Conch Blue Hole.
Below right: Rob Parker (left), myself (centre) and Julian Walker (right) rush to meet a dive deadline.

Above: Ray Stead (left) and myself at the diving base in Chamber 9, Wookey Hole, prior to the deep diving operation in October 1982.
Below left: A section of rapids in Chamber 24 at Wookey Hole makes access to the further reaches difficult.
Below right: A typically beautiful section of cave discovered in Crag Cave, County Kerry, August 1983 after a very short and easy dive. One mile of passages was discovered – a cave diver's dream!

These were pre-revolution days and in Tehran we were based at the British Institute of Persian Studies, a large building in a select area of the capital just down the hill from the Shah's palace. By comparison with the cold, damp weather in Britain, it was summer, though not completely devoid of wintry reminders. Above the clear air of the upper city the beautifully snow-clad Elburz Mountains towered majestically, as though but a stone's throw away. In the other direction we could look out from the tranquility of our little haven on to the haze, bustle and noise of the grimy third-world city.

'Must be an alcoholic, this producer' I thought, as Alan Bell started unloading six bottles of whisky.

'Sorry lads this stuff's earmarked.'

Two days later the booze had gone but all the gear had been freed from the customs; corruption seemed to be everywhere. The rest of the film crew had yet to arrive and leaving Alan, efficient and pragmatic, to sort things out, Anthony, Richard and myself set off for the mountains in advance.

We disembarked from the immaculate first-class train at Doorood, a large town whose one and only claim to fame, apart from the being the last real stop before Abadan, was its hideous cement factory. This belched out smoke and dust around the clock and was plainly visible for miles around. It reminded me of Mervyn Peake's Industrial Factory in *Titus Alone;* a steel and concrete hell house. The sooner we were away from here the better, but first we had two days to kill.

Just about the only interesting feature of the town was the place we referred to as 'Al Capone's'. This was a most unusual establishment; it was situated a short distance from the railway station and each time we walked by, it further aroused our curiosity. The front possessed two huge plate glass windows, one either side of the door, and both white washed. There were no signs up or produce on display. Adding to the mystery was the fact that the only people who ever seemed to enter or leave were really shifty, sneaky-looking individuals.

The day after we arrived we were having an ice cream nearby when coming from the direction of the station we noticed a chap walking towards the place who was obviously trying to make himself inconspicuous; he stood out a mile. He was walking at an erratic pace, furtively looking over his shoulder and nipping in and out of alleys and the like. When he reached the door of the mystery building, he knocked gently a couple of times and jabbered away in a low voice to someone behind the door. The next second the door was opened fractionally and he slipped inside. Instantly the door closed.

'What is that place Anthony?'

'That's the local booze store; booze is illegal here because the religion forbids it.'

'Do you reckon we'd get in?'

'Probably, we're westerners.'

That was it. Anthony went off to see some local government official and we strolled along to the saloon. A few moments later the door creaked ajar and this squat, seedily-suited Iranian, type-cast for a '30s Al Capone movie peeped out at us. Richard motioned for a drink and we were speedily ushered inside to join the three or four other shady-looking customers. Even before we'd reached the counter three heavy bolts had been secured across the door and 'Al Capone' had taken a seat. I looked at Richard.

'Bloody hell, we've been locked in!' I whispered.

Looking around the place it had more the feel of a dairy, or perhaps a slaughter house, than a bar. The walls were painted glossy white and the floor consisted of reddish brown, glazed ceramic tiles. There were a couple of circular tables made of steel and again painted white, and perhaps a dozen cheap looking seats. The choice of booze was vodka, vodka or vodka; all the same brand, all imported from Russia.

It was a very strange, unnerving, experience. As we quietly sipped our drinks 'Al Capone's' beady eyes maintained a constant surveillance from the seat by the door. The other characters chatted among themselves, every now and again casting suspicious looks our way. We didn't stay long and we didn't go there again; I could just imagine us being robbed, getting our throats cut, and our bodies being cast into some concrete blocks a short distance away.

Later the same day we found that we had been allocated a personal guard, or liaison officer, who it would appear was instructed never to let us out of his sight; not even for a moment. Whether this was anything to do with our visit to the bar was impossible to say, but our shadow took his duty so seriously that we couldn't even go to the toilet without feeling that he had his eye on us. About six feet tall, he looked the part with his polished boots, a reasonable green khaki uniform and a flat-topped hat to match — that is until you noticed the untidy stubble on his chin and his crude rifle. He never went anywhere without it, the barrel of which was always stuffed with some multicoloured rag (had it been a pistol then we might have been forgiven for thinking it was one of those toys which discharge a little flag with the word 'BANG' emblazoned on it when it's fired). With this slung over his shoulder he proudly marched around, at least in Doorood, a few paces behind us. Ammunition-wise he possessed just five bullets which he counted every day, each bullet individually wrapped in a small pouch.

The two days we stayed in Doorood were two days too long and we were greatly relieved when the necessary clearance to proceed came through. With enough provisions to last us a few days we caught a train deep into the mountains. The route followed a deep and twisting gorge, which was carved into the most rugged limestone scenery I'd ever seen. Whether it was good limestone for caves seemed doubtful; all too often the rocks appeared contorted and broken, a result no doubt of the frequent earth movements that occur in Iran.

Anthony was always talking; if not talking then picking at any bit of food that happened to be available. His particular forte was relating anecdotes and surprising us with bits of unexpected information.

'The Germans constructed this line you know, back in 1937. What a feat of engineering; there must be 30 miles of tunnels along this one stretch down to Abadan. And the irony is that the Russians used it against them during the war!'

In fact it had been two German engineers who had first stumbled on the blind cave fish during the construction phase and since that time no one, until Anthony had bothered to check up on the siting.

After a couple of hours we disembarked at the small hamlet of Tang e Haft that seemed to be set in the middle of nowhere. A hot gruelling walk of over three miles took us from the railway line up a small tributary valley towards the diving site, but after the barren wastes to which we had become accustomed the contrasting colours and magnificent proportions of the scenery were refreshing. It felt extremely isolated: the nearest road was back in Doorood and the rail link at Tang e Haft was the sole form of communication.

Just prior to the diving site we entered a settlement of mud huts and the scene that now met our gaze was like something from the Old Testament. The people who flocked around us were wearing clothes that their ancestors might have worn back in Biblical days. Anthony, who was recognised from his visit the previous year, greeted everyone warmly — and for a while our way forward was completely blocked. Then suddenly an aged, white haired old man with a turban created a path for us — it was like a scene from the big motion picture 'The Ten Commandments' — and we witnessed the return of the prodigal son. If only the camera had recorded this! Anthony seemed to be enjoying his role enormously as out of his knapsack he carefully produced a mounted black and white print of the headman himself, taken the previous year. This was duly presented and from then on we were treated like royalty.

It was impossible to refuse the invitation to take *chai* (tea) and very shortly we came to appreciate exactly how these people lived. The head man's house was typical, crude and basic. Rectangular in shape there was but one main room, with a simple staggered approach to the door. Constructed of mud and stone, the walls were almost a metre thick with a virtual absence of windows. Inside was almost like being in a cave: cool and dark, swarming with flies. The only light penetrated via the open door, through which ran the occasional chicken, frightened perhaps by some quarrelsome guard dog outside. The roofs were flat on all the houses, and were of considerable thickness and supported quite literally upon tree trunks laid horizontally from wall to wall. The walls themselves were constructed of branches, straw and caked mud. Inside the room had little embellishment, save a small picture of the Shah or some religious leader, and a large chest. There was no other furniture.

We sat on the floor, on a carpet that was specially laid out for us, and took tea from a small glass about the size of a large egg-cup or small whisky glass. There was no milk and the ritual involved popping a lump of sugar straight into one's mouth and then sipping the tea through the sugar. It was quite normal for our hosts to consume four or five lumps per small glass and as fast as the wooden sugar bowl was depleted more lumps were cut to size, using a machete, from a large solid block. The whole while countless flies circulated unhindered between the doorway, the lumps of sugar and our glasses. No one seemed to mind so neither did we.

It must have been a good two hours later before we reached the flooded cave. As we approached the pool, down a narrow trench-like gorge, Anthony turned, his face beaming:

'There it is lads,' he said proudly.

'Bloody hell, is that it?' I muttered to Richard.

Our guard yawned. For once I almost sympathised with him. He couldn't see what the hell anyone could find of interest in this wilderness, and was staring somewhat disbelievingly at the pool.

'It doesn't look much like those photographs of yours Anthony,' said Richard.

That was the understatement of the year! The picture we'd been shown gave the impression of some lake nestling at the foot of a large cliff, something like the resurgence pool at Wookey Hole or a more watery version of the rising at Malham Cove. I'd never have believed that a camera was capable of such misrepresentation. The site that now confronted us was an elongated pool about two metres wide by four metres long and it wasn't as though it looked all that promising.

'Looks good that,' said Richard.

Richard was being positive. We'd had a free trip to Iran; the least we could do was to look enthusiastic, although to our experienced eye it was an acute disappointment. After all to Anthony it was a flooded cave full of blind fish.

Shortly afterwards it was time for Anthony to make his way back to Doorood as he still had arrangements to make concerning the film crew. We were delighted at being left to our own devices but soon found we were rather limited with regard to our activities. Somehow we had managed to come all the way from Tehran without any caving gear, not even a hand torch.

The next day Richard, the guard and I set off on a recce of the upper part of the valley. Everywhere around us was limestone; surely there must be some decent caves. We trudged on; our limbs felt like lead; the heat of the day and our lack of acclimatisation were beginning to tell. En route we received a further warm welcome from a group of Lure nomads, and again we were to marvel at the simplistic life of these peoples.

Everything depended upon pastoralism. Sheep and goats rummaged about in the endless search for food (if it was spring now, goodness knows what they lived on for the rest of the year) and in a corner a tightly woven bamboo enclosure served as a pen for the kids and lambs at milking time. Young girls performed the latter task, sheep and goats alike standing perfectly still, untethered, while the milk was collected in a plastic bucket. Chickens ran clucking to every corner of the tent and were occasionally shoo'd away by the women. Beautiful little chicks scurried between our feet and like the hens nibbled at the bread, which in Iran came in sheets about the shape, size and consistency of a slightly soggy newspaper. These people had very few possessions and the few they had would be carried by the mules and donkeys when it was time to move on to greener pastures.

By our standards the nomads and villagers alike lived in abject poverty, yet they were among the friendliest people that we had come across. What little they had they were quite prepared to share. There was no envy, jealousy or begging that one encounters so often in third world towns or cities. The people appeared genuinely content with their lot in life. The men tended the flocks, or the few rudimentary fields of corn, and occasionally travelled to town to buy or sell other commodities. The women milked the animals, ground corn, carried water and performed a multitude of household tasks beyond the comprehension of housewives back in Britain. The latter included spinning yarn from raw wool, dying it and weaving it into carpets using methods unchanged for centuries.

In the mountains hospitality to travellers seemed to be a time honoured tradition. Often, as with the nomads, we would be presented with a drink as we arrived at their camp. This normally took the form of a metal tureen containing a milky looking substance called 'dough'. Whenever it appeared our guard's eyes would light up, but to us the whey-like drink was totally nauseating. The natural desire was to regurgitate the liquid and after a mouthful or two we would express humble gratitude and pass the communal bowl on to someone else. Our guard could drink several pints in one go. It had a vaguely minty flavour, it certainly quenched our thirst, and after a while we got used to it.

About this stage an enquiry would usually be made by one of the villagers of our companion. Then we would see his eyeballs roll upwards and watch as he shrugged his shoulders. We could well imagine the conversation.

'Mad Englishmen, they've come out here to look at little fish and holes in the ground. By the grace of the Almighty I had to laugh this morning. Him with the golden hair; he crawled down into a porcupine hole. I've never seen anyone move so fast in my life. The world must be going crazy.'

At meals bread and a thick yohurt-like substance, *mast,* was always provided. To us it was more like bread and lard; the white sticky substance was completely tasteless. No cutlery or crockery was used, a piece of bread was just broken off and dipped straight into the lard. Fried eggs, and rice pudding (unfortunately minus any sugar) seemed to be the only delicacies. There were no luxuries here; this was a subsistence economy tempered with a small amount of trading for commodities like sugar and rice.

But change was in the air. The odd teenager possessed a new radio. Did they know about the mounting political crisis in Tehran? Did they know that all around them events might well be moving towards a Third World War? Did they care? This was a land where life went on regardless, a land where man had left no mark, and where he and nature co-existed in relative harmony.

But the aesthetic qualities of an April existence in this idyllic setting were countered by acutely distressing sights. Men of no great age stumbled around with cataracts, others with deformed limbs. It could not be our choice of lifestyle. The experiences were savoured, photographed and memorised.

How could we ever forget, for instance, the night which we spent on the head man's roof? From early evening we sat around on carpets on the mud surface, together with all the men and boys of the village. Amid endless cups of *chai* we chatted away as best we could. The main conversation was with the elder boys who were learning English in Tang e Haft, although their knowledge of the subject was little more advanced than our knowledge of Iranian. As the evening wore on it was clear that the women were excluded from any such events. They stood around below and talked among themselves. At a suitable hour we petitioned for leave to make our camp, but our friends would not hear of it.

Then we realised: the two of us were to have the honour of sleeping on this roof, using the carpets as mattresses. At some stage in the evening our guard had disappeared. What could this mean? 'Perhaps he's nipped off somewhere to see a friend,' said Richard. It was suspicious anyway.

Before settling down for the night we climbed down a ladder and strolled off to relieve ourselves of all the excess *chai*. What a sight met our eyes. All the neighbouring roofs were covered by scores of sleeping animals, mostly sheep and goats. Getting to sleep was difficult. The occasional bleat or bark rent the air and our sleeping bags were uncomfortably hot. Shortly we began to itch.

Morning came early, heralded by a veritable cacophony of noise and activity. Cocks crowed, dogs fought, an incessant bleating emanated from the other stock, while all about children screamed and shouted. Emerging from our bags to join our hosts we found ourselves covered in small red lumps that were obviously flea bites; so it wasn't heat rash that had kept us awake after all. We looked one hell of a mess. Our guard looked fairly amused when he saw us — perhaps that's why he'd disappeared. He was getting his own back; he knew we'd get bitten. Being thoroughly prepared for all eventualities we realised that we hadn't got any first aid equipment. For a day or two we were worried, but slowly it became a joke; we grew to live with our newly acquired parasites.

The day came when we had to return to Doorood and while we were sorry to leave our friends we were both looking forward to an improvement in our diet. Strolling in to the one and only restaurant to await the full team I noticed three crates of Coca Cola at the far end of the room. This was just what we needed and I walked over to get a couple of bottles. Reaching down I suddenly realised that Iranian Coke was white!

'Ugh, it's that dreadful stuff *dough.*'

Expecting something palatable and western, it came as a great shock. We sat down and made do with a few *chais*, some hard boiled eggs, bread and some nasty-tasting cheese.

It wasn't long before Anthony arrived, closely followed by Alan Bell and the 'World About Us' team. As soon as he saw our bites he burst out laughing.

'Oh I had that last year; lasts abour four days! Animal fleas probably; can't live on humans for more than a few days.'

With the exception of Alan, the rest of the team instantly backed off. We never even got a handshake and they refused point blank to sit at the same table. It was a poor welcome.

'Ah the British are such a civilised race, so tolerant, caring and friendly.'

'Don't worry about it,' said Anthony. 'How did you get on otherwise?'

We gave a full breakdown and in turn got an update on the plans.

'Look at that,' exclaimed Richard suddenly.

'Christ, what a star!'

On the next table the sound technician had broken open a tin of Ambrosia Cream Rice, and was proceeding to eat it direct from the tin.

'Oh he won't eat anything else until we set up camp and our food's unpacked,' said Anthony casually. 'He's got that brief case full of them.'

There was no question of them being shared.

Alan Bell's efficiency was impressive. He saw to it for example that a 'mini train', a sort of maintenance vehicle suitable for transporting half a dozen people, was placed at our disposal, and despite all the prevarication and bureaucratic red tape he always seemed to stay on top of the situation. There was little doubt that he was out to make the best possible documentary.

The next day as the cameras whirred, we rattled perilously down the line. Our role, for the purpose of filming, now became that of two friends of Anthony who had accompanied him to Iran to study the fishes' habitat.

Base camp was situated next to the railway line at the bottom of the tributary valley. This soon became a 'little England', with its regimented row of tents and reflection of British tastes and cuisine. By night a generator flood lit the scene enabling us to work on the maintenance of equipment, play card games, read or whatever. It was all very civilised.

It was also an interesting insight to the glossy world of television. Other than Bell, there was a camera man, a sound technician and a fourth chap who would normally have been responsible for lighting, but who seemed to have little to do. With the exception of Alan and Anthony a bloody minded attitude seemed to pervade everything the crew did and there was little team spirit in the camp. Our food was never prepared for us along with that of the crew and we had to fend for ourselves. When I considered that they had every conceivable catering facility at their disposal, and we had next to nothing, it was clear that for them the meaning of common courtesy had been lost.

Our walk through the village near the diving site now became quite impersonal. We were working to a schedule and as such were forced to snub our villager friends. The crew had no inclination to take *chai* and had they seen the flies swarming about the sugar bowl it was almost certain that they would have refused the hospitality. In none of our conversations did the Iranians warrant a comment; in the eyes of our fellow countrymen these people were squalid, flea-infested wretches. I felt sad. Anthony had experienced all this before and he had become quite philosophical about it all. To him the 'unfeeling', discourteous behaviour of the crew was just another facet of human nature. He upheld his own values while at the same time maintaining a shrewd business-like attitude with the crew; after all this was his bread and butter.

The day of our dive was a real carnival. It was work as usual for our lads but the local Iranians had a real treat. Like an overgrown schoolboy Anthony rolled his trousers up to his knees and waded gingerly into the pool, clutching a kiddie's fishing net in one hand and a perspex container in the other. From our position, kitting up a few metres away, all we could see was Anthony's hefty backside bobbing around like an upturned duck. About twelve little tiddlers were netted, filmed and subsequently transported back to London. By this time scores of Iranians lined the crags above like a herd of inquisitive mountain goats. How on earth they got up into some of the positions without falling or dislodging some of the many loose boulders I don't know.

Eager discussions now took place between crew and director. I could just imagine the chat:

'As union spokesman we insist on danger money to carry on filming. We haven't had our lunchbreak so I think you should clock us extra time tonight as well.'

It was only about 1.00 pm but the sound technician was beginning to grumble, the cameraman started to scratch and the lighting technician came around the corner moaning about a laundry allowance or something; apparently he'd just stepped on some sewage. The Iranian huts possessed no latrines and people simply went outside in the open. Our guard, who'd been keeping a low profile up till now, also saw the funny side. He turned to an Iranian at his shoulder, gave a wry smile and pinched his nose, indicating that the lighting technician was smelling.

Alan Bell probably promised them the earth to keep them working and now it was our turn to provide the amusement. To my mind we were only lending a few minutes of suspense to the documentary; there didn't seem much possibility that the sump would go.

About four metres in I reached a flooded pot. This was uncomfortably restricted so I carried on down feet first while Richard held the line in place at the top. Eventually, in a total blackout, a depth of 18 metres was reached. Here the dive was aborted. We surfaced and related the findings. The B.B.C. had their film and we'd had our dive, all ten minutes of it. Later that day our six cylinders, which we had compressed the previous night, were emptied once more ready to be freighted home.

Programme-wise everything had gone relatively smoothly and now it was time to pack. On such projects it was normal to have a couple of days in hand, days which could be spent touring, just relaxing, or haggling over some souvenir. But there was no spark of life in this crew; they were going to fly straight back home. Richard and I had earmarked one day for travelling down to the plains on the west side of the Zagros, near Abadan. However permission for this was not forthcoming from the Iranian authorities.

In our search for caves several entrances were found near camp but by day these were inundated by large numbers of bats. The creatures swooped menacingly, as thick as a swarm of bees, and the furthest point reached was only about 75 metres. Here the stench was nauseating and the atmosphere stifling. Above and around me bats as big as jackdaws squeaked and circled; below all manner of creeping insects turned my stomach. Beads of perspiration ran down my face and back. This I recalled was a prime spot to contract the tropical disease 'Histoplasmosis' and of an instant the exploratory urge was to wane. I chimneyed back up the guano slope and left. There were caves to be explored therefore, including another sumped resurgence downstream of Tang e Haft, but the area certainly did not have the potential that we were hoping for in the summer.

The next day we caught a third-class train back to Doorood. What an appalling contrast this was to the mode of transport we had used previously. It was more like a cattle wagon than a passenger train; people were crowded in more densely than animals. The rank stale smell was impossible to describe, despite the open windows on either side. Women openly suckled babies while grubby little children hung out the windows hurling abuse and rubbish at wayside travellers. Chickens and goats shared the benches. With heavy bags we shuffled along the corridors until we found a corner wide enough to stand. The crew were horrified. The journey seemed like an eternity and the prospect of Doorood was none too welcoming. The 'Hey meesterr, 'ow are you,' which every Iranian knew by heart now got us down and we were glad to be leaving. It was a very strange mixture of feelings that we harboured on that last gruelling journey.

From Doorood Richard and I decided to catch the night express back to Tehran. Strangely I cannot remember even saying goodbye to the crew. Three days later we flew over the northern part of the Zagros Mountains at an altitude of 30,000 feet — bound for Rome. Below and clearly visible through the clouds lay high mountains blanketed with snow. Somewhere down there was Kuh-e-Shahu, our mountain, waiting.

6

The Ramshackle Expedition To Iran

IN SEARCH OF A DEPTH RECORD

Within a short while of returning home Richard withdrew from the main expedition; he had some personal problems that demanded urgent attention. This left us in a bit of a predicament. Who was to be leader? At the next meeting there were two immediate nominees for the post: John Elliot from the Royal Forest of Dean Caving Club and myself. I excused myself owing to the fact that I was taking along my fiancée, Sally, which might have provoked a reaction at a later stage, especially as she was the only woman on the 18-person team. Bob Lewis who had already done so much towards the preparations was another possibility, but he declined 100 per cent; he was too much of an individualist and he didn't want the responsibility. John Elliot therefore assumed the role of leader while Geoff Richings took that of treasurer.

The team list included John Elliot, Bob Lewis, Pete Glanvill, Geoff Richings, Mike Jay, Andy Dawe, Chris Hannam, Tony Madison, Doug McFarlane, John King, Barry Weaver, Dave Viggers, Phil Rust, Steve West, Dave Morris, Pete Francis, Sally and myself.

Through June and July of 1977 preparations for the big event continued with ever pressing urgency. At the same time it became increasingly obvious that a good proportion of the team had never seriously undertaken any SRT work. Considering that we were after a world depth record, and that everything we were likely to find would be vertical, such apathy was hard to comprehend. Getting to grips with a new technique was not something to be relished high on an isolated mountain 3,000 miles from home. For many this was to be the one big trip of a lifetime; the one for which jobs were to be sacrificed and savings spent; for a few it appeared to be an extended holiday, not to be taken too seriously.

We knew that there were caves on Kuh-e-Shahu because a small party of French cavers led by M. Jean Farcy had sent us limited correspondence on the place. The site of greatest potential was Cyrus Le Grand, explored by Farcy to a depth of 185 metres from an entrance at a supposed altitude of over 3,000 metres. Considering the location and the considerable fall to the valley below there was a cave depth potential of 2,150 metres.

But what had the French done since their trip in 1974? Had they been back? Was the cave still going and was this the reason for the lack of communictions? Even if we did not know the answers to these questions at least ours was not the uncertainty of the first expedition to Kuh-e-Parau; at least we knew that there were caves and we knew that we had that all important potential for a record breaker.

At our meetings of this time other caves were also listed while the main difficulties of porterage, heat and water were also outlined. Some of us began daily runs and training sessions to ensure that we would be fit enough to see it through.

Possibly the greatest unknown in this preparatory stage was the vehicle that was to take us over: an ex-Bristol omnibus, circa 1954. This I reflected was almost as old as I was and the subject was so 'hush-hush' anyone would have thought it was some top secret weapon awaiting its great unveiling. 'Somewhere in Bristol' and 'being completely overhauled' was all we ever seemed to hear.

'Don't worry chaps, it'll be ready' came Mike Jay's reassuring voice at each meeting. How would such a coach cope with a twisting mountain track or with ferrying equipment high on to a mountain? Some of us had a pretty shrewd idea. Why on earth we never had a trial run in the thing to see how it performed, get to know each other and do some SRT goodness only knows.

Then came the great day; the day the Welsh contingent were picked up in Cardiff. The quiet cul de sac erupted into life as our transportation rumbled in. From a distance it sounded more like a chieftain tank than a bus and what an eye catcher it proved to be. Every household turned out to view the thing. It might have been a float from a carnival or a political rally; none of us had ever seen anything like it. Stuck all over the outside and on some of the windows were multicoloured symbols denoting the extent of our sponsorship. It seemed almost criminal to subject it to the abuse that was inevitable over the ensuing weeks; it should have gone to an exhibition of contemporary art. We began loading up.

One of the first things to go on board was the food. As food officer Pete Francis had amassed an incredible amount of provisions; wherever we ended up we certainly wouldn't go hungry. Gradually as we humped the stuff on board, I became aware of something odd.

'You got shares in Goblin Foods Pete? Half this lot must be tinned beef-burgers!'

'We got a good discount there,' came the proud reply.

For months after the trip I still had nightmares about beef-burgers. We must have had about a quarter of a ton of the things and they were on the menu daily. At the end of the expedition we still had two cases left and these were stashed inside a cave at the last high level camp ready for the next expedition.

With the gear all stowed at the back of the bus and everyone safely on board the engine was started and in a cloud of smoke and dust we thundered off. Travelling east at a speed of 40-50mph, Mike assured us that she was 'running like a bird'. The rest of us looked at each other; by comparison with a normal bus 'croaking fit to die' might have been a more appropriate description.

That night it was a very jovial crew who gathered at the Hunters Lodge, to relish and savour those last few pints for which we would all be pining in a couple of weeks. The bus eventually returned to Bristol for the night while the revellers dispersed among the various caving huts.

Come the dawn problems arose. News arrived early that a half shaft on the bus had gone just outside Bristol. We knew that the matter was in capable hands so the rest of us began to amass and sort gear for packaging. It was hours before the bus arrived and when it did everything was frantically piled in. In no time at all the expression on Mike's face became serious and then he began shaking his head.

'We're right down on the springs chaps — that's it.'

With loads more gear still to be packed it was clear that certain things would have to be left behind. The scene now became chaotic and our leader's voice rang out above the din.

'Priority equipment first lads.'

Amusingly everyone had his own idea of what constituted

priority gear. Those experienced with SRT removed the ladders at one end of the bus while almost incredulously the 'ladder men' wrought similar havoc on the rope stocks at the other end. Matters became so confused that only Bob Lewis seemed to have any idea of what was happening. He seemed to be everywhere at once and it was impossible to ignore his heart felt pleas.

'Leave those steel carabiners behind. Those peg hammers can go as well.'

All manner of items were eliminated.

After many more hours had elapsed the load was deemed to be tolerable. The press took their pictures and we were left in little doubt that we stood no chance of making our Dover ferry booking. To stop over for one more night seemed to be the only answer.

In Bristol the following morning we stocked up with additional half shafts and then it was on to Dover. Here we missed another ferry booking. Eventually, as the sun began to set, we caught a boat to Ostend. At last we were on our way and in the time honoured tradition this was the moment for celebration, and what a celebration it was. Too much was consumed too quickly and for the latter half of the sailing the youngest member of the team, Steve, could be seen hanging over the side being violently ill.

Landing in Ostend it was evident that like some of its pasengers our coach was 'hung over'. 'Mutton dressed up as lamb' was one description I heard as delays followed closely, one after another. These were all teething problems that could better have been diagnosed and treated in Britain. Central to the whole problem was that of the cooling system. This was grossly inadequate and lengthy stops were necessary just to let the engine cool. Fortunately the weather was superb and in high spirits worries were suppressed, although gradually it became obvious to everyone that if we couldn't cope with the heat here in Europe how on earth would we begin to cope with the soaring temperatures of Turkey and Iran?

Some miles from Frankfurt and about the fourth time that day the vehicle was forced into a service area to cool and we met a British transcontinental truck driver. He didn't rate our chances very highly. After the chat there were no smiling faces, rather looks of despondency. It was almost a case of smelling salts for Bob who looked as though he was about to pass out at any

122

moment. But with true British spirit we limped on to Frankfurt in the forlorn hope that we might cure the problem with the addition of another radiator. A campsite was found and the engineers set out in search of a scrap yard. That evening beaming faces told the tale. They had purchased not one but two radiators, 'just in case', for a price of around £5.00. The first of these was soon plumbed into the existing system and the next day our dual-radiator coach rolled on down the E5, her passengers slightly more confident than hitherto.

But the calamities were by no means over and late one night, ascending the Phyrnpass in Austria, another bout of excitement came our way. Everyone was feeling tired after a lengthy stop-start day and several people had nodded off to sleep. I was sitting fairly close to the front when Mike's head peered out from the driver's cab. Quite casually he called back.

'We're on fire chaps.'

No one reacted. Surely if there was a fire there would be a note of urgency? The coach ground to a halt and Mike repeated himself a little louder. Instantly there was a rush for the door. Outside, keyed up as ever, our action man, Bob Lewis, was demonically dashing back and forth with the extinguisher trying to find the source of the flames. In a few minutes the emergency had passed. The flames leaping from the underside of the vehicle, had been safely put out. Mike was still unruffled as he pointed to the source of the problem beneath the discoloured side panel.

'It's that diesel drip tray; I was expecting it to overflow one of these days. I guess the exhaust system underneath it was getting a little hot on that ascent.' Bob's face was a picture. You could read the reaction.

'. . . expecting it; my God!' There was no doubt about it, Bob was spent; he was a nervous wreck and we hadn't been going more than five days.

Having seen flames licking up around the windows as we stopped there was an immense feeling of relief on everyone's part that the damage hadn't been more serious. So easily could it have been disastrous; there we stood, outside the coach without a possession in the world, thankful that we hadn't lost the lot. Last to leave the sinking ship had been our leader, who amid the confusion had taken the opportunity of carrying off all his valuables.

So that's what a captain does when a boat goes down! That was initiative.

In view of the cooling problem Mike had paid very close attention to the temperature gauge all along, but we were constantly amazed at the dogged enthusiasm he possessed with regard to the driving. For over twelve hours a day he coaxed and carefully nursed the bus along; possibly an excessive responsibility for one person.

Istanbul and the Bosphorous were reached on the eleventh day after we had left Britain. Now would come the real test for the vehicle: the high passes, extreme summer temperatures and the unmetalled road surfaces. A half a day into Asia Mike pulled in to a wayside park and made another of his nonchalent announcements.

'She's getting a little warm, we'll have to plumb in the third radiator.'

Cavers are nothing if not resourceful and if the original coach makers could have seen the bodging that ensued over the next couple of hours they would have been horrified. The second radiator had been fixed directly in front of the first; now the third was set some distance along one of the sides. It was a real lash up with bits of tubing being attached to one another by any possible method. But it worked and that was all that mattered. Water was now circulating all over the place and a couple of days' slow travelling suggested that we might just get there.

Gone now was the civilisation that we knew. This was Turkey with its needle-like minarets breaking the skyline of every settlement long before we reached it. From the top of these structures horn-shaped amplifiers wailed to the holy five times each day. Noisy buses covered the villages with dust, while oxen carts gathered by the frequent waterpipe oases; the animals unperturbed by the gathering forces of the twentieth century.

Great care was now being lavished upon our coach. With the approaching danger of a boil we would pull in and take a rest. In fact the drive out, if one ignored the frustration of the breakdowns, was highly pleasurable. The coach was spacious and with a few sleeping bags thrown out on to the kit in the back three or four people could easily sleep in comparative comfort while we travelled. Dave Viggers had brought his hammock and this, slung between the luggage racks, likewise proved a popular spot.

For those a little more intent upon activity there was the usual choice of cards or chess while for those of us who liked playing with cameras there was always the odd crash to watch out for; Turkey must have the worst drivers in the world.

Equipped as we were with two sliding roof panels, superb views were obtained from the roof while we were actually in motion. Perched on this lofty seat, high above any other form of transport, and with the sun and wind on our faces it was an invigorating way to travel. Travelling on the roof also gave the added advantage of cultivating a good sun-tan and it was interesting to note that no one was to use sun tan cream extensively after about three weeks. With red hair and fair skin I had a nasty habit of burning each and every summer back home, but with careful acclimatisation I was to use no cream at all after our arrival in Iran.

We normally cooked our main meal of the day in the evening, while it was still light and then pushed on for a few hours into the cool of the night. But in Turkey travel after dark was rife with additional dangers such as pits, ramps and unmetalled roads, which seemed to be endemic. Having usually been on the road since 7.30 in the morning the days were long and when Mike decided that enough was enough we were always grateful to throw out our bags on to the roadside verge and just crash out. Despite the fatigue, the starlit skies inevitably commanded attention even for those who knew nothing of astronomy or the actual constellations. Every few minutes, or so it seemed, someone would point out the ephemeral trail of another earth-bound meteorite as it blazed across the sky. Then gradually the exclamations would die away as one by one we fell asleep.

By day 15 we reached the Turkish-Iranian border and suddenly there was a flicker of hope; we were going to make it after all. And three days later the sight of the massive limestone scenery just before Kermanshah was something magical. This was an outlier of the mountain on which Ghar Parau was situated and everyone started jabbering at once. Huge limestone crags towered above us, dazzling us in the morning sunlight; our minds boggled at the scale of it all. Like ship wrecked sailors cast adrift after some horrific ordeal it was as though we had at long last seen land. After 18 days of uncertainty when it had seemed so often likely that the bus wouldn't make it and that we would

125

have to abort the trip, we were there; we were on a caving expedition once more.

Hardly had we arrived in Kermanshah than we were invited to the home of an English couple, Ken and Frances Skjonnemand. The offer of a clean up and swim was impossible to turn down; this was the first real opportunity to have a good wash since we had left home and goodness knows how long it would be before we would get the chance again. Our luck had turned. The meeting was more fortunate than anyone could possibly have realised at the time, for by the end of our stay in Iran these kind people were to be of immense help to us.

The evening we spent with them was memorable for our 'taster' of night life in the city. Ken supplied us with directions and about half an hour's walk saw us at the International Club. There was a cordial welcome and we really began to feel at home, especially as the drinks were free. It was an enjoyable evening for all concerned and at about 11.30 pm the last of us set off to happily walk back. About an hour later we realised that Kermanshah was a big place, and that we were lost. Navigation above ground has never been my strong point; it was the same old story — it all looked the same. There was a regular grid pattern to the layout of the city, but the area in which we now found ourselves didn't seem to have any street names.

'Why don't you ask somebody?' suggested Sally. 'You've obviously got us completely lost.'

'Such confidence.' I thought.

Matters were then complicated slightly when I asked Pete for some information.

'That's bloody marvellous,' he replied. 'You mean you don't know Ken and Frances' address? Or even their surname?'

'Bit of an oversight that!'

We looked at each other. Now we were really in a mess, and not being conversant in the language we didn't know how to go about asking directions for a 'big bus' or 'many English people'. We walked on. As we did so we gradually became aware that somewhere nearby people were whistling signals to one another. We began to get edgy; if these people decided to mug us there was no one else around to come to our rescue. It was an unnerving experience and we were all glad when about fifteen minutes later a car suddenly appeared and drew up alongside us. The tension was

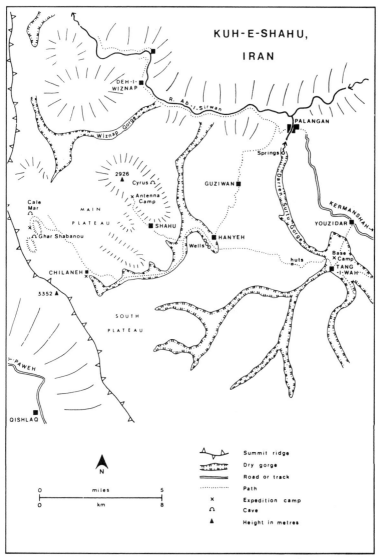

KUH-E-SHAHU,
IRAN

DEH-I-
WIZNAP
R. Ab-i-Sirwan
Wiznap Gorge
PALANGAN
Springs
2926
Cyrus
GUZIWAN
Darreh Suru Gorge
Antenna
Camp
Cale
Mar
MAIN
PLATEAU
SHAHU
KERMANSHAH
Ghar Shabanou
HANYEH
YOUZIDAR
Wells
huts
Base
Camp
CHILANEH
TANG
-I-WAH
3352

SOUTH
PLATEAU

PAWEH

QISHLAQ

N
miles
0   5
0   8
km

Summit ridge
Dry gorge
Road or track
Path
×   Expedition camp
∩   Cave
▲   Height in metres

broken. Two uniformed characters motioned us to get in. Everyone was still subdued and by means of explanation someone
timidly muttered 'English'. The Welsh nationalistic pride had
gone. We sped off. I expected to spend the night in gaol but the
next thing we knew we were delivered right to our hosts'

127

doorstep. It was all a trifle embarrassing; the police laughed and drove off.

The next day we set off for our mountain, a good 65 miles to the west north west. The last 25 miles were along a tortuous track and there was real concern that having got so close our vehicle would now let us down. With limited ground clearance the countless gulleys were a serious threat. Consequently people were forced to walk, push, dig and fill in as the need arose. The back bumper was completely torn off but by midnight we had arrived within a stone's throw of Youzidar, the village which the earlier French party had adopted as their base.

Early the following morning we set about negotiating a spot for our base camp and trying to hire some mules to carry our equipment. Fortunately for us the French had been through this routine before and after an interesting game of international charades, considerable waving of hands and lastly the production of cash, a deal was sealed with the spokesman for the villagers — a friendly looking man called Kareem. With an infectious smile that stretched from ear to ear he assured us he would see to everything.

It was about one and a half miles from the track to our chosen camp site and the journey was to cost the best part of £2.00 per mule. Everything now went smoothly apart from the fact that a couple of people were ill. Steve West who had not recovered from the Channel crossing was so weak that he had to be carried into camp on the back of one of the animals. Sitting on a make-shift saddle one didn't know who to feel most sorry for — Steve or the mule. The former was clutching a plastic bucket in one hand and a box of paper tissues in the other. Judging by the bed-raggled expression on the mule's face this was probably the worst load he'd ever transported. But the comical touch came in the form of the smiling, bubbling Iranian who led the pair into camp. Tugging away at a lead much longer than that held by the other muleteers you could tell at a glance what he thought of his unsavoury cargo.

From base at about 1,000 metres we planned to establish our advance camp on Antenna Ridge, at 2,900 metres, where the French had been based. This would be an ideal staging point for our assault on our prime objective, Cyrus le Grand. High on the mountain, lack of water would be the greatest problem but on the ridge we hoped to be able to obtain an adequate supply from compacted snow and ice, mined from deep shakeholes.

Having hired a team of mules, six of us made the first trip to the ridge early the next morning. Other teams were to follow at intervals of several days. After three hours' hard walking from base we arrived at Hanyeh Wells and a village. This arid, rocky landscape was about the last place on earth I could imagine people choosing to subsist. There was a complete absence of trees, what soil there was could better be described as dust, and the only things that seemed to grow in the inhospitable waste were thistles.

The settlement was evidently a temporary summer camp. While the animals grazed on the mountain, fodder crops were being harvested on the comparatively fertile lowlands. Over 100 people lived here in amazingly spartan conditions. Each family occupied a primitive, dry-stone-walled compound, partially roofed with flimsy branches. Timber and everything else had to be transported from the valley far below. From our point of view it was a photographer's paradise. The women for example were dressed in fabulous colours and often wore skull caps. Attached to these, by virtue of holes drilled in them, were dozens of Iranian coins. Whether they were purely of a decorative nature or intended as an indication of wealth was difficult to ascertain. The wells were picturesque. Here the girls lowered rusty biscuit tins into the narrow shafts, hauled out the water, filled their large black goatskin containers and then wandered off, with the heavily bloated loads balanced somewhat precariously on their heads.

The water from these wells (which were reputed to be the highest source of water on the mountain), made a refreshing break. Another gruelling trek led to the ridge were Kareem took us to the site of the French camp. Having made ourselves at home our porters soon realised that we intended remaining there on our own. Suddenly they all began jabbering at once.

'Ali-ba-ba... Ali-ba-ba,' and other indecipherable sounds.

If that wasn't enough to unnerve us Kareem gestured that we would get our throats cut staying there by ourselves and that we should be on the look out for bears and tigers.

'Do you have a gun? Where is your guard?'

We did our best to reassure them that we were not afraid, but as they set off for the valley and everything went quiet we looked apprehensively at each other.

'Ah, they're pulling our leg,' I said.

'Well they had big cats on the Ghar Parau expeditions,' said Barry, 'and the Iraqi border is just over there; there's been a bit of trouble round here lately.'

'There are definitely bears on these mountains; we'll have to keep a careful look out,' said Pete.

That was it. We spent the next few hours constructing a dry-stone wall, not that it provided any real protection — one good growl and the lot would have collapsed — but it made us feel better.

As the last of our well water was consumed we started looking for snow. Due to the method of extraction we expected to have to tolerate grit and earth, but what we hadn't counted on were the flies and human faeces that seemed to be everywhere. When melted, the new supply was refreshing but given an hour or so to warm up the brown liquid almost made us retch. It didn't seem to matter if it was boiled, sterilised with tablets, filtered through toilet paper or whatever, the detestable sewage-like taste remained. In the days to follow almost everyone fell victim to chronic stomach and bowel complaints; illnesses exacerbated by heat, dehydration, exhaustion and altitude.

The morning after our arrival on the ridge Dave Morris, Tony Maddison, Pete Francis, Sally and I set off down Cyrus le Grand. Despite the heat and having to carry 400 metres of rope and several water containers, everyone was cheerful and hopeful that we were on to something big. Pitches of 115 metres, 8 metres, and 40 metres led quickly through mixed ground to the awkward drop which our predecessors reported as being unbottomed. This was 16 metres in depth and led almost immediately to one of 86 metres. Next came a 6-metre drop and the excitement was very real. We were well into new territory and it seemed as though nothing could stop us. Dave was chattering away non stop when suddenly we rounded a corner and passed an awkward squeeze, only to encounter a severe blow. Staring us in the face, almost unbelievably, was a continental-style rope tied off to a bolt hanger. A stream of exclamations and abuse poured forth none of which was complimentary to the French.

'Bloody Frogs are less co-operative than the Yorkshire lot,' muttered somebody.

'It must mean one of two things,' I said. 'Either they are coming back to push on from where they've left off or this is intended as some sort of jibe or mockery to any subsequent party, and it marks the end of the cave.'

There was only one way to find out; one after the other we slid down the muddy rope. I was expecting the worst and sure enough by the time I unclipped at the bottom of the 22-metre drop Tony had discovered that the rift tapered impossibly in either direction. This was indeed the end of the cave.

After a quick snack and pouring further abuse on the French we began the laborious task of detackling and desperately trying to extricate ourselves from the confines of the termination. Sally meanwhile had started ascending the 86 metre pitch and had just reached a height of 60 metres when she discovered that both her Jumar ascenders were plastered in mud and slipping. The note of panic that filtered down to our ears was impossible to ignore and in my struggle to get to the top of the last pitch I lost my spare carbide lamp, which clattered into the depths. This had to be abandoned as I frantically attempted to sort out Sally's predicament. The only solution seemed to be that she should stay exactly where she was while I tandemmed up the rope with a spare ascender. She would then have one secure point of attachment and be able to remove each of her Jumars in turn and clean the teeth on the cams.

About 25 metres up both of my clamps began to slip but rather than waste time using the spare ascender I slowly worked my way up for a few more metres until I could struggle onto a wide, watery ledge. But no sooner had I crawled to the backwell than the spray falling from above extinguished my carbide lamp. Fortunately Sally had our spare electric light which she shone down the shaft so I could see to clean my Jumars.

By the time Tony arrived at the bottom I was rather concerned as to our predicament as a whole and I called him up to join me. Then with all my problems sorted I set off again while Tony held the rope in to the back of the ledge. If we slipped now at least we wouldn't go all the way to the bottom! I had nearly reached Sally when both my Jumars went again. This was definitely a bit of a crisis as more mud was continually being plastered on to the rope. Another considerable delay followed but eventually we continued to the top.

131

The rest of the exit proved to be thoroughly exhausting and it was over 16 hours before we reached the entrance. There seemed little point in waiting around as the others would be down for quite a while so we returned to camp. The hours ticked by and from the comfort of our sleeping bags we watched the dawn fast approaching. Where were they? Unknown to us they were really having fun. Both Dave and Pete were using Jumars and were having one hell of a time while Tony who was using Gibbs ascenders (which were relatively unaffected by the grease) was having to pass these from one to another so that all three could shuffle their way up the muddied ropes. Eighteen hours after entry the last man was out. Dave led the way back but to add insult to injury he managed to get them lost.

'It's around here somewhere,' repeated Dave as they staggered around on the wild goose chase. Neither Tony nor Pete had the strength to argue and all three were on the point of collapse when they reached us.

'What kept you?' I enquired.

'Got lost boy.'

Tony just looked; Peter slumped onto his bag and passed out.

Cyrus had gone to a depth of 308 metres, but that was it; we were bitterly disappointed. Other teams now arrived from base only to find us spent and dejected.

By now all of us, bar Sally, were severely ill with sickness and diarrhoea and unable to make any contribution to the ongoing explorations. Under the circumstances it seemed best that our group should return to base camp and recuperate. The newcomers proceeded to examine the remaining French leads. In these instances the information that Farcy had given was accurate, but as none of the sites displayed any promise this might have been expected.

To the west of Antenna Ridge lay a plateau, three miles across, absolutely riddled with dolines, the examination of which was a laborious, protracted affair. It was a wilderness; a contorted, fractured landscape of grey rock and dull green thistles; a hellish frustrating wilderness. Phil Rust and Dave Viggers in particular made several long sorties to the foot of the main Summit Ridge but the story was always the same 'Too much broken rock,' and 'Shafts blocked by breakdown.'

132

A distinct pattern of activity became established, namely a rapid turnover in teams working from the high camps. Illness took its toll and after just one week everyone was back at base, disillusioned and rather the worse for wear. The Doc, Phil and crew had finally been forced to quit the ridge when they had run out of petrol for cooking, depleted the medical supply of pills and used up enough sterilising tablets to keep any normal team going for months. But the conditions on Antenna Ridge were far from normal; they were the worst that any of us had ever experienced. Leaving the gear unattended the last group departed in dire straits and by the time they reached the village of Hanyeh Wells, Phil was so weak that he collapsed. As the entire party were on their last legs our doctor, Pete, judged it prudent to leave the casualty in the care of one of the villagers with help to be despatched from base as soon as possible.

Down at base the afternoon was so hot that it was a real effort even to put on a brew of tea. But despite this and severe personal exhaustion Pete instantly tried to muster some of us together to go back and pick up Phil. Angrily he moved from one group to the next stamping his feet and waving his hands high in the air.

'I've got a casualty up there... he could be dying. He must be brought down now... Do you hear me, now!'

But no one budged. To attempt to walk up to Hanyeh in the heat of the day was insane. We made plans for the evening and like the Iranians kept in the shade.

Just as a group were about to set out Phil arrived. After a rest in the shade he'd recovered slightly and for the equivalent of £5.00 had bought a ride back to the valley. Once again the mule had a very sorry look on its face but fortunately by the time they reached base Phil had no more liquid in his system to lose.

With its supply of clean water and abundant medication, base camp helped us make a speedy recovery. We were learning though — I was to find for example that my system could cope with conditions on the mountain for a matter of three or four days but after that severe bowel problems would occur and I would have to return to base for a day or two. Some like Phil and Geoff Richings who tried to combat the ailments on the mountain spent a miserable existence until they were forced to admit defeat. It was understandable that being ill one didn't feel like the long walk down but it proved that no recovery was possible while one continued to drink the snowmelt.

Base itself was no holiday camp. Temperatures often reached over 120°F during the early afternoon and at these times it was all we could do just to sit in the shade preparing endless drinks. Occasionally 'dust devils' would develop, sweeping dirt and possessions in all directions. The stream by which we camped harboured all manner of pests and I had never seen so many frogs in my life. Ants and flies roamed everywhere while a constant nuisance was the hoard of curious Iranians who laid seige to the big kitchen tent. They would turn up in dribs and drabs and just squat, quietly absorbing our every move. They had to be watched at all times, particularly the children who had the mischievous habit of picking things up and walking off with them. Although the people were friendly I never felt that we were as welcome as we had been in April. Perhaps they were suspicious of our numbers or indeed our motives. Whatever the case they were certainly to make good money out of us and to fully avail themselves of our medical facilities.

Of immense satisfaction to our Doc, who clearly enjoyed reminding us how well he had prepared for the trip, were the periodic visits made by the equivalent of the 'Iranian Health Service', who arrived each week to distribute anti-malaria tablets. For us 'Daraprim day' was a Tuesday and taking this tablet was one of the few routines that kept us in touch with the passage of time.

The success of the expedition hinged upon a reasonable water supply, something that was virtually non existent on Antenna Ridge. Having also established that the caving potential was poor in this area it seemed obvious that we should move to a new high level camp. Somewhere close to the main summit ridge seemed to be the best bet. Over the following days we disbanded the Antenna site and transported everything to the Iranian summer camp at Chilaneh. Within a few days of our arrival at the other side of the plateau the native population departed and we moved in to their abandoned accommodation. Despite a better supply of snow the story was the same — virtually everyone who arrived succumbed to illness.

I remember vividly the evening I discovered a promising hole directly beneath the wall of one of the huts. A considerable amount of energy was spent enlarging the cleft sufficiently to allow entry. This done I was feeling rough but even so keen to see if it went anywhere. About 22 metres down the shaft the 'runs' were imminent; what a palava! Fortunately I could get off the rope on to a ledge and then commence the desperate struggle to strip off the sit harness. Beads of perspiration broke out on my forehead as the muddied buckle refused to loosen; every muscle was tensed and it felt as though a dam would burst at any second. Squirming, heaving and cursing I finally got out of the harness, the one piece oversuit and undersuit. Fortunately I'd remembered the toilet paper! Outside the caves there was never any water to spare for washing and experiencing an 'accident' was not a very pleasant thought. By now all my energy was spent; I felt so weak I had to get out. Kitting up once more I had just set off back up the rope when I was violently sick. A cold sweat had broken out, my arms were like lead and my stomach was retching fit to burst. Ah, the delights of caving. I got out alright and someone else polished off the hole.

Barring illness nights spent at this new camp were interesting. Marauding pests like mice and gerbils regularly woke us up as they scampered, rustled and gnawed away at our food supply. They seemed to be especially curious when it came to any sort of container; amazingly some drowned themselves every night in one or other of our water bottles.

The caving prospects in this area suggested initially that things were looking up. Many caves were soon explored but all were of limited horizontal extent, and with a maximum depth of 125 metres. Bob Lewis found an interesting pot nearby which in his typically eccentric way he pushed down several shafts to 78 metres depth . . . but using hand-held lighting and without a helmet. At such holes people like the Doc, with their brand new gear, learned SRT. He and Barry were surveying Bob's Hole one day when Barry gave Pete a ticking off for dropping things on his (Barry's) head. It was only later when they reached the surface that they noticed that one of the two nuts holding the chest box together was missing. One of the offending projectiles had in fact been part of the Doc's SRT gear.

After a full week at Chilaneh most people were back at base again; illness and a visit by Ken and Frances, who were bringing fresh provisions, being the principal reasons for the evacuation.

The luxurious goods, the first real delivery of outside goods, came in the form of an individual ration of two small packets of real milk, two hard boiled eggs, a tomato and two small bottles of fizzy lemonade — absolute heaven after our dried foods and tinned beefburgers.

But even this couldn't raise our spirits more than temporarily — by now morale was rock bottom. This was plainly evident by the deterioration in standards around camp. Washing up and dirty utensils lay strewn around and soft pink toilet paper occasionally wafted past in the wind from the direction of the latrine. At the outset we had agreed that 'nice' foods like peanut butter, Angel Delight and confectionary should go up the mountain for use by those on the sharp end but now we discovered that people at base had sorely depleted the stocks. With its shortage of clean water, base camp might not have been the most idyllic situation but to sustain an assault on a mountain like Kuh-e-Shahu it was essential that people follow the code.

Inter-personal relationships had worsened and lack of motivation could be read on many faces. Some people like poor Steve West were quite literally trapped at base for the majority of the time by ill health; others like Chris Hannam seemed to thrive on it. Bob's antics were about the only thing that kept everybody amused. He seemed to have adopted an air of independence, and would disappear on his own for days on end. On one of these ventures he set out for the furthest reaches of the plateau provisioned with just a packet of digestive biscuits, a box of Alpen and a pint of water. He was eventually 'returned' by the Iranian authorities suffering from an acute bout of dysentry and being suspected of spying! On the positive side however Bob was a good antidote against base camp apathy and in the process of his wanderings made a useful reconnaissance of areas otherwise untouched; among other things Bob established the location of the main risings around the base of the mountain.

On rest days the gorges near base were thoroughly covered and the existence of any resurgence systems ruled out. Five miles down the valley at Palangan for instance lay some huge risings where water welled up from impossibly small fissures at an altitude of just below 1,000 metres. Judging from the geological setting and the cold water presumably the flow originated at considerable depth — hopeless!

There was no doubt that Ken and Frances' visit came in the nick of time but even so it was obvious that something had to happen and soon. The day after our friends' visit the Doc, who seemed to have gone from strength to strength, Dave, Sally and I returned to Chilaneh for what we viewed as possibly the last week's effort. Next day we went to the North Summit (3,385 metres), with the intention of exploring any holes along the ridge to the north. Towards mid afternoon we were forced to descend towards a low col and here we found an area riddled with deep caves. As if this wasn't excitement enough, when we walked over the brow of a hill a sight that was to change the whole course of the expedition greeted our eyes. There in front of us was a living miracle: issuing from a scree slope was a small stream of clean fresh water. This trickled over the surface for 6 metres before plunging into a deep shaft, occupied by an enormous snow plug. With gay abandon we poured away our snow-melt and drank our fill. Instantly our spirits were revived.

Next day our small advance team departed the flea and mouse ridden Camp 3 and taking all the tackle we could carry, struggled three miles along a twisting path to the new area. Dave and I could hardly believe our good fortune as we started to rig the deep shafts. Doc sherpa'd for us, satisfied himself that this was the long sought after location and then rushed off triumphantly for base; clearly we would need a lot more in the way of provisions and the organisation of this was his prime objective.

For a couple of days we pressed on alone. After the hardships that we'd overcome we were floating on a cloud; we had everything we wanted. Like the lead climbers on a major expedition Dave and I had reached our peak of fitness at just the right moment.

One could not wish for a better person than Dave on this sort of venture. He too was a member of South Wales Caving Club and we had operated together as a close knit team for the past couple of years. Dave had made tremendous progress; if only his mates in the Wolverhampton Caving Group could have seen him now.

I'd first really got to know Dave Morris on a visit to Fermanagh with Pete Francis back in October 1974. At the time Dave was a constant source of amusement to his Birmingham clubmates and it didn't take us long to work out why. Like flies to a

137

spider's web he had the amazing knack of attracting disasters. As one of the Birmingham lads once said 'Dave's an accident looking for somewhere to happen.' As Pete and I found out Dave was funny. When normal people were played out, exhausted, and hours from exit in some cave one little witticism from Dave would act as a stiff tonic. The anecdotes were legendary.

Dave's first car for example was a battered old three wheeler, 'The Plastic Pig'. Whilst driving down the A38 in Birmingham one day an abnormally powerful roar, simultaneously accompanied by a loud clatter, indicated that the exhaust system had fallen off. Naturally enough he pulled in to the side of the road to retrieve it. But before he could move more than a couple of paces from the car lights started flashing and bells ringing. Dave stood transfixed as a fire engine on an emergency call came thundering towards him. The exhaust was completely flattened; not worth picking up.

On another occasion while driving home from work the braking system failed. As would anyone else he pulled in to the curb, discovered the oil reservoir to be empty and proceeded to top it up. Clearly there was a leak at some point and the fluid was running to waste. He was only a short distance from home so he decided to carry on, using the brakes as sparingly as possible. At rush hour in Birmingham brakes are essential and in no time at all the reservoir was empty again. There was only a mile or so to go and being an optimist Dave decided to chance it. All went well until a set of traffic lights turned to red almost immediately ahead of him. A stationary car now occupied the nearside lane and traffic was proceeding thick and fast directly across his path. Tugging desperately at the hand brake had little effect and quick thinking was necessary. In a split second he thought of the pavement and took to it. The three wheeler filled this space and scraping along from railing to railing, cruelly gouging the passenger side of the car, Dave quickly came to a stop directly alongside the bewildered motorist in the other vehicle. In a typically casual manner he looked across, smiled and just sat there unperturbed. When the lights changed he nonchalantly bumped off the footpath in front of the other motorist and continued on home.

Granted he had saved himself a hefty insurance claim but he must have petrified the local inhabitants. As we came to appreciate in a short time such occurrences were not abnormal events but an integral part of his day-to-day living. 'It could only happen to Dave' became a stock phrase. Normal people would have been quite daunted by such adversities but not Dave. he was never ruffled, always ready to shoulder another load, and as time was to prove, he was an exceptionally good caver. His humour, incredible physical strength and indefatigable personality were features that few could ignore.

Our success story over these first days in the new area was the major system which we called Shahbanou. The 125 metre entrance shaft was always menacing from the danger of falling rock but thereafter a couple of squeezes led to steeply inclined, sporting rifts. By 300 metres depth we had picked up a small stream and it seemed that at long last we had a cave to rival Ghar Parau. But in caving frustration is a constant companion; at 308 metres we encountered a localised area of collapse. An apparent by-pass was found and we crawled down in to an obvious way on. Then came a cruel blow. A constricted watery duck blocked the path, beyond which the route looked negotiable. It was anyone's guess what happened around the next corner. Shahbanou was a prime site of immense potential but the blockage required a crow-bar to shift and items such as these had been jettisoned back in Britain!

The first few nights were also memorable at the new camp. Transition from a permanently dehydrated state to having all the clean fresh water that one could wish for was interesting physiologically. The bladder seemingly could not cope with all the liquid and never before, not even after a long boozy party, had I been forced to quit my sleeping bag so often — as many as four or five times in one night!

A disturbing incident occurred shortly after we moved in. Sally and I were woken in the middle of the night by a series of whistling calls. These originated well off on the mountain from two or three sides. No one in their right mind would go wandering about high on an isolated mountain in the middle of the night; what the hell was going on? A loud whisper came from Barry's sleeping quarters.

'Did you hear that Martyn?'

'Yes, it's been going on for a while now.'

Bandits? Rebel Kurds?; if so we were virtually surrounded. All of a sudden from a few yards away the Birmingham burble rent the air with an almighty 'Yoo-hoo.'

'Christ Dave, shut up; you'll get us all killed!'

A minute or two later a bunch of wild looking Iranians peered over the low stone walls of our compound. We were scared stiff. There was little doubt that they were armed and considerable stress regarding their intentions. Cowering quietly in our sleeping bags we mustered what courage we could. I greeted them and made an offer of food, trying to hide the fact we were all on the verge of a nervous breakdown. The newcomers had us at their mercy. But after making a few more indecipherable comments they collected bits of our kindling wood, lit a small fire and made some *chai*. Then, as mysteriously as they had arrived, they slipped quietly away. Who they were or what they were up to we never found out but the next day a few of them returned around mid morning. Once again they offered those around camp no threat and left within a short while. The whole event was most suspicious particularly the fact that the barrels of their rifles were carefully wrapped with a dark, non-reflective tape.

The numbers at the top camp slowly grew and all manner of sites were tackled. Superb snow sculptures were found at Crystal Pot, close to camp and these extended all the way to the bottom of the cave at 86 metres. Several other sites were found and surveyed by Geoff Richings, Andy Dawe and Barry, while the Doc, Bob and Dave Viggers were engaged at the lengthy Ghar Se Rah. The latter group eventually extended their system to a link with Shahbanou at a depth of 125 metres. The overall depth of the cave was not appreciably increased but the length now reached half a mile.

Immediately after the disappointment at Shahbanou Dave and I set to on the impressive cave next to camp, Ogof Bendwr. This was the system into which the small stream sank and once down the entrance shaft and through the glistening depths of the snow plug, we emerged into a spacious passage that augured well. A succession of small pitches in a wide rift slowed exploration but it again gave the impression of being the sort of place that could so easily become the 'deep one'. However, at 190 metres the floor levelled off, a fine sediment coated the walls, and it became apparent that there was some sort of blockage ahead. Within a short distance we came up against a massive fault; the small stream filtered in to a muddy alcove; the cave just ended.

It was a frustrating finish but equally obvious that further exploration of any one of these holes might pay off. Ten consecutive days were spent at our top camp before Dave, Sally and I decided to go down for a change of scenery. Rumour had it that we were expecting another consignment of goodies from Kermanshah and the lull in activity on the mountain seemed to be a good opportunity to take advantage of the situation, have a wash and take stock of morale at base. A fair number of people had yet to do anything. This was of no great concern providing that they were pulling their weight at base. But hardly had we arrived down than it was evident that a study of life here would have been a psychologist's dream.

One particular caver, renowned for his prowess at the Hunters Lodge had undergone a total degradation. He was unbelievably pathetic and reminded me of some poor dog after frequent beatings. For hours on end he lay in the swirling dust outside the kitchen tent, occasionally uttering some short, pathetic moan. His long hair was a matted, disgusting mess and he seemed as though life had lost all meaning for him. When he could muster the energy to crawl under cover he made a point of ensuring that people noticed that he was taking pills. It didn't seem to matter what pills; any pills that he could get his hands on seemed to do. Tragically sympathy for this creature was almost impossible; everyone seemed to have washed their hands of him. After all we were running a caving expedition, not a holiday camp for psychiatrics or hypochondriacs.

The atmosphere about base was sickening. If only we had a land-rover; if only! It was late in the afternoon and we had just washed our clothes when a small group arrived back from Kermanshah. As if things weren't bad enough the expression on their faces was a clear indication that the worst was yet to come.

'Bad news; it's the coach. The engine seized in the outskirts of Kermanshah... somebody stole a radiator cap and the thing boiled dry.'

We were dumb founded. Apparently a new engine was required and there was some talk of bussing it back home. As it would be a while before any definite decisions could be made it was proposed that we carry on as normal! 'Carry on as normal'?

We just looked at each other. How we could ignore the fact that we were stuck in Iran with no transport home goodness knows.

There was still plenty to do but this blow was enough to deter the most enthusiastic among us. Nearly half the team were now at advance base which, all things considered, was a much better environment than that in the valley. There were plenty of people at base to sort out the mess so less than 24 hours after arrival Dave, Sally and I were on our way back up the mountain.

How to break the news to Bob was a nagging issue on the day-long trek. We had visions of him tearing his hair out or hurling himself down the nearest deep shaft. In the event Bob just stood there, transfixed and ashen, muttering repeatedly 'My God, My God'; even he had resigned himself to the continuing saga of expeditionary disasters.

Ironically possibly the most interesting hole of all was now discovered. Cale Mar or Snake Pot was found and pushed by Bob and Doug McFarlane. This was a typically British system involving long, sinuously meandering rifts and short drops. However at about 77 metres depth it opened onto a far more mature, long abandoned fossil passage and here over a kilometre of passages were discovered, all of which ended at major chokes.

On a photographic trip down Snake Pot we took a look at the main choke. This was a real jumble of blocks down through which cavities beckoned mysteriously in what looked to be something of a shaft. I took the precaution of sending Dave off to check out a promising side passage, vested complete authority in the Doc to prevent him from following and then wormed my way slowly downwards. Boulder chokes I had long regarded as a more adventurous game of chess, and playing one as a team was most definitely out of the question. If experiences before and after, both above and below water, were anything to go by, Dave was indestructible; he didn't seem to mind boulders crashing around his ears. He was indefatigable digging chokes and I had plenty of confidence in his excavational ability — providing I had a clear exit from the field of play and at least a minute's start.

Spiralling downwards, around and beneath some particularly airy boulders I was amazed when I broke out into open passage. Two 9-metre pitches followed before a 4-metre, completely undercut drop had me beat. From a good vantage point on a ledge I could see on down a vast rift, and stones hurled into the distance echoed tales of great promise. Jubilant I carefully rejoined the other two and we set off out to organise a major assault.

A few hours later Barry, Geoff, Phil and John Elliot went in equipped with a plentiful supply of ladders for the short drops beyond the choke. Dave, Doc and I fell asleep with visions of a momentous push on the morrow, continuing from where the night team left off. To beat the 740-metre Iranian depth record set at Ghar Parau would be something; it was still well within our capabilities.

Unfortunately at 1.30 am our ambitious dreams were shattered. The exploratory team had returned. It transpired that they had followed my route through the choke and passed the last pitch. Beyond, an easy rift led off at an easy gradient but after a hundred metres and less than 16 metres below the point which I had reached, a second choke was found at a depth of 136 metres. The first choke was highly dangerous and no one felt overly enthusiastic about the second. So, that was it.

In the dull and distinctly chilly light of early morning our spirits were low. It was agreed that while Dave and Tony surveyed the section below the first choke Sally and I would make a photographic record; if nothing else turned up we were to detackle on the way out. In the event nothing did turn up. I managed to ease my way for 24 metres or so along the left-hand wall of the choke but at this point it felt prudent to retire. The cavities continued beyond; with a little time, a crow bar and support, this obstacle would quite probably have yielded. The site certainly had good potential but it wasn't for us; Snake Pot was detackled.

On the 23rd September, one whole month after setting up the Antenna Ridge camp we packed to leave the mountain for good. The whole place had long since been abandoned by the summer-dwelling Iranians and although during the day conditions at altitude were those of a cool summer's day at home, by night the temperatures fell to a few degrees above freezing point — without a good sleeping bag cold enough to be uncomfortable!

Wandering back along the mountain path we were filled with a strange mixture of feelings. Paths that just a few weeks before had been bustling with the activity of children tending flocks of sheep and goats, muleteers chastising stubborn animals, lone travellers with heavy loads and hermits living in cave entrances, were now empty. There was a deep, almost religious serenity about the place and it was as though we people were an irreverent element in the landscape. It felt right that we should be leaving. Instead of human prints the dusty tracks now showed clear evidence of bears and big cats. Previously these had kept well clear of the mountain highways; but now the mountain was theirs and in a way we felt like trespassers. We saw neither bear nor cat but we did hear noises around our camp on several occasions. With reflection though, since our camp was sited at what appeared to be the only water hole on the mountain, it was only natural that it should be visited by the animals of the area.

The following days were ones of grim uncertainty. All hope was ruled out for the bus which had been towed away rather ignominiously to the local customs' pound. We had visions of a few score Iranians already in residence; Mike Jay's pride and joy reduced to a doss house for vagrant Kurds.

Time lay heavily on our hands as we waited for news, any news, from the group in Kermanshah. In this instance it was abundantly clear that no news was bad news; we had to accept we were stranded 3,000 miles from home with no transport to anywhere. With everyone fearing the worst, camp became an amazing market place with scores of Iranians in constant attendance. Each of us now sought to sell off whatever was deemed surplus to requirements, or whatever would be too expensive to freight home. An interesting discovery was that the local women laid great store by our copper coins. They weren't particularly interested in the more valuable silver ones, just the dull low value variety which we sold for about ten pence each. Somehow or other someone let slip a desirable 5 mark German coin which the purchaser quickly learned was a lot more valuable than he'd thought. After one or two of us had casually tried to buy it from him our friend took great delight in parading it around camp, over and over again, just trying to establish how much he could get for it. As he had probably bought it for about 20 pence he derived great amusement baiting us. But he never did sell it.

As it worked out we might have been a little unscrupulous in the respect of coinage but the Iranians certainly struck good bargains when it came to such things as shoes, clothes and cooking utensils. Dave always seemed to captivate a much larger audience than everyone else. Whether it was because his prices were more competitive than the rest or whether he was more fascinating as a person was difficult to tell. The Iranians were always babbling humorously as they came away and Dave became rapidly the possessor of less gear than anyone else in camp. In fact one day he became so carried away by his own salesmanship that he sold his last pair of shoes by mistake and had to buy another pair from one of us in order to get home!

Kareem, the well dressed entrepreneur of the village, was always at hand when there was money to be made. It was nearly always he who settled the transport arrangements and acted as 'go-between'. During the course of our stay it was obvious by the constantly improving standard of dress that he was making a fair amount of money for himself. I had noticed on the April trip that cameras in particular seemed to sell well and when I put my second-hand 'Zenit E' on the market (Worth about £20 in Britain) Kareem was there eagerly outbidding everyone else. The offer rose to £60, £70, then £80. Kareem was hooked. Some people on the trip were desperately short of money but I didn't need to sell this camera. On the other hand Kareem was so much better off then the other villagers and he really wanted to own it. I thought I'd hold out and see just what he was actually prepared to pay. Suddenly he flashed an almighty wad of notes in front of my eyes and I weakened.

'£80' said Kareem.

'£100' I replied, at the same time thinking 'I must be stupid.'

Disappointed Kareem motioned that he would return on the morrow and walked off. That night a group meeting decided that we couldn't wait any longer for news from Kermanshah and the next morning we hired a few horses for the communal gear, packed up and left for the city — and I lost the chance of selling the camera!

In our multi-coloured Bristol omnibus we had arrived at Kuh-e-Shahu in carnival style. We left like a bunch of dishevelled vagabonds in an old lorry shared with six dead goats and a live one. As on arrival it was smiles all round but this time occasioned by the thankfulness of departure; at long last we were on our way home.

The expedition might not have ended quite as planned but it

was certainly no anticlimax. Everyone had their share of excitement en route back. A couple of lads for example were robbed of most of their possessions when they attempted to sleep rough in the centre of Tehran (they were probably lucky to get away alive). Sally and I attempted to 'thumb' only to be told by a young student who eventually picked us up that waving a thumb at traffic in Iran was the same as giving the 'V sign' to cars in Britain — we wondered why it had taken so long to get a lift! After nearly ending up in the gutter late one night in the slums of down-town Tehran we opted to bus it back to Europe — the way that everyone else had taken.

Had the expedition been a success? It had certainly been an amazing experience — but a success? At a personal level I felt that I had done all I could; we had bottomed the deepest caves so far discovered on Kuh-e-Shahu but we were still left with an overriding feeling of frustration — frustration at not having gone really deep and frustration at being stopped in the way in which we had. If only we had had a landrover, base camp might have been set in slightly more salubrious surroundings. If only we had had a crow bar and a little more time then the story at Shahbanou and Snake Pot might have been altogether different.

Little did we appreciate the intense undercurrents of discontent prevalent in Iran as we bused it home. Less than twelve months later the Shah had been deposed, the Ayatollahs were supreme and Iran had closed its borders. The high limestone peaks were left in peace, but I wonder to what extent life actually changed for the people of the mountain areas. Flocks of sheep and goats would still be taken to the upper pastures in summer, weary travellers with heavy loads would still commute along the dusty paths; hermits would still appear with a tureen of minty dough. For these people life would go on as normal. The problems of the world would be secondary. Once again caves would be places merely for the extraction of snow and ice, places whose length or depth would be unimportant. But one can well imagine the flow of anecdotes related by Kareem and friends sitting beside some smoky fire on a long winter's night. Tales of the crazy English struggling up the mountains only to climb down again inside the rock. What were they looking for that was so special and why did they go down there?

It is inevitable that some time in the future the most isolated

146

limestone areas will come under the caver's close scrutiny. Our findings would indicate that Kuh-e-Shahu certainly holds the potential for a world depth record, but how long will we have to wait before Iran once again opens its doors to the easy going adventurers of the western world?

7

Explorations in the Peak District

P8 AND PEAK CAVERN

Roger Solari and I had begun our explorations in the Peak District in 1973 at a time when, from the exploratory point of view, the area was extremely frustrating. There were about half a dozen prime sites waiting to be tackled in the area but almost unbelievably the majority of these lay in privately owned caves — caves whose owners refused entry to cave divers! Speedwell, Bagshaw and finally Peak Cavern were all out of bounds after 1971. At each the prospects were excellent, merely awaiting a determined assault.

The only accessible site offering significant potential was P8, a fact that had not gone unnoticed by my old rival John Parker. And with a flare that seemed to typify all his explorations Parker 'blitzed' the cave in 1971 and 1972. Over a series of trips he and Jeff Phillips passed Sump Four and continued to a point 100 metres in to Sump Nine, a total of 550 metres from Sump One and involving 365 metres of diving. It was a dramatic advance.

To enthusiastic cavers like Roger Solari (his death at Agen Allwedd was to occur one year later) and I, P8 now appeared all the more challenging; the way on was wide open. But knowing that our Welsh colleague was a little touchy about 'his' caves we waited about nine months before mounting our push.

Colin Fairbairn was recruited for the weekend and everything went like clockwork all the way to Sump Nine. Excited by the feel of the place I reached Parker's limit and tied on my own line, very optimistic of the route ahead.

The passage was now easy going despite thick accumulations of light, oozy sediment. My only concern was the state of the reel which had been damaged during the carry and which threatened to fall apart at any moment. I laid out the line carefully. At about 136 metres from the start of Sump Nine an airbell was reached. This was more than welcome but the water was deep, there was nowhere to rest and the walls were smooth. After paddling hard to assess the bell I sank heavily back to the floor, suddenly feeling very isolated and vulnerable. The visibility was less than an arm's length; the stress level had shot up.

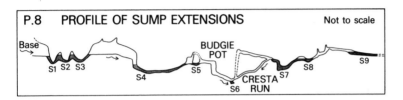

'Perhaps the passage will surface a little way further,' I told myself. I bumped forward in a muddy fog and after a few metres icy blue water led on at a depth of four to five metres. By now I knew that I was cold and that physically I was approaching my limit. Mentally however the mind was strong.

'Just a little further; a little further.'

Suddenly, somewhere in my numbed head an alarm sounded.

I was now over 150 metres from Sump Nine base and the side of the reel had just broken free. I watched it disappear into the light ooze and loops of line sneak off the spindle. The brain was so lethargic, but the alarm was automatic, tuned in for just this sort of eventuality.

'Entanglement imminent... retreat.'

There was nothing obscure about this message even if the other mental functions had closed down.

I let go of the reel. Of an instant the whole scene was hidden in a thick blanket of mud cloud. The reel disappeared; the loops of line disappeared, as did the few remaining hopes of a break-through. The imaginary line between hope and panic that was so fine had now tilted against me. In my mind I could see the line spreading, twisting, writhing, like a giant cobra all set to pounce and ensnare. That was it. I backed off in as controlled a manner as possible. It was just like being face to face with some savage dog; I dare not turn and run lest the animal would sense the panic and rush in for the attack. Here the line was the adversary; I had to establish a distance between myself and it — then turn and get out. I was scared.

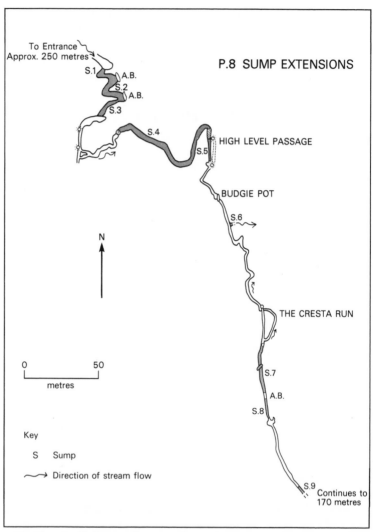

To Entrance
Approx. 250 metres

S.1
A.B.
S.2
A.B.
S.3

S.4

P.8 SUMP EXTENSIONS

S.5
HIGH LEVEL PASSAGE

BUDGIE POT

S.6

N

THE CRESTA RUN

0   50

metres

S.7

A.B.

S.8

Key

S   Sump

⌒→ Direction of stream flow

S.9
Continues to
170 metres

Feeling half frozen I groped back towards safety, emerging from the water almost in a state of collapse. As I possessed no gloves I was totally unable to feel or use my fingers. The others could guess the state I was in and as ever Colin was quick off the mark.

'Here get some of this down you.'

He unwrapped a Mars bar and held it to my lips.

I looked down and between the shreds of neoprene my right knee was blue. A patch had also come adrift on the other leg and the last of the water was now trickling from the holes at the elbows.

'This is stupid,' I told myself. 'That's the last time I'll borrow a suit from Neasden. He knew we had a big trip on and this is what he gives me; the bloody thing's perished.' How I wished that I could afford some decent gear!

As the circulation slowly began to get moving again I related the events. This was the most ambitious undertaking that I had made to date and I was certainly ill-prepared for such a push. With just a single source of lighting and a totally inadequate wet-suit I was at my physical limit. The tangle of line at the furthest point would pose a most effective obstacle to any subsequent exploration; to continue further in this sump very careful preparation would be required. I looked elsewhere for my next project.

I had no wish to get involved in any deep diving escapades so Giants Hole was ignored. Shallow dives were the best bet and Bagshaw Cavern was the obvious choice in the area. A couple of diplomatic visits were made to Mr Revell's show cave in 1976 and eventually, after a considerable amount of friendly badgering, and a present of some transparencies, he was persuaded to let us have a crack at the Mainstream Sump. We got a date fixed for the push and I recruited a small group to help with the carry.

Our scheduled dive was just over two weeks away when, out of the blue, I got a phone call to say that another group of divers had got permission to dive the Mainstream Sump as well. The first reaction was one of indignation.

'Bloody cheek, the first crack ought to be ours after all the groundwork we've put in. I just hope they don't mess things up.'

'Murland's diving next Sunday,' the call went.

'Hm,' thoughts were racing. 'Well all's fair in love and war; how about getting in there on Saturday?'

'That should stir the buggers up; you're on.'

Laughter erupted down the line. The trip was arranged.

We turned up at the cave the next Saturday morning sniggering at the thought of our little coup. But now we found ourselves in a slightly delicate situation. Clearly Mr Revell had been thinking things over and he could see that there was a new demand on

151

his cave. It didn't take a lot to read his thoughts. 'Two groups of divers on one weekend, hm. If cavers are prepared to pay 50p a head to have a look around the cave, surely it must be worth £1.00 a head to a diver?'

We had travelled up from South Wales especially for this trip. How could we argue? — after all this was the first time that a diver had got in since 1971.

'Paying to carry a diver's gear! You nearly ended up carrying the lot on your own there,' said Bomber, as we parted company from Mr Revell at the end of the dry section of cave.

'I've got faith in you lads,' I replied. 'Nothing like it to test the loyalty of your porters!'

The previous exploration of this site, by James Cobbett in July 1971, had extended the cave a distance of 200 metres. Both Sumps One and Two were short while Cobbett had terminated activities 45 metres into Sump Three. Supported by Colin Edmunds and Dave Morris I now carried on into the final Sump for 136 metres, reaching, surprisingly, a terminal depth of 26 metres. In crystal visibility the passage was observed to descend steeply beyond.

Sump Three was tricky; there was no way the 'Sunday group' was going to push it. Despite the cave's rebuff spirits were high back at base and someone jokingly suggested that we leave our colleagues a little message; something calculated to raise a few expletives. Having paid to get in and carried their gear all the way to the sump they would be a little hot under the collar anyway; we could just imagine the fury. I donated the writing slate and the next thing I knew we were all rolling around in the mud; in fact we chuckled all the way to the pub. The real touch of genius was Dave's in signing the message, which basically said 'Don't waste your air', with the name of an eminent member of the Northern Section of the C.D.G.

I must admit that I did feel quite guilty about it the next Monday when the long-distance call came through.

'What do you think you're doing? ... We struggled with all our own gear down there, bla bla, bla, ... waste of time, bla.'

'It was only a joke, honest; I apologise, honest; it won't happen again honest.'

To date no further penetration has been made into this promising site.

In 1979 another assault was mounted on P8. Since the push in 1973 no one had been further than the start of Sump Four; surely the cave wasn't that bad? But, as with several other places, time had erased the memories of any difficulty in the system and had replaced them with an overwhelming urge to continue the exploration.

Dry, stable weather conditions were essential for any trip to the further reaches as the cave was extremely flood prone beyond Sump Four. From the earlier visit it was abundantly clear what the main obstacle would be, namely the so called 'Sump Six'. This was the place where the mainstream disappeared into a gravel-choked fissure, and which we by-passed in favour of a high level passage leading to the next dive — Sump Seven. Sump Six was like some partially blocked plug hole. If the input of water increased the sink-hole would not be able to cope and the whole thing would back up. The trouble with P8 was that the level had to back up at least 12 metres before the excess water could flow off through Sumps Seven, Eight and Nine; virtually all the cave beyond the first few sumps was flooded in the process.

Our first attempt early in June found Sump Five so silted that it was impossible even to push one's foot into the hole. We knew that this section was less than 10 metres in length, and via an aven in the roof we could actually hear the stream flowing away on the far side. However, to gain this aven we would need climbing gear.

The next visit a few weeks later was also destined to reveal a few surprises. Dave Morris and I dragged a heavy haul sack apiece through the first set of sumps. We were carrying just about everything, ladders, ropes, hammer, bolts and all manner of other gear. Conditions were about the same as on the previous trip but the big turn up for the books came on arrival at our destination. Sump Five had been flushed out! Now it was easily diveable, even wearing two sets of diving apparatus; a very pleasant surprise.

There was no need to climb the aven so we abandoned the sacks and moved on to the next obstacle, Budgie Pot. Peering over the edge I was horrified to see that the water had backed up, all the way from the Sump Six outlet, to within three metres of the top of the pitch. Hopes faded. It seemed almost incredible that we should encounter such difficulties trying to retrace the earlier route. We had come so far and pinned such hopes on Sump Nine that we could hardly just turn around and leave. There was also a high powered desire to show up the comparatively pathetic attempts by other divers to 'push' the first three sumps. At least we were putting everything into a real attempt rather than doing it for the sake of a couple of lines in some caving magazine.

I knew that the way on lay in a flood over-flow passage above and beyond the normal 'Sump Six'. Perhaps this new sump could be dived? I estimated that the submerged section ought to be about 30 metres, but the visibility was virtually nil. If only we'd laid a line through this passage back in 1973.

The pitch was rigged and I climbed down under a torrent of water. Then, standing chest deep on a mound of silt, Dave slowly despatched my gear. Neither of us was optimistic and judging by the difficulty I was having it seemed best that Dave should stay put at the top. It took two dives before I got any distance and in the process a lot of valuable air and line was used. However, about 45 metres out from Budgie Pot I eventually surfaced into the dry passage which led on towards Sump Seven, known as the Cresta Run; another obstacle had been passed.

With nowhere to tie off the diving line I crawled on up the winding, ascending tube, throwing the reel on ahead. During the passage of years my mind had cast aside all memories of this tortuous, horrible place and wearing twin 47-cubic feet cylinders I quickly found myself in a series of sharp bends which required all sorts of contortions to pass. I wished Dave was here to help but he was on a lonely vigil above Budgie Pot. In places the route was a flat-out crawl and soon I found myself sweating and panting with the exertion. The three thicknesses of neoprene that a reasonable job had afforded and which clearly was essential on long dives did nothing for manoeuvrability. Several times I attempted to de-kit, only to find that the cylinder clasp buckles had somehow slid around to my back. It was all very annoying, though it also served to intensify my determination; it was Sump Nine or bust. After what seemed like ages, and still throwing the reel ahead, a low section had me beat. There was no chance of getting through fully kitted. I rolled around and around again. The resonant 'clang, clang', echoing in the confined space, interspersed with long winded pants and moans. My trusty high pressure cylinders were being abused yet again, but I was being extremely mindful to take care of the fragile breathing regulators and contents gauges. Somehow the buckles were released and with two journeys Sump Seven was reached, lying only about eight metres beyond the squeeze.

Time was getting on — it was about 5 o'clock but I'd come so far and invested so much effort that giving up was unthinkable; there was no way I was going back without having a crack at Sump Nine. Ominously the water here was almost as cloudy as that in the mainstream sumps. In 1973 these high level sumps had been crystal clear, at least for myself in the lead; now visibility was down to one metre. Fortunately the old line was still intact and in no time I was through the 65-metre sump, across the waist deep airbell and into Sump Eight. This was about 25 metres in length but just where it broke surface there was a cursed, flat-out silt-and-gravel slope up into the final extension. Half in, half out of the water I thrutched awkwardly upwards on my stomach; it really is desperate trying to push yourself along wearing fins. The grovelling was much easier said than done for with each forward movement the unconsolidated shingle and gravel slumped backwards, almost a case of three steps forward, two back.

Within a couple of metres of the sump pool I entered a chamber where I could stand but which led immediately to yet another longer slope. 'It was never like this in '73!' I was absolutely furious at the resistance the cave was putting up. The next slope was even lower than the first and I had to de-kit completely and dig out something of a trench before it was any good even attempting to drag kit up. At the head of this obstacle a short length of passage led to an awkward slippery traverse. Here at last the passage regained fair sized proportions, almost two metres in diameter. This point was probably 10 metres above the mainstream sump, and probably 16 metres above the Sump Six level when the water is low. Beyond the high point a low step dropped me back into the continuing tubeway, now trending south-east. From Sump Eight to Sump Nine was about 110 metres but about halfway the roof lowered to an area of crawling and stooping. This necessitated two carries to get all the gear to the destination.

On the second journey I was about 15 metres from Sump Nine

when I heard an almighty booming sound in the distance. My heart stopped, and panic stricken I was rivetted to the spot. Everything had changed. Determination had been replaced by confusion, anguish and despair.

'Think . . . Think; What the hell do I do?'

A message came through:

'Kit up.'

I ran the last couple of metres and frantically started assembling the gear. The base drum continued with its steady doleful beat. It was like some tribal summons to battle. My heart was racing.

Slowly rational thoughts returned. What the hell was happening? What was the weather doing outside? We'd checked the weather before the trip and there was a high pressure ridge over the country — it couldn't be raining out there could it? Rain. I realised that if a flood pulse was about to overwhelm me I stood no chance of getting out; the whole place would be flooded to the roof and Dave would most probably be done for as well. Frantic thoughts occupied the space of about five minutes but not for a moment did I stop kitting up.

As the noise abated an immense feeling of relief came over me; I lay down, flat out; nervous energy all spent. There was no wall of water or even a resurging stream. Calmly I tried to think what the noise might have been. The answer seemed to be that of breaking air pockets in Sump Nine. But was this something of an omen and if so, should I turn back? Even if it was I decided to carry on.

When fully composed and rested I dived off laying a fresh line. Visibility was much the same as in the preceding sumps. Occasionally, at floor level, the odd patch of clear water was entered; a weird and frustrating phenomenon, serving only as a taunt, showing what conditions might have been. The boundary between this and the overlying poor visibility was very distinct. After 100 metres however the overall visibility started deteriorating rapidly. At about 125 metres the conditions were terrible and it was evident that I stood no chance of sorting out the entanglement at the previous limit. The shock waves had dislodged the fine sediments lining the walls and roof. There was nothing for it; much against my natural inclination I tied off my line and made a slow demoralised exit to my loyal partner. The time was not right for P8.

156

It was to be the winter of 1980/81 before Derbyshire again captured my attentions. The occasion was to be the opportunity of fresh exploration in Peak Cavern. Access had been regained to this system in 1979 but for the first 'trial period', from October to Easter, only the local divers, of the Derbyshire Section of the C.D.G., were allowed in. The rest of us were green with envy but quite prepared to give them the first crack of the whip as it had been their efforts that had reopened the cave. The two prime sites here were Ink Sump and Far Sump. Treasury Sump was also very important as this gave clandestine access to the lower section of streamway in Speedwell Cavern, a system to which unfortunately both cavers and cave divers are still officially barred.

Just as expected significant penetrations were quickly made at both Ink and Far Sumps. Ink was to capture the main attention especially after an airbell was reached 220 metres from the diving base. A boulder choke lay just beyond and during the 'close season' — April to October — when the Management wished to concentrate on the more lucrative 'show cave' trade, plans were devised to explode a charge at this site.

When access was renewed the prospect of a breakthrough looked good at Ink Sump but at Far Sump there was almost a total lack of interest. A penetration of 250 metres had reputedly been made here the previous season but from the nature of the diving reports the place sounded intimidating. The passage was low and heavily silted; Jerry Murland had seemingly reached his limit. This was borne out by a minor advance in January 1981.

Friendly relations had been established with the members of the Derbyshire Section for some time and in mid February I was grateful for the opportunity for a 'push'. Anticipating a few awkward moments in the low sections it came as a very pleasant surprise to be able to pass them with ease. And once beyond the notorious 'squeeze' in the second sump everything was straight forward. The passage was low (1 metre high by 1.75 metres wide), but in crystal clear water perfectly comfortable.

I had borrowed a very heavy reel containing 200 metres of thick line. This was difficult to transport and as a consequence my speed of movement was painfully slow. The amount of silt that was kicked up was disturbing but by the time I had reached Murland's limit my confidence was soaring. Not for the first

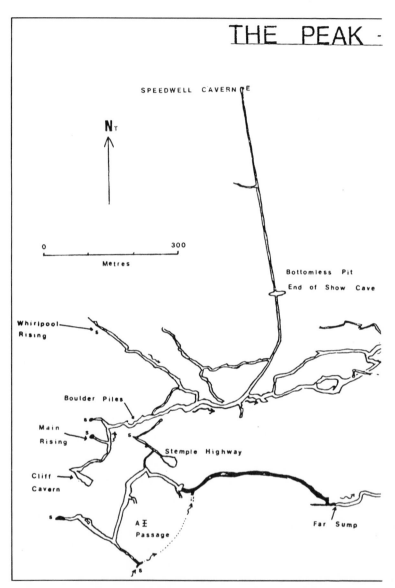

time had my predecessor been prone to a little exaggeration and this was a classic. The distance supposedly explored was wildly out; my estimate put it at 120 metres — less than half that quoted by Murland. A similar discrepancy accompanied the question of

158

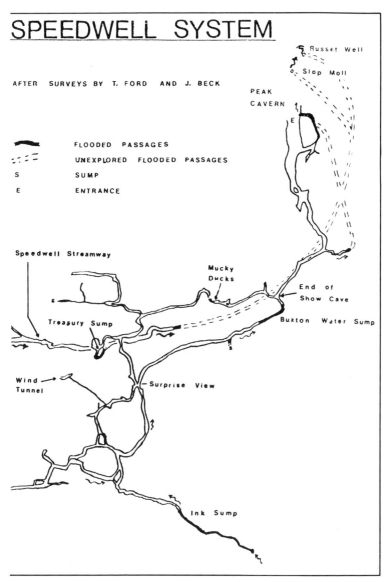

SPEEDWELL SYSTEM

AFTER SURVEYS BY T. FORD AND J. BECK

Russet Well

Slop Moll

PEAK
CAVERN

E

▬ FLOODED PASSAGES

- - - UNEXPLORED FLOODED PASSAGES

S SUMP

E ENTRANCE

Speedwell Streamway

Mucky
Ducks

End of
Show Cave

Treasury Sump

Buxton Water Sump

Wind
Tunnel

Surprise View

Ink Sump

depth. By my gauge the deepest point along the route had been seven metres, just beyond the squeeze, and thereafter it had made a gradual ascent. I tied on my line and continued. The depth was only 3 metres.

Confidence was now inspired by the use of my new 'safety tag' system. This involved separate yellow and black tapes wrapped around the line, in the same sequence, at five metre intervals. If for example you were unfortunate to lose sense of orientation, then providing you still had hold of the line you could quickly establish which way was out. No matter which direction was taken at the first set of tag marks all would be clarified, as the black tapes are always sited away from base. So, if you met a yellow marker first the direction taken would be further into the sump.

I bumped clumsily forward. The passage meandered slightly but overall trended north-west, then more towards west. At 285 metres from base I reached my safety margin with just about five metres of line remaining on the reel. Ahead lay a low muddy area, the depth only 1.2 metres. Feeling very pleased with the progress, I made an uneventful exit.

The second assault was to take place on March 1st. I had travelled up from South Wales on the Saturday evening with Chris Howes and Tom Sharpe. To break the journey and ensure a good night's sleep we had stopped off in Stoke on Trent to stay with Bomber. Sunday morning dawned grey and heavy. It was raining and my voice had just about gone. Considering my cold and the fact that there'd been a heavy snowfall on the Peak the preceding week the prospects were poor. I plied myself with several spoonsful of Benolyn and took a few pills; anything to try and subdue the itching in the throat. If we did manage a dive then I certainly did not want to risk the dry bottle air giving rise to a fit of coughing a long way underwater.

We all piled into Chris' mini and set off North. There was little doubt in any of our minds — entry to Peak Cavern was becoming increasingly unlikely.

'If we have to spend the day in the pub it'll be good for relations,' I said.

'Murland's never ever going to buy you a pint!' retorted Chris.

The previous week I'd received a most indignant phone call from the self-appointed leader of the Derbyshire Section.

'I hear you've been in Far Sump?'

'So?'

'I think you've got a bloody cheek.'

160

'Why's that?'

'Why's that?' . . . the phone almost deafened me 'After all the hard work put in by the Derbyshire Section?'

Murland proceeded with a long diatribe to which I muttered the odd 'Yes,' or 'No,' into the phone. When he'd finished I mentioned the exaggerated dive reports.

'That's just my literary expression,' he said.

The conversation eventually ended and somehow I'd forgotten to inform him we were coming up again today.

Amazingly when we arrived in Castleton the water level was found to be extremely low, but floods were inevitable later in the day. 'We've got until about 4 o'clock,' stated John Beck 'Don't hang around.

It was a strange feeling as our group made its way up the streamway which was as low as ever it could be. I had every excuse not to dive, but as we'd come so far I was committed. Another good dose of Benolyn had been taken before going underground and my throat, realising what was expected of it decided that it might as well play cured — at least for a few hours.

Hot and sweaty we arrived at the sump. Bomber, efficient as ever, assisted me to kit up while Chris and Tom took a few 'record' shots. I wore a 3-mm vest, 5-mm trousers and jacket and a further 5-mm over-jacket. The previous dive here had lasted about 35 minutes and I had emerged warm and comfortable wearing the attire. The cold was the least of my worries. Would the cave rise to break surface? This was the number one question. Judging by John Cordingley's survey and John Beck's knowledge of the local geology everything looked favourable. I set off across the chamber when a voice rang out.

'Hold it. Everything's working now. Can we get a couple of shots before you go?'

It wasn't Chris's day. I'd never seen so many bulbs going off, tripods falling over and cameras malfunctioning before.

'Are you sure Chris?'

'Yes, honest. I didn't think the other two cameras were right after the last trip.'

'Well, be quick.' I was anxious to get away.

A few moments later three flashguns went off simultaneously, and Chris hadn't even wound on.

161

'. . . hell.' shouted Chris.

'Sorry.' muttered Tom in his broad Scottish accent.

Then a fierce argument broke out; hands waving and voices raised. I took advantage of the situation to slip quietly away. Who'd be a cave photographer's model!

Confident that the passage would surface in a short distance I decided to travel light, taking only 125 metres of line and a few lead blocks. Feeling comfortable and warm was almost a novel sensation and the fact that the sump was virtually guaranteed to 'go' almost dismissed the normal stress factors. Cruising along in a slow and relaxed manner I could unwind.

Peering ahead occasional puffs of silt cloud drifted towards me that had dislodged from the crest of some mud bank just ahead. The experience could be likened to one of those rare summer days when intricate chains of white cumulous rise from some distant skyline. But here the terrain was barren and lifeless, the ground an ever shifting confusion of miniature sand dunes laced with a brown edging.

On the straight sections aching neck muscles could be relaxed. Instead of craning my head well back to view and assess the route ahead I could maintain a more normal pose. The field of vision now assumed a different complexion. A finely rippled floor which one might expect to contain little of interest suddenly seemed to be hiding a monster. The spots from my two aquaflash units seemed to pose a pair of eyes while my Nife cell beam, adjusted to shine rather glow, formed an open mouth. It was as though some alien wished to make its presence felt; a slightly disturbing and eerie sensation that I had to quickly and forcibly dismiss. This was no time for fantasy; my concentration had to be complete.

I reached the previous limit and tied on my fresh line. An awkward manoeuvre lay immediately ahead — a wriggle around the side of a mound of silt, which almost completely obstructed the route. This was quickly passed and I chugged on expecting to surface at any moment. The depth gauge continually read one metre. My neck muscles were beginning to ache from scanning the low ceiling, searching for those tell-tale silvery surfaces which would herald the approach of an airbell. Two airbells were in fact reached after the 335 metre mark. At neither was there any dry land and at both the water was waist deep.

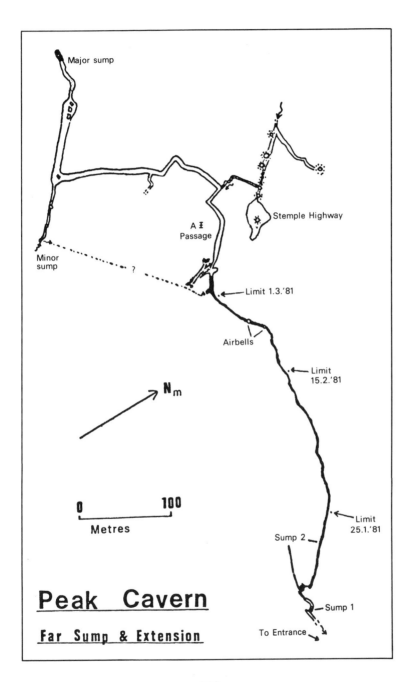

Major sump

Minor sump

A ⚚ Passage

Stemple Highway

Limit 1.3.'81

Airbells

Limit 15.2.'81

N_m

Limit 25.1.'81

Sump 2

0   100

Metres

Sump 1

To Entrance

Peak Cavern

Far Sump & Extension

My expectations were high but at 410 metres the line ran out. A block of lead was then used to weight the line at this point. The lure of the continuation — crystal clear water, depth about one metre and a tubular shaped passage — now proved overwhelming. I swam on, consciously breaking one of our cardinal rules of safety 'Never dive without a line'. After 10 metres I arrived at an underwater junction. To the left, due south, the route went deeper while in a north-westerly direction a low muddy continuation led on at the same depth. In just the few seconds that it took to establish bearings on the two passages lying ahead swirling mud cloud rolled in, blotting out the perfect conditions and simultaneously destroying any remaining confidence. Further progress without a line would have been reckless so I groped carefully back to the security of my leaded line and made a rough survey en route out.

For my third dive, the next week, I set off with another 200 metres of line and even more air reserves. At 345 metres I was grateful to bob up into the first cramped airbell as several critical problems had developed. The strap on the harness of the 82 cu/ft cylinder had worked loose resulting in the bottle sliding around to my stomach; a fin was hanging off (and wearing so much neoprene I was having difficulty in bending down to replace it); the strap on the depth gauge had worked loose, and to aggravate the situation even further the line reel had started to shed some of its loops. With head and shoulders out of the water I spat out the gag and slowly remedied everything.

The dive proceeded. Water levels were higher than the previous week and the second airbell was missed completely. Reaching the junction a choice of routes existed. The main flow appeared to originate from the left while the shallow muddy passage on the right seemed to suggest that it was the main continuation. The latter was more or less geologically 'up dip' and this swayed the balance. Moving forward the passage was now lower than hitherto with thick oozy mud on the floor. Confidence was ebbing when suddenly at 435 metres the passage surfaced. Just ahead I could plainly hear the echo of a waterfall. Far Sump had been cracked.

Within a few metres an inlet was found spouting into a chamber from a height of five metres. The kit was quickly dropped on a convenient mud bank and the climb was assessed. While searching for a belay point for the line another piece of exceptionally good fortune arose — a large passage was discovered beyond an awkward boulder obstruction at water level. This was the continuation of the sump passage, trending once more north-west. The inlet climb was abandoned and feelings of excitement grew with every step.

About 90 metres from the sump the passage regained proportions similar to those downstream from Far Sump, that is about three to four metres in diameter. At this point an inlet passage made its entry at roof level, two metres up on the right-hand wall. With compass and formica slates to hand I continued to chart my way upstream along an abandoned water course. Fortunately the terrain proved kindly and it was only rarely that my wet-socked toes were stubbed against the odd boulder.

The next section was orientated south-west when 200 metres later a large 'T' junction was reached. To the right even larger passage proportions were illuminated by my three light units. Thoughts of the exit suddenly assumed a priority and of an instant it seemed a good idea to erect a small cairn. There was a prominent boulder at this point and before I could place a rock on top of it something odd became apparent, scratch marks? A closer inspection indeed revealed the splintered marks inflicted by a small pick hammer. At my left elbow I then noticed the stunted remains of an old candle, unquestionable proof that I was not the first to tread this route. The Derbyshire 'Old Man', some long forgotten, probably unrecorded miner had been here before, searching for that elusive mineral wealth secreted in the depths of the Peak District — lead. But I had seen no other evidence of man in the passage so far, so where had my predecessor come in? What seemed certain was that he had had the same idea as myself, to mark the route for his own safe exit.

By now I was hot and sweaty but there was no question of calling it a day just yet. Taking the larger passage, north-west, I wandered on hurriedly jotting down distances and bearings. The odd footprint testified that my friend had also trodden this route. How long before? Had he come from Speedwell Cavern or some other long lost mine? Thoughts were racing and time was short. I slipped and slithered through a shallow muddy lake and shortly after arrived at a massive boulder which effectively blocked the passage. It was just possible to slide up through a squeeze at the left-hand side. Again I was not the first to travel this way. Less than 15 metres beyond, a sheer 5-metre precipice confronted me revealing a huge green lake at the foot. There was no way around, in fact there was no reason even to a attempt a traverse. By my spot lights the only way was down, into the unknown depths of a vast sump pool. I hurled a rock into the centre and watched the ripples die away. There was something rather spooky about this place. 'It'll be some time before that's dived,' I thought and quickly I retraced my steps to the junction.

The other passage led via two large solutional bells to a steep sand slope where water could be heard flowing. Unfortunately less than 70 metres from the junction the route again terminated at a sump. Evidently in times of high water the passage issued a fair sized stream which flowed off along my route of entry, to Far Sump.

The question again arose as to where the unknown miner had made his entry. A return was made to the inlet about 90 metres from Far Sump. Here an easy scramble gave access to a low tube along which a sluggish little streamlet made its way between mud banks. I followed this eagerly despite it lowering gradually to a crawl. Suddenly, after 50 metres a length of blackened and rotting timber was found lying in the mud. I had reached the foot of an aven. Gaining my feet I peered up and there 10 metres above the floor, wedged from one wall to the other, lay countless rotting stemples; varying lengths of timber which the original explorers had carried in and jammed securely between the walls to serve as a form of climbing staircase. A short crawl gave access to a second aven above which a similar sight met my eye. I reflected that this climb would be easy to make in boots before continuing a very short distance to the end of the passage. Here the little stream gushed from an aven. Somewhere above, the miners' passage led on in a north-westerly direction. The rotting stemples were also found to continue in a south-easterly direction along a spacious passage that appeared easily negotiable at floor level.

Time was running out and it was essential to give no cause for alarm. One mystery at least had been solved. Returning towards the sump the letters AE were found inscribed on a muddy boulder. Were those the initials of that early explorer or just a miner's term indicating that this series of passages held little of interest? Perhaps we shall never know. Up above, another large passage led on to a boulder choke close above the waterfall at Far Sump.

With my brain sifting through the countless details of the 500 metres that I'd just explored, I began kitting up. After spending under three hours away I gurgled merrily back in to base. People seemed to have drifted in from all over the place, all curious to know what was going on. My small crew of three had swollen to ten or more and it was beaming faces all round. For once the carry out didn't seem that bad.

By far the most memorable incident however occurred after we got out of the cave. Returning to the T.S.G. hut the bombardment of jokes was inevitable.

'I wouldn't like to be in your shoes when Murland finds out.'

'He'll have to change the name of the sump now.'

But the funniest thing of all was the hilarity that arose when Chris Rhodes came up with the suggestion of letting Jerry know right away. Agreeing it was a good idea, a small crowd promptly paraded around the corner to the nearest telephone box. Thinking that it would be better entertainment if Chris made the call the rest of us squeezed in tightly, eager not to miss a thing. To the local residents we must have looked like a class of giggling schoolgirls.

The coin clanked into the box, and instantly the joviality ceased.

'Hello, Chris Rhodes here Jerry.'

'It's Far Sump Jerry, it's gone.'

An interval developed and Chris attempted to adopt a stern face, while letting slip the odd giggle.

'Half a mile and still going.'

A longer interval.

'Couldn't stop him Jerry. He just turned up with his lads and went in.'

We could all imagine the scene at the other end of the line. Jerry would be hopping mad. In minutes he would be on the phone, writing letters, desperately attempting to keep his imaginary empire safe from thieving Welshmen.

The conversation ended. Chris replaced the receiver and turned to the door.

'He says he's going to fix you.'

Another burst of laughter and we all returned to the hut.

Floods effectively barred entry to the cave for a couple of weeks and the final opportunity to continue the exploration of the new extension, before the end of the season, came on 28th March. On this occasion Jerry was at the hut, his curiosity having got the better of him. No one else fancied the dive through to the new extension so this second visit was again a solitary affair.

By this stage the sketch survey of the new discoveries had been drawn up and its relationship with the rest of the Peak-Speedwell system scrutinised. The results were highly interesting. Far Sump and its extension were on a convergent course with the furthest upstream reaches of Speedwell Cavern. The huge and impressive Major Sump was, if anything, located further west than Speedwell Main Rising, the latter situated about 200 metres to the north. The most significant feature however was the fact that the north-western passage of Stemple Highway was virtually on a straight line for the Boulder Piles in the Speedwell streamway. The separation between these two points was something of the order of 100 metres. The question was obvious: was there a 'dry' connection with Speedwell?

Equipped this time with a pair of boots I was quite confident that the passages heading off from Stemple Highway could be entered and explored. Wearing smaller capacity cylinders than hitherto the dive itself was a relatively pleasant experience. The squeeze had been slightly enlarged by the recent floods but the current was quite strong. It was a smooth 25-minute journey to a new world — a world which for all the others knew was but a figment of my imagination — except for the occasional feeling that perhaps I was not alone. I kept imagining I was being watched by the spirits of those long dead miners whose realm I had invaded, and something inside continually warned me to keep a careful watch on the surroundings — even though another part of me kept telling myself not be so stupid.

Making quickly for the Stemple Highway the passage heading south-east was the first to be followed. A short climb, then descent, gave access to a reasonable sized chamber with the remains of a stemple stairway leading up for 9 or 10 metres. The climb was just too wide to bridge and the rotting timbers, although well niched into the wall in their day, were no aid. A small pile of stones was erected but this proved no answer. Having explored a mere 8 metres further than the last visit I had to admit defeat and turned to the passage heading north-west.

At the second aven, where previously I had been optimistic, the climb also appeared daunting. It seemed to be only 10 metres or so to the top but even wearing boots the walls were treacherously slippery. By a traverse/chimneying action 7 metres height was quickly made. Here the mud was glutinous and cracks had to be excavated before any use could be made of them. By a combination of   layback and some confident bridging another metre or so was gained. The crux was just above. A large boulder lay wedged in the mud. This looked as though it could well be the top. But the movement required to reach it necessitated total commitment. A slip in a similar clean washed aven would not worry me in the least as I could throw out my elbows and wedge in ... but not here. With slimy walls and a suit now plastered with grease any fall would be critical. Several strategies were assessed and tentatively tried before resting and cursing. Why hadn't I at least brought the diving line? It was pretty thin but perfectly strong enough to rig a footloop in which to stand, or indeed with which to lower myself back to the floor. The descent from here was bad enough. It might even have been possible to lasso the boulder. But the more I thought about it the more annoyed I became. 'Easy to climb in boots' I'd said after the last trip; how wrong you can be.

My left leg began to tremble again and it was clear that either I did something or gave up. Eventually the gamble was taken, banking heavily on the fact that within a couple of metres I should be able to wash off in the small stream. If I couldn't I was under no illusion that I was in trouble. Slowly I eased myself out of the crack — an almighty stretch gave the required handhold — and I heaved myself up on to the big boulder. With an immense sigh of relief I leaned on the walls for a moment. I had made it. Just as well though; there was no rescue from here.

But things weren't over yet; the rift seemed to continue diagonally upwards. A traverse and another five-metre climb and I reached an impressive roof tube, over two metres in diameter. Could this be the way the miners had come in? I was getting excited. I washed my hands, pulled out the formica survey slate and strode on. Unfortunately after 60 or so metres the large tube shrank to a much diminished rift and the little stream flowed from a small sump; big enough to dive but not on this trip. A side passage led on generally in the direction of Speedwell, only to terminate at the foot of a high aven. This was frustrating. I'd only found 150 metres of additional passage and there was nothing vaguely reminiscent of a 'connection' with Speedwell. I guessed that I had to be close to the Boulder Piles in the upper section of the streamway but to make the link I had to find something heading downwards; here the only ways were up.

For the first time in the extension I located a mineral vein. There were no signs of any extensive digging just of a tentative prospecting amid the associated non-commercial crystals. From articles dealing with the old records of this area it was interesting to recall that £3,000 worth of lead ore had in fact been brought out from Speedwell Cavern in the late eighteenth century. Such a sum in those days would have been a considerable amount by today's values and would surely have represented a substantial quantity, or volume, of ore. The more I thought about it the more obvious it seemed to become that no lead had ever been taken from any of the passages that I had explored so far. As the ore was heavy one would expect a lot of trampling on the mud-banks, bits of ore scattered about where they'd spilt some, or debris littered beneath an excavated fissure — but there were none of these.

All the cave passages that I had covered appeared to have been 'checked' by the miners but nowhere could I say 'This vein appears to have been dug commercially.' The only logical solution to this question is that the ore was obtained from some point that I had failed to reach, either from one of the three high avens or from the south-easterly continuation of Stemple Highway.

I was no expert on the archaeological side by any means but a few other questions were nagging. They obviously had ladders in the eighteenth century so why, if they were only checking out this area, did they not use them, or even two ladders strung together, on the longer vertical sections? Surely in terms of speed, cost and safety it would be infinitely more preferable to use ladders rather than have to carefully place each individual stemple. But could it be that access to this extension was difficult, a restricted crawlway perhaps, and that ladders were impossible to use? Then again stemples may have been used because manpower was short or because they were prospecting in secret.

So where did the miners come from originally? All the literature and the close proximity between the two caves, clearly suggested Speedwell. But even this idea was far from convincing. In the first place the true Speedwell Cave section had been intercepted by a completely artificial tunnel; driven, due south, for a distance of half a mile in 1781. It has long been presumed that the original excavators drove this in the hope of meeting one or more of the rich lead veins which were known to exist deep under the mountain. But was it purely a coincidence that having mined that half mile, absolutely horizontal, that they should then enter the natural cave complex exactly at floor level? To me this was unbelievable. A couple of metres up or down and they would have missed it altogether! The more I thought about it the more logical it seemed to be that the natural cave section of Speedwell was already known; discovered some years before by some high level route now lost or inaccessible. In turn this may well have originated in one of the 'lost' mines of the neighbourhood. Quite a number of these were covered or 'capped' when the underground work ceased. The mystery was as puzzling as ever.

Retracing my steps along the high level passage one small aven was scaled for 20 metres near the new sump, only to find a boulder constriction at the top. The miners had climbed this as well, without any apparent aid and I was left with an overwhelming respect for these explorers. They had covered every nook and cranny in their quest for lead.

I covered all that was possible, washed off, and made the all committing move. Luck was still with me and in a few minutes I was safely back at floor level. All the other dry, open passages were now examined more conclusively than on the previous visit but little additional passage was added. Back at Far Sump a large, structured cairn was erected directly in the sump pool and after a quarter of an hour or so the Waterfall, or Inlet Passage was entered. This led for a mere 17 metres to a complete boulder choke where yet again pieces of timber gave clear evidence that it had also been examined by the miners. Having made the descent I contemplated one last objective — a dive at the Minor Sump.

Regrettably I failed to muster the enthusiasm for the carry. So, four hours after leaving Bomber and friends back in Peak Cavern I was out and the season was at an end.

The following winter, 1981-2, the mystery as to the miners' point of entry to the extension was still unsolved. There seemed to be one last hope of an easy solution; that of climbing the terminal aven at the south-easterly branch of Stemple Highway.

Carrying a full set of vertical gear, rope, ladders, pitons and bolts, two solo climbing trips were made before success was achieved. At the head of the 9-metre aven an airy vantage point gave an incredible view — an immense chamber — the walls of which merged imperceptibly with distant blackness. Laddering down for 7 metres the expectations of another major extension were high — but disappointment lay in store. The chamber measured 28 metres by 24 metres and the only way out was a large 30-metre-plus aven, situated almost centrally in the roof. Here an elaborate trail of stemples disappeared from view after about 25 metres. The chamber is by far the largest in the Peak-Speedwell complex and I felt confident that this, at last, was the elusive point of entry made all those years before.

Over the two years the four trips to the Far Sump Extension had yielded just over 700 metres of dry passage. In retrospect this was not all that it might have been but as a venture it was certainly one of the most enjoyable solo explorations that I had undertaken. Not only was there scope for continued efforts in the future but it was a wholly unique experience rediscovering and shedding new light on events of the past.

8

The Mysterious Blue Holes of Andros Island

The word Bahamas is synonymous with sun, sea and sand; with beautiful bikini-clad females soaking up the sun; with ice cold bacardis; in short with luxury and holidays.

'Well it sounds just my cup of tea,' said Bomber. 'I'm fed up waiting around for you, freezing to death in caves over here ... a suntan, plenty of booze, water at 28° centigrade is just what I need ... but who's going to organise this holiday?'

'Expedition Bomber; think positive!'

I flashed the relevant chapter from Bruce Sloane's book *Cavers, Caves and Caving* again and drifted into a beer-fuddled dream of mystical caves or Blue Holes drowned by the sea some 14-15,000 years ago and stretching god-knows how far. We looked at the pictures.

'Bloody hell, they're not even wearing full wetsuits!'

'Piece of cake, I reckon, if we could get there.'

We supped on and the women shook their heads 'More ridiculous schemes!'

Some time later Rob Palmer took the bait and instantly sold himself on the project. Organisation was never my forte and at our first informal meeting we were more than glad when Rob's eyes suddenly brightened. His chest inflated and an assured confident announcement greeted our ears.

'I'll organise the trip if you like.'

That was it. From then on there was no restraining him.

'We'll need a Patron you know. I'll try Prince Charles. The book and the lecture tour should fund an ongoing project for years to come. Think of it — we could get hold of some 're-breathers', set up an underwater habitat and live down there for a week at a time.'

Yes, Rob was keen all right. If we'd learned anything about

him since he'd migrated from Yorkshire it was that he had an
unparalleled enthusiasm for organisation. Obviously this could
be his finest hour.

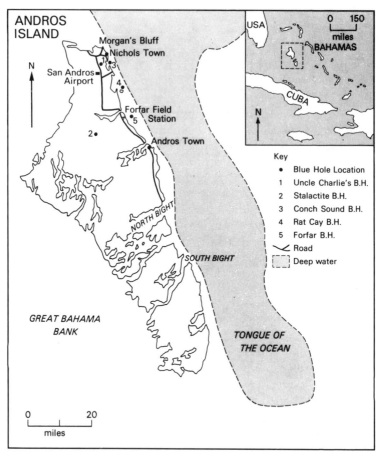

The expedition to tackle the mysterious Blue Holes of Andros
Island would be a new departure in British caving. It would be one
consisting of 100 per cent diving, in other words there was no
chance of discovering any dry extensions whatsoever. There was
ample opportunity for things to go wrong on such a venture; after
all we were following in the footsteps of people such as Jacques
Cousteau, who with every facility at his disposal had been on two
expeditions to the island in 1970. Dr George Benjamin who had

174

written the chapter on cave diving in Sloane's book had long captured my imagination after publishing an article in *National Geographic* back at the time of Cousteau's visit. This amazing character had also produced a film detailing his major discoveries. We managed to procure a copy from him which gave us the flavour of what lay in store. The Blue Holes were unique. Originally these water-filled caverns once lay high above the sea and were subjected to all the processes of cave erosion and deposition that occur in any normal system today. The Blue Holes then are remnants of great cave networks that were formed during the Pleistocene era, more commonly referred to as the Ice Ages. During this time much of the planet's water was trapped in the form of glaciers further north and the sea level was as much as 150 metres below its present level. But with the close of the Ice Age, some 14-15,000 years ago the ice melted and the sea rose. In the process the great cave systems in the Bahamas were flooded.

Benjamin's film *15,000 years Beneath The Sea* set the scene well enough but it also gave our friends at the National B.C.R.A. Conference the wrong impression of our proposed expedition entirely. It reinforced their preset ideas of sun-drenched beaches, a tropical paradise and all the rest. But having seen the film few would ever forget it. Benjamin had a very strong German, more precisely Latvian, accent, and this combined with a commentary enriched by understatement, and pregnant with dual meanings proved to be just the sort of entertainment that British cavers thoroughly enjoyed.

Most people, for example, fear sharks sufficiently not to go seeking them out. To do so in the murky confines of a cave passage would be madness. But Benjamin set out to film such an encounter. Just imagine the scene in the film with several sharks dodging artfully between thickening mud clouds, biding their time, the diver becoming more and more apprehensive and the ever understated commentary running:

'I didn't mind the one in front of me that I could see. I was more worried about the one that was sharing this cloud of muddy water with me. Suddenly I could swear that something was nibbling at my right foot, and just at that moment it didn't matter whether it was a shark or my imagination.'

But possibly the most frightening thing to the lay public was the extreme depth and the apparently nonchalent way that this came over:

'I was still 200 feet from the surface but I knew that the line would guide me . . . I was moving straight up, fast . . . I had well over three minutes of air left — plenty of safety.'

There were plenty of examples of dead-pan humour too. Later in the film when the team prepare for a dive the commentary ran:

'We are ready; all the systems are go. It looks like rain; let's get straight into the water before we get wet.'

Our caving audience were incredulous; the whole lecture room roared with laughter, again and again.

After showing the film, which incidentally we had just received, it was a wonder that we got any sponsorhsip at all. Scepticism was rife. Could we achieve anything worthwhile in an area in which we had little or no experience? Benjamin and Cousteau had all the backing they needed, every facility at their disposal; by comparison we were impoverished British amateurs. All this tended to intensify the pressures upon us and certainly nurtured personal doubts to a disturbing extent. I tried to justify it to myself on the grounds that it would be an essential preliminary trip, a recce, for a stronger expedition in the future.

The quest for sponsorship on any expedition is difficult and ours was no exception. Despite good support from the Sports Council and the Royal Geographical Society it was difficult convincing people that we had a legitimate or genuine aim. Occasionally the response to letters would be downright annoying. The following extract from a letter from Pennine Boats was perhaps the most pointed:

'I must say that I admire your style! As a B.S.A.C. Second Class diver and Training Officer of the local branch I have every admiration for a group seeking to obtain finance for what is basically a thinly disguised holiday, albeit a rather special one!

'Regrettably we are not in business to act as a charity . . . The undersigned has in fact twice visited the West Indies on diving holidays, the second time in a fulltime instructional capacity. If you are short of expedition members I would be interested to know — in which case we may be able to offer some worthwhile discounts on materials and equipment.'

Matters eventually took an upturn: Spirotechnic, one of the largest 'sport diving' companies, loaned us all the underwater equipment we needed while a professional diving, North Sea company, Comex Houlder Ltd, came forward with a direct cash grant of £1,000. Financially this saved the day and combined with the fact that H.R.H. the Duke of Kent agreed to act as Patron, gave our image a tremendous boost.

But the more we submerged ourselves in the project the greater became our doubts and pressures. The deep entrances to the Blue Holes lie in the sea floor just off the east coast of the island and lead to extensive cave networks stretching for an unknown distance both seawards and/or inland. There was no deceiving ourselves: the prospect was of long, continuous deep diving. Could we cope with it and the problems of decompression?

Psychologically the Blue Holes were a new frontier. Were we up to the challenge? Not only were there obvious dangers such as sharks but there were also the mildly disturbing legends of sea monsters and the like which inhabited the entrances. Benjamin had laid the majority of the latter to rest supplying some colourful anecdotes in the process. To the islanders for example the Lusca was a terrible creature — something like a huge octopus — which ensnared the unwary and dragged them down in to the depths.

Just imagine the scene with Benjamin on one of his first trips hiring a local boatman to take him out to a Blue hole for a dive. A few weeks before this same Bahamian's boat had drifted from its mooring out to the blue hole, and a lusca had supposedly pulled it down; whatever had happened, the boat had vanished. As the boat was anchored over the hole and Benjamin started assembling his gear the boatman started to panic.

'You go down dere and lusca, him of de hahnds get hold of you; you dead mahn!'

Whether the boatman was really concerned for the welfare of this crazy eccentric, or whether he was more concerned for his second boat was difficult to establish; one thing was for certain, he was in deadly earnest. In no way would Benjamin back down and when he dived he was rewarded by the discovery of the lost boat. That same day he probably immortalised himself in local folklore as being the first to enter the lusca's lair and more important come out again — together with a flooded outboard motor.

Benjamin had managed to squash the local legend of an actual monster but there was little doubt in everyone's minds that it had

177

been based on something real and awesome — the oceanic blue holes possessed some exceptionally strong currents.

Our expedition posed so many unknowns. Benjamin and Cousteau had used all the technology available including 'torpedoes' (Diver Propulsion Units). Everything we planned to do we knew would be done the hard way. Special equipment, lighting, for example, had to be constructed for the job. Here Bomber's ingenuity was something to marvel at. Together with Geoff Attwood he devised a system of 50-watt, head-mounted units that would last for one hour — unquestionably the finest lights known. But all this involved tremendous expense and each of us frequently asked ourselves if we could actually afford to go. This was probably the most organised trip I'd been on and the torturing self enquiry refused to end. What if it turns out to be fiasco? How could any of us ever go to the Sports Council in the future, or to anyone else for that matter if all we had to show was a sun tan? The entire expedition hung in the balance even as we boarded the Miami-bound 'Skytrain' from Gatwick.

Final team members were to be Rob Palmer, who had gone out over a week in advance of the main group, myself, Bomber, and Dr George Warner — the divers. Apart from exploration, survey and photography the programme incorporated a strong scientific content: George was to make a detailed study of blue hole ecology, Dr Mel Gascoine planned to continue with his stal dating activities while assisting Simcha Stroes with water sampling. We were also joined by Dr John Fish who supplied invaluable information regarding the island's fresh water resources. Completing the team list as base camp organisers were our two wives, (Bomber's and mine), Pam and Sally.

A night's stop over in Miami and the next day we flew on in a specially chartered light plane to the small airfield at the northern end of Andros Island. Our first view of the place, from the west, filled us with apprehension. The island seemed to be totally deserted, there was just a level carpet of greenery with no indication of human activity; an island 100 miles long and 30 miles wide forgotten or abandoned. Gradually what appeared to be a mere cutting in the monotonous terrain transformed itself to an airstrip, and a few minutes later we bumped along the weed infested runway; San Andros at last.

We disembarked amid the sweltering heat of early afternoon

178

wondering when, or if, Rob would come to collect us. Base was to be the Forfar Field Study Centre at Stafford Creek, about 20 miles due south. After sitting around for about two hours we got the feel of the place. The airfield was the hub of a minute settlement consisting of a single, diminutive terminal building, a hotel and a couple of houses. Just nothing seemed to go on. A few taxi drivers chatted away but since there were no arrivals, or departures I wasn't sure what they were waiting for. With a pained expression a young customs official eventually arrived from somewhere, eyed us up and down most suspiciously and duly stamped our passports; this was hardly the welcome we'd anticipated from the tourist brochure.

The reality at San Andros quickly asserted itself. Rob arrived and we all bundled into the back of an old pick-up. Hurtling along the unmetalled road (which we learned was the main north-south arterial highway), all we saw were pines and mangrove swamps. 'This place must be desperately poor' I thought to myself; it was certainly no tropical paradise. If we thought things had started a little disappointingly, worse was in store.

Forty minutes later we arrived at Stafford Creek and a few minutes later the pick-up spluttered to a halt outside what appeared to be a chicken shed.

'This is it; the International Field Study Centre' said Rob avoiding our gaze.

We were all a little shocked. The parking lot looked more like a scrap yard: it was overgrown with weeds and sported several derelict wagons in various stages of dismemberment. Even as we were standing there land crabs scuttled between our feet, clawed their way all over the timberwork of the shed and peeped out at us from the inner recesses.

'It's all right here,' said Rob reassuringly 'we've got everything we need.'

We were ushered into the adjoining shed. Barely had we been introduced to the resident staff and we were coming to grips with the prospect of a spartan existence, when the topic of conversation got around to our accommodation.

'Oh yes, I forgot to tell you,' said Rob, 'for the first week we'll be camping; bit of a misunderstanding on bookings.'

Camping! bloody hell; we just looked at each other. We'd read all about the traumas of life under canvas in the tropics, and

179

knew all about the sandflies and mosquitoes that could make things absolutely unbearable.

'It's only for a week and then we'll be back in the cabins up here.'

We were in no position to argue.

Next on the agenda was news of the diving and again a nasty surprise was in store for us. A few hours earlier the remains of a diver's body had been found in Uncle Charlie's Blue Hole. By this stage nothing else Rob told us could surprise us anymore. Although none of us cared to air our thoughts openly, the discovery of a cave diving fatality on the very day of our arrival had to be a rather disturbing quirk of fate; especially so since to everyone's knowledge there had only ever been one other cave diving fatality on the island — that of Frank Martz in a blue hole off the southern part of the island, in 1971.

The day after we arrived we went to inform the Chief of Police. The local authorities knew nothing of any 'lost' diver and it was immediately apparent that apart from a morbid curiosity the case held no interest for them. Having involved ourselves it seemed best that we did what we could to solve the mystery. We agreed to try and make a better identification of the remains a couple of days later and possibly obtain a photograph.

At 12.30 on the allotted day we met our friendly Chief at the nearby settlement of San Andros. He was still none the wiser as to the identity of the individual and I seriously wondered if he had done anything more than just enquire of his subordinates in the local station. Clearly the easy-going lifestyle on Andros had more concern for the living than the dead.

The temperatures were well into the 90s and even the Police chief thought we were a bit crazy, when we began preparations to dive. Why hadn't we dived a couple of hours sooner when it was relatively cool? Fully kitted in our new wetsuits and packing a pair of heavy 80 cu/ft cylinders apiece the sweat was running off us as we staggered through the jungle towards the blue hole.

'Don't touch that stuff!' came a sharp voice from behind as I ploughed forward along a winding path desperate to get in to the water.

'It's poisonweed; brings you up in horrible blisters.'

The little shrub that Rob was referring to had a leaf very much like a laurel and looked innocent enough. But by all accounts it was responsible for the majority of first aid accidents at the Forfar Centre. We'd only been here a couple of days but George had already presented us with a tarantula spider and a scorpion; poisonweed was just one more item to join the list of hazards.

The still blue pool beckoned invitingly. It was a perfectly circular area of glassy water screened secretively by the canopy of jungle. Were it not that Rob had been shown the site by the unsuspecting centre staff who used it regularly as a swimming pool, we might never have found the place. Despite the fact that the island rarely rose more than a metre above the high tide mark it was almost impossible to try to penetrate the dense undergrowth immediately off the roadside. We heard for example that the pilot of a light plane which had crashed just a couple of miles off a road nearby spent two days covering that distance, during which time he was half eaten to death by mosquitoes and other tropical nasties. If we thought that the midges of Scotland were bad then mosquitoes on Andros were to give a completely new insight to the word torture.

Carefully lowering ourselves over the vertical one-metre drop in to the water the relief from heat, exertion and surface hazards was unbelievable; such a contrast. One moment you felt it was all too much, you were going to flake out; the next you were floating, relaxed in a warm bath of pure shimmering delight.

Our portly Bahamian 'Mr Plod' had been educated back in England and as he mopped his brow at the water's edge it was obvious from his expression that the comforts of his air conditioned little office were calling; either that or an ice cold beer.

With the gear organised and plans discussed, Rob led off laying the line. From Benjamin's correspondence and the film we knew of the curiously localised band of water, the sulphur layer, to be found at all the inland blue holes, but even so on each dive we were to make through its murky barrier it always presented sinister forebodings. The depth at which this localised sulphur layer is encountered varies from hole to hole but its essential characteristics are a brown or slightly purplish colour, an evil taste and an evil smell. It forms a sharp interface between the predominantly fresh water above and the salt water beneath. From a diving point of view it presents atrocious visibility of just a metre and effectively cuts off all daylight to the deeper water.

At Uncle Charlie's Blue Hole the evil layer coincided with a dramatic narrowing of the shaft and at this point the steeply sloping walls were 'padded' to a depth of 0.3 of a metre by copious quantities of light coloured organic debris. As we brushed or bumped in to the side the mass exploded, and flecks of what might have been mushy newspaper or decomposed human flesh floated frighteningly around our masks. I held the line fast, and thankful for the powerful light, groped down into the world of total darkness.

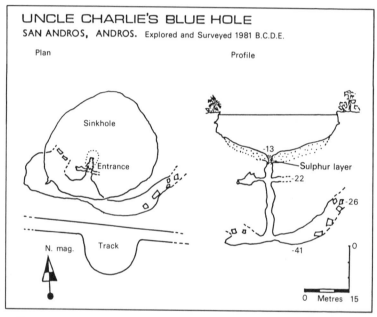

Down, down, down and between the regular surge of expanding bubbles that raced towards me I could see that the grey walled shaft maintained a constant two metres diameter in the crystal water. At a depth of 40 metres we reached the floor, at which point a huge trunk passage led off in either direction. I was confused; a passage at 18-21 metres Rob had said; this was well below the level of the side tunnel where the body lay.

The flash on my photographic outfit failed to operate and by gesturing to each other it was decided to surface. The situation was discussed and the camera outfit dumped. What did the Police Chief think? To an onlooker we could hardly have appeared efficient; we felt we had to make a second dive.

Diving back in and passing once more through the curious sulphur layer at 10-13 metres depth we started groping around in the vertical funnel. The blackness of the water was now well fortified with silt and scouring every nook and cranny down to 24 metres depth was a laborious job. Again it seemed a fruitless task. On the way up, at 21 metres, I somehow managed to pull myself up under an overhang and glimpsed the crystal blue of open passage. How on earth Rob had stumbled through the restricted opening to this without noticing the main shaft disappearing in to the depths neither of us could make out. I retreated momentarily, grabbed Rob, and as he still had the reel, pushed him in the required direction.

I manoeuvred my bottles carefully into the elusive side passage. Ahead the visibility was crystal clear while behind the water looked like a thin unwholesome porridge. Instantly I recognised the place from Rob's description; then he turned and made the 'O.K.' signal; no longer was there any doubt in his mind. We both knew what this meant; this was the passage. Less than 16 metres from the main shaft he veered off to the left, and simultaneously, with an ominously outstretched arm, he motioned up to the right. There it was — the body; he hadn't been hallucinating after all. What a way to start an expedition.

The remains were lifelike as they floated or wedged themselves precariously in a crack in the ceiling. Apart from a couple of leg bones which lay on the silt directly beneath, the body was distinctly intact. Leaving go of the line I moved in for a closer examination, with Rob perhaps two metres behind. In the clear water the detail was gruesome. Around the waist of the fully wetsuited diver were three or four weights, hanging clear of the now empty shell on a grey webbing belt. A black handtorch with a bulbous head was attached to part of an arm, a valve something like a 'U.S. Divers' hung from above. To the left, part of a large grey air cylinder (80 cu/ft or more) could be discerned protected by a black tank boot. Stripes of red had been immediately apparent and this was the remains of a red and white A.B.L.J. or B.C. (buoyancy compensator) as the Americans preferred to call it. Both fins of the 'Jet Fin' variety were now aligned in very unusual positions and only remained attached to the wetsuit legs by virtue of the fact that both were partially propped against the walls. On one of the legs a sturdy knife lay unused in its sheath.

My bubbles were disturbing all manner of silt from the alcove above and any moment I was worried that perhaps the disturbance might cause the skull or some other part of the body to break off. I backed away, motioned 'Out' to Rob and finned off along our line . . . a line which would unquestionably have saved the life of this diver. He must have groped around panic stricken on his ascent, accidentally passed under the small overhang in the main shaft and found himself in the side passage. Once into the larger dimensions inside and without a positive guide back to the surface he was doomed.

To lesser experienced divers than ourselves a discovery such as this at Uncle Charlie's might possibly have served as a severe deterrent. In this instance we were able to adopt an objective, detached attitude. There was no question of being flippant about the matter; it was just that we had been more intimately involved in tragedies, occasionally personal, before. Just a short while before leaving Britain I had virtually relived the Agen Allwedd tragedy of 1974 by continuing the exploration of the downstream Sump Four. A long period had been necessary to achieve the psychological strength to tackle the site and it was no surprise when a small part of Roger Solari's remains was discovered. The previous winter again I had been involved with the attempted rescue of another good friend David Woods, at Pollnacrom in Northern Ireland. His body had to be left where it was found. Sadly perhaps we had trained ourselves to suppress any emotions aroused by these and other encounters; perhaps it was nothing to be proud of but the body of a totally unknown stranger such as that at Uncle Charlie's Blue Hole seemed of comparatively little consequence and left us unmoved.

We decompressed, surfaced and outlined our findings. The Police Chief was anxious to get away and rather than rush a description on the spot it was thought better that Rob should write out a report later and drop it in to the local station. While we'd been down the others had informed him of the general objectives of the expedition — namely to dive as many blue holes as possible. A final word of warning was issued to us: stay away from the isolated inland sites — there was a real danger from armed smugglers; a number of people had been waylaid of late!

It appears that ever since the days of the renowned pirate Henry Morgan, who incidentally had loaned his name to the island's highest point, a mere 18 metres above sea level, smuggling and piracy seem to have been a natural way of life. The island's great advantage in this context is its geography: it is riven by lengthy creeks and bights, into which a boat might sail and there unload its valuable cargo well away from prying eyes. It also forms an ideal staging post to take advantage of its proximity to the United States. In the Prohibition Era of the 1930s the trading was in alcohol; today it is in drugs ... in transit from South America to the lucrative markets of the northern hemisphere.

Back at the Forfar Centre the resident staff filled us in on the island's incredible economy. Just a few months before a small group of them had found themselves spread eagled on the floor with shot guns to their heads; they got a clear message that nosing around inland was not very popular. More recently the Forfar lead diver had discovered a bale of marijuana stashed near another of their haunts. As he said the safest answer was just to leave things well alone, not get involved, and give the particular area a wide berth for a few weeks.

By now it was evident that like some distant outpost the Centre was virtually a little patch of America, provisioned weekly with supplies and new clientelle by air, from Fort Lauderdale in Florida. The staff typified the best of southern hospitality and always took great pains to help us out. But there was a limit to which even they could ease our time spent at the campsite. By day everything was fine but at dusk we plastered or sprayed every lotion we could get hold of on our bodies. Then, until it was time for bed we sat, repaired gear, chatted and read, the whole while itching, swatting here, swatting there, cursing and swatting again. Our sleeping bags gave little respite to the agony. It was too warm to slide deep into our bags so we generally lay on top of them, lightly wrapped in just a sheet. As the sleeping quarters were large communal tents devoid of mosquito netting or even sewn in ground sheets all manner of nocturnal visitors came our way. A high pitched whine in the ear inevitably heralded another hungry mosquito while all night long land crabs busied themselves scratching and scuffling all around the tent, in, under or over our sleeping bags.

Falling asleep has never been a problem for me and as long as the mosquitoes weren't unduly noisy I wasn't too concerned; the

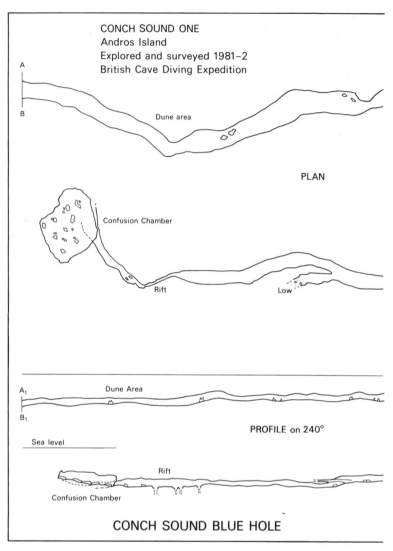

CONCH SOUND ONE
Andros Island
Explored and surveyed 1981–2
British Cave Diving Expedition

PLAN

Confusion Chamber

Rift

Low

Dune Area

Sea level

PROFILE on 240°

Rift

Confusion Chamber

CONCH SOUND BLUE HOLE

land crabs were harmless until they tried climbing on your face. My biggest problem was the other inmates of the tent. Bomber spent hours, or so it seemed, scouring the tent ejecting the creatures, but as the crabs were more familiar with the tent than its human occupants five or ten minutes later they, or their friends, were back. Despite sand and stones being piled onto

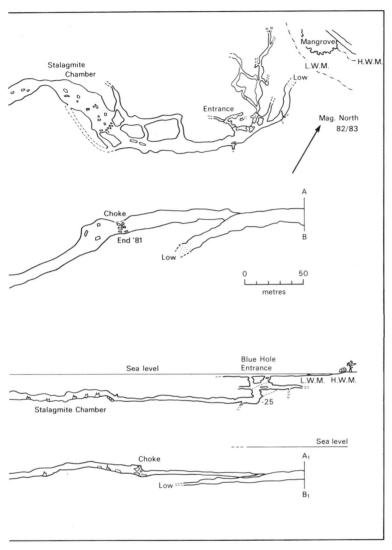

every conceivable crack or entrance nothing seemed to stop them and as a result Bomber lost more and more sleep — continually mumbling and cursing as only a northerner knows how. Anyone who has spent a night in a large dormitory of a caving headquarters learns to turn a deaf ear to snoring, moaning and the like; what is impossible to ignore is the sudden unexpected jab in the ribs from someone who insists on sharing their miseries.

'What did I pay all this money for to be half eaten by mosquitoes and kept awake all night by crabs?'

'Yes dear.'

I rolled over, crushed some poor little creature in the process and passed out again.

From Benjamin's literature and a very brief recce by Rob before our arrival, Conch Blue Hole was to be our prime objective. This lay in the extreme north east of Andros close to the settlement of Nichols Town. The site was superb, less than 60 metres from the shore and with good vehicle access.

Just as the trip to Uncle Charlie's Blue Hole tuned us in to the nature of inland blue holes so our introductory trip to Conch Blue Hole was to give us the full flavour of the offshore blue holes. The unusual hydrology of these oceanic blue holes, certainly the intensity of the currents (reaching three knots or more) would seem to make them unique. For over 80 per cent of each day the currents 'suck' or 'blow' from the openings and effectively preclude any safe underwater activity.

Why should such a hydrological pattern exist? Quite simply the few oceanic blue holes that line the shallow waters off the eastern side of Andros are linked with a large number of inland blue holes, via a maze of interconnecting passages. As the tide rises water flows into the oceanic blue holes and surges beneath the island. The inland blue holes then react to the tidal influx but the actual variation in water level at these sites is dependent upon distance from the sea. Uncle Charlie's for example, only half a mile from the coast, might rise and fall by 30 cm or more while another site several miles inland might only rise 3 cm or so. When the flow is sucking in on a rising tide a vortex can often be seen to form and it has been known that a diver's exhausted bubbles will be pulled downwards; one could well imagine an unwary diver also being sucked in, and then the older islanders might insist the lusca had claimed one more victim.

As the tide falls the reverse action occurs and something of a 'mushroom effect' can be distinguished upon the surface of the sea where the water forces, or 'blows' its way out. At certain sites entry is utterly impossible at such times.

This cyclic effect is clearly dependent upon the rise or fall of the tide but there are further complications. The currents in the blue holes do not reverse at exactly the same time as the tides. Thus when the tide reaches its low point and starts to rise water continues to flow out of the Andros holes for two to three hours. Similarly, when the tide first starts to subside, water in the caves is still flowing inwards. The most plausible explanation is that during rising tide seawater is forced into the restricted blue holes and distributed underneath the island through the maze-like passages of the intertidal zone. During low tide the pressure is released and the direction of the flow reverses. In simple terms the island water table acts like a piston in a supersize cylinder.

Rob's calculations concerning Conch Blue Hole made high tide somewhere around 11.30 am. We arrived at the beach an hour later. Our plan seemed sensible; if we dived in at slack water and were down for any length of time we could have assistance from the 'blow' current on the way out. Nothing could have been simpler, had it not been that Rob's calculations were slightly out.

After an initial snorkel around above the entrance it was considered that the current was sucking in a little too well. We adjourned to the shore. The logistics of the trip were basic: Rob and I were to dive together, each carrying 100 metres of line which we hoped to be able to install as a preliminary to a major penetration at this site. Bomber and George decided on a less ambitious familiarisation dive and weren't intending going very far. After a suitable interval we kitted up fully and made our way out. Again the current was too strong and we postponed entry for another half an hour. After this second delay we were both confident that slack water was imminent and our excitement overruled a further wait.

Rob led off while I followed a short distance behind. The line was tied off to a boat which had sunk at one of the interconnecting entrances and we swooped on down into a passage below. Despite the odd bits of weed and debris that were still moving inwards with the current, conditions near the entrance gave no cause for concern. The current seemed weak and the visibility was well over 10 metres.

At 17 metres depth the gradient eased and a large dark tunnel loomed ahead. Glancing back towards the surface countless fish swarmed to and fro in an area suffused by a beautiful green glow; a mystical sight spelling safety and relief. A few more feet into the tunnel and all light was lost; we switched to the powerful 50 watt head lights. I still could not get over the temperature of the water; it was superbly comfortable wearing our new 3-mm wet suits, with no need at all for the use of a hood. Never before this trip had I appreciated how restrictive, indeed claustrophobic, was the effect of a tight fitting neoprene hood. Without it I felt so much more at ease; breathing was much less of a strain and the medium somehow felt infinitely more hospitable than that back home.

Rob continued reeling out while I followed. The passage seemed to narrow slightly over the next 48 metres and here the current intensified. There was hardly any need to fin at all. Despite the route being spacious and the immense confidence inspired by our lights, in no way could I say that I felt happy. An inbuilt survival mechanism seemed to cast doubt after doubt. This was quite probably the strongest current that I had ever experienced in a sump and there was always the nagging worry that it might get stronger. Several times Rob stopped and periodic checks were made to ensure we could in fact move out against the current — we could, just! At such times it was all I could do to hold onto the taut line and avoid being swept directly into him. We'd dived together enough times to gain a mutual appreciation of the other's feelings and I derived a strange comfort from the fact that he too felt uneasy about the inexorable force that swept us on down the passage. Without the reassurance of such a heavy 5-mm line, which we could use if necessary to pull ourselves out, the conditions would have been downright intimidating.

When Rob's reel ran out the depth had levelled off at 23 metres. In the cold murky waters back home a sustained depth like this would generate more than enough anxiety; one could literally watch the needle on the pressure gauge fall back with each breath. We knew from experience that the air supply here would be used up three times faster than at the surface, giving a life expectancy of just 25 minutes per bottle, as opposed to 75 minutes which we might expect in shallow water at home — a disturbing realisation if one cared to dwell on the fact. But lulled and relaxed by the warm clear water and the towing effect of the current it seemed that the depth factor was not so important; an insidiously deceptive situation.

190

The dive was certainly an amazing experience, my first ever in the sea. Diving off the British coast had never raised any enthusiasm and my only recollections were of abysmal disasters or so it seemed. While on my basic air training for example, in university, I remembered vividly the feeling of panic as I snorkelled through a heavy storm-driven swell across a Gower beach — water continually swamping my snorkel tube as wave after wave rolled by. The fact that I had an inflatable life jacket on, and therefore had little cause for concern, somehow didn't register. My next attempt came in 1978 when we planned an assault on a submarine resurgence off the coast of Co. Clare in Ireland. On that occasion we spent 20 minutes battling against a ferocious incoming tide getting bowled over again and again until we finally had to admit defeat — losing our line reel in the process.

A profusion of life was the striking aspect of our new environment; something never noticed in Britain; Near the entrance the most obvious form was that of the shoals of fish and hydroids. The latter looked like a type of fern and floated or wavered like long discoloured streamers with the current. Away from the entrance there seemed to be no fish at all but virtually every boulder or cleft concealed a lobster or crustacian. I'd never seen a lobster in its natural habitat before and here in the total darkness of the passage seemingly they had no fear; if anything I was far more worried than they were. Singly, or in pairs, they just stood there, bigger than life, eyeing us up. But it was the slow, deliberate movement of their amazingly long tentacles that appeared so menacing. I could almost imagine a swift whip-lash action with the lobster deftly removing my mouth piece, snipping through the air supply hose and just waving two tentacles at a horrified, purple faced diver. We left them undisturbed and cruised quietly on. By 100 metres the various life forms had thinned out appreciably but even so the roof, walls and floor displayed a heavy encrustation, the resultant build up of countless years of marine organisms.

The second reel was tied on and it was my turn to follow the current on its mysterious course. The 50-watt light was magnificent. At a glance characteristics of the huge tunnel could be noted and shortly stalagmites began to appear. In fact from about 125 metres they were common-place. What a discovery, and on our first dive! George Benjamin had searched the South Island area for almost 10 years before making such a find.

At 200 metres the reel expired and the depth had reduced to 19 metres. And it was here that we entered a vast chamber with stal in every direction. Rob cruised up and like myself he could barely contain his excitement. In big letters he wrote 'STAL' on my slate. I felt like writing something sarcastic on his like 'Brilliant' but managed to refrain and gave a nod and an 'O.K.' sign instead. But what a turn up for the books; we'd come all this way and located probably the finest grottos discovered to date, on our very first attempt.

But our elation wasn't to last. No sooner had we turned around than the seriousness of our predicament became evident. The current was as strong as ever. Each fin stroke required a determined effort and suddenly the entrance seemed a long way away. Rob led carrying the two empty reels while I followed surveying from marker to marker, set at 10-metre intervals. The temptation was clear; abandon the survey and head on out as fast as possible. This was a situation that required a cool, level-headed response. The journey in had been so deceptively easy that we had been lulled into a false sense of security. But there was little doubt now. We certainly couldn't hang around and wait for the current to reverse. All senses were at red alert. So little air had been consumed on that graceful journey in; now we were paying the price. The needle began to fall — fast. Thoughts of the diver in Uncle Charlie's stole their way in to my head increasing the rate of breathing. It was essential to alleviate the anxiety and in this, doing the survey helped by keeping me occupied on the journey back. The task was completed satisfactorily but all things considered the exit was a bit of a rout. Having made a brief decompression stop we surfaced and firmly resolved not to make a habit of misreading the tides.

When we reached the others we told them what we had found and learned that George had also had an adventure. George Warner is one those quiet, affable sorts; easy to get on with and great company on such an expedition. He also happens to be a British Sub-Aqua 1st Class diver and as such we had immense respect for his ability. However George had never been on a cave dive before and we mistakenly believed that he would progress at his own pace, as he slowly gained experience in the new environment. After Rob and I had set off into the cave George thought that he would follow along our line, equipped with just a single

70 cu/ft bottle. Unknown to us he became totally absorbed with the marine life and was lured ever further along the passage. By the time he consulted his pressure gauge he was over 103 metres in and down to 55 atmospheres, compared to 130 when he had started out: he had just 10 minutes worth of air to get himself out. A cave diver would have started on the exit when he had reached 87 atmospheres (one third of the air used en route in, two thirds for the journey out), but the conditions had deceived George as well.

Finning and pulling his way along against the current he remained cool but was soon aware of breathing heavily. Anger, at having been so stupid, filled his thoughts as did concern as to how his family would fare without him. Fortunately George's lung capacity is quite astonishing; by remaining cool he made it — as the last of his air gave out. It was just as well that he did not require decompression! As he lay on his back, all energy spent and floating above the entrance, all Bomber could get out of him was 'bloody hell, bloody hell, bloody hell.'

George learned a lot that day; so did we.

'You should have been stricter with me. You should not have respected my 1st Class diver status and should have insisted that I wear a twin set — and did precisely as Bomber said. Not that it makes it any less my fault — but us naive open water divers just don't know the score.'

We had made a bit of a mess of our first dive at Conch Blue Hole. It wouldn't happen again. By the following morning we were psyched up to try and lay another 200 metres of line on to that already installed. We now knew the exact time of slack water and provided that we dived to schedule then we ought to have more than sufficient air. The plan was simple. Just to make sure of our safety margins we opted to dive in for approximately 110 metres breathing off a spare hand-held set which would then be deposited for the exit. Florida divers regularly adopt this system which they refer to as 'stage diving'.

The daily routine at the centre was far from smooth; flexibility of approach was essential. No matter how organised the staff might be some aspect of Bahamian life would upset the best laid plans. One day there would be a fuel crisis affecting the whole island; then the vehicles would break down. This particular day for some reason or other we were palmed off with the most beat up station wagon that anyone could possibly imagine. It was quite literally falling apart. Ever since our arrival this wagon had stood in a patch of weeds consigned, or so we thought, to scrap. Not one of its tyres had any tread, most of the windows were missing and huge rust holes characterised the bodywork. The wiring was a maze of bright green leads which wove all over the place like rampant bind weed. Needless to say few of the electrical fittings actually operated.

Barely had the vehicle juddered across the parking area than a puncture occurred. This would have been a comic situation were it not for the fact that we had to drive thirty miles to dive. Timing didn't matter particularly in Britain; here it was of paramount importance because of the tides. I was getting more and more agitated.

'Don't worry about it,' shouted the centre staff. They had seen it all before, but this was no consolation to us. The heap rolled hazardously out on to the track now minus a spare. Then, belching fumes and with a noise like thunder it careered north. The suspension, like the syncromesh in the gear box, had ceased to exist back in the 1930s, not that this worried Rob in the driver's seat; we had to make up for lost time. With 10 clanging cylinders (only one of which needed to explode to wipe us all out) and six of us huddled on the back, it was probably safer combating the currents in Conch rather than riding on this wreck. Much to everyone's relief and apart from bruised back sides, the journey passed uneventfully.

As on the previous day hoards of curious youngsters gathered round, by now asking more and more questions. The girls usually managed to keep an eye on them, chatted and kept them amused. It was amazing what these kids came out with. A general enquiry about for example a cabin cruiser with long radio masts moored out in the bay yielded an astonishing reply.

'Dat ma uncles; it faster dan anyting de coastguard got.'

The conversation moved on to guns — all manner of armaments, and these kids were ready and willing to make comparisons and even suggest where we might get our own.

'I know arms dealer; he fix you up.'

Yes, we could well imagine getting fixed up alright. All this was becoming too much. We couldn't risk 'heavies' coming round to sort out the nosey foreigners so the conversation was switched to school, family and the like.

194

The dive itself went like clockwork. From the previous day's limit we proceeded at roughly the same depth through grotto after grotto, occasionally belaying the line around convenient stals on the floor. From 350 metres to 410 metres we traversed what could only be described as a lunar-like landscape. Here the passage had a width of about 22 metres or more and vast quantities of light sediments quilted the floor. All too soon our line was gone. Once more I surveyed out while Rob took the reels and collected biological samples for George.

Amazingly even 300 metres in there was marine life, crustacians, eels and the odd anemone; all surviving in a delicate balance and dependent upon a food supply carried in the current. Just how the crabs and the like managed to catch their prey in the dark was anyone's guess but they certainly seemed to make the best of the situation.

The inevitable occurrence finished the day when we had a puncture. With an almost non existent telephone service on the island, certainly Forfar Centre had no phone, we either had to drive slowly on the smouldering flat or walk. Dusk was rapidly approaching at which time we would fall prey to the rapacious mosquitoes. It was a rather ignominious return for our leader as the wagon limped into camp like the sole survivor of some western ambush.

On the third dive at Conch Blue Hole, about a week later, we decided to use an extra back-mounted cylinder as well as a stage unit. By now we were beginning to feel confident, not only of our loaned 'Spiro' gear but also through familiarity with decompression procedures. The depth averaged 22 metres to 410 metres, which even by British standards was not unduly deep. After ten days we were also thoroughly conversant with the vagaries of the currents and were now utilising them to our best advantage. Having planned a dive carefully we could for example dive in at the tail end of the sucking current, explore fresh ground during slack water and then exit assisted by the outgoing current. Meticulous planning and observation of the current pattern at each individual site was essential for blue hole diving.

By this third exploration I was intrigued with my own attitude towards such diving. I had never enjoyed cave diving back in Britain, it was purely a means to an end — a way, albeit incorporating greater risks — of discovering new caves. Dive explorations such as those at Keld Head had never really appealed to me. We had come to Andros to try something different and I was amazed at the fact that this was actually pleasurable.

Beyond our previous limit I laid out the next 100 metres of line. The entire distance was characterised by an enormous passage, devoid of stal, where frequently the powerful 50 watt beam failed to reveal the walls either to the left or to the right. The line expired at a convenient boulder jutting from the fine silt. I tied off and lay on my side to rest. Out of idle curiosity and a desire to conserve the life of the batteries I switched off my light. Darkness was only momentary however as peering generally in the direction from which I had come I was in time to experience my own personal sunrise. Piercing the blackness, a beautiful blue glow foretold Rob's approach, deepening steadily as the beams from his lights encompassed an increasing area of my vision. To have captured the scene on movie film would have provided a surrealistic, unforgettable record. Then Rob came homing in, lights ablaze, like something of a pioneer space vessel, and the image was over.

Rob led on. As the second of our cylinders reached its one third safety margin almost nonchalently each of us swapped to a different mouthpiece. Back in Britain exchanging mouthpieces was something that I had only rarely undertaken. I preferred the idea of keeping my teeth firmly in contact with the air supply. It was all very well on training sessions in the pool; in a sump it is altogether different. Here in the warm water there seemed to be plenty of time and our fingers were supple. The fear that we might bodge the delicate manoeuvre was lessened and after a few dives the swap was undertaken with no qualms whatsoever. In the context of changing mouthpieces, sticking to the 'third rule' is essential. There are so many things that can go wrong in a sump, for example a valve failure, a broken harness, cramp, losing the line, bad visibility — the list is endless. Only by maintaining an adequate reserve in all cylinders can you stand any reasonable chance of averting a crisis; the diver with inadequate reserves is a liability not only to himself but especially to his companions.

By the time Rob's line ran out we were 609 metres from the entrance. However the depth now registered 28 metres — not a place to hang around. The journey out was uneventful until the last leg. Rob was ahead, as normal, and the current was well into its 'blow' cycle. Each of us had been carrying three lights but on this trip I was conserving batteries and only using one unit at a time. Suddenly I was pitched into complete darkness as, with no warning, the light just cut out.

The first hourly unit had long since expired but by my reckoning there was at least another half an hour's light expectancy from the one that had just failed. Grinding to a halt, releasing the spare hand-held stage unit and holding fast to the line feelings were tense. I could probably get out if need be in the dark but as I quietly worked away at the problem I was amazed to discover countless luminous specks racing by in the current; another unique phenomenon of the blue holes? It was as though I was cast into the eternal darkness of outer space, flying at vast speed past endless chains of cosmic bodies. A few hefty thumps and the light was restored; instantly these minute organisms, or whatever, became invisible.

Blue hole ecology was certainly to prove complex. The community of organisms growing on the walls of the passages seemed to be nothing like that in the neighbouring reef habitats. Sponges of various colours and small corals were abundant. In the stalagmite chambers, deposit feeding sea cucumbers appeared to be common — looking like chubby sausages crawling around on the floor. But beyond 400 metres life diminished significantly until by 555 metres even the sighting of a crab was noteworthy. Occasionally in these deeper parts a snake eel might weave its way off to one side, or standing on its head excavate frantically downwards quickly disappearing in a small puff of sand.

We were well pleased by the progress made at Conch Blue Hole and lesser discoveries at other sites, but the expedition certainly had its problems. The freight for example did not arrive until the third week of our stay which meant that we were limited with our activities. Being leader might have been prestigious but again it meant that Rob lost out on several explorations. Looking back the most enjoyable day of our trip in fact occurred while Rob was way-laid in Nassau, sorting out the freight. The previous evening we had all been to a party and everyone was suffering with a hangover. At dawn Rob dragged himself off to the airport while George woke bright and cheery muttering about us joining the Centre staff for a deep 'Wall' dive.

197

The 'Wall' is the local name for an incredible oceanic cliff which borders the entire length of the eastern side of the island. It is in every respect a wonder of the diving world — a vast, sheer precipice that descends hundreds of metres into a deep trough, known in the Bahamas as 'The Tongue of The Ocean'. The top of the 'Wall' lies at a depth of between 30-40 metres below sea level, and about a mile offshore.

In view of the fact that the limestone strata of Andros are estimated to be over 4,300 metres thick it has long been hypothesised that the cave systems which formed on the island tens of thousands of years ago once drained to resurgences in the actual face of the 'Wall'. It had always been one of Benjamin's aims to locate such a cave and his team spent a considerable number of dives on the project. There was a certain fascination with this type of exploration; working at the limits of technology and in the process establishing unsurpassed depth records. But working at the limits the risks are high and Archie Forfar who had established the centre at Stafford Creek, and contributed so much to cave diving on the island, died on a world record depth penetration, to 147 metres, in December 1971.

During the time spent exploring the upper parts of the 'Wall' a now legendary site 'The hole in the Wall' was discovered. This subsequently featured in one of Cousteau's adventures as, ever the showman, he actually took a mini-sub on a through trip.

We had been to 60 metres depth attempting to find the 'Hole' before and the opportunity of a second dive here seemed too good to miss. I was feeling rough, dead rough, and in a bit of a dilemma. The day's main objective was a final push at Conch Blue Hole. Time was definitely running out and one had to consider very carefully the changeover time between the 'suck' and 'blow' cycles. High tide was a half an hour later each day and therefore the period of slack water was becoming progressively later. In a day or two a long penetration would be totally out of the question, as a night diving operation was too inconvenient. Against my befuddled brain George's arguments and clear logic met no resistance.

'You're not diving in Conch til 5.30 pm; you can fit in both dives easily.'

It was game, set and match. We left for the 'Wall'.

As on the other occasions the half hour boatride out past the reef made me feel dreadful. My head had stopped spinning but my stomach felt as though it was working overtime. To get off the bobbing boat and into the water sounded a simple operation but every time I went to kit up I felt sea sick. Keeping my eyes fixed on the horizon seemed to be the only way of alleviating the symptoms but it meant I had to stop everything. Getting into the water was a long job, but an indescribable relief.

The anchor rope led directly to the edge of the precipice at a depth of 40 metres. Below the black craggy abyss looked ominous. At the same time it possessed unique photographic qualities. I promptly set off down to 60 metres to try a couple of shots of the others silhouetted high above. I still felt uneasy after the night's drinking and having taken two photographs made a hasty ascent back up to 35 metres. For the first time in my diving experience I became aware of strange and disturbing feelings. My brain was telling me that I had been down for a half an hour or more; a feeling of panic welled up. I desperately tugged back my wetsuit sleeve to consult my watch. My breathing rate was almost a state of panting and it was an immense relief to see that just six minutes had elapsed since leaving the surface. I knew what this meant alright — the 'narcs', or nitrogen narcosis. Having identified the ailment I felt reasonably confident of my ability to overcome it, especially as I'd been to 60 metres with no symptoms on the previous dive.

A few minutes later I opted to swap mouthpieces. What a shambles. I got a neckstrap caught across my mouth and as a result half a mouthful of water. Matters were getting out of control but strangely my brain was cool and clear. A quick cough and splutter, a momentary shot of panic and the whole exercise had to be repeated; this time infinitely more cautiously.

As I made to close up on the others who were oblivious of my condition I became aware that everything had become slow motion — so incredibly slow as to be unreal. It was very, very strange. I could analyse the situation perfectly in a snappy instantaneous sort of way yet my brain was unable to speed up my perception to what it should be. I told myself to get a grip but even so the symptoms continued.

The rest of the dive was maintained on the edge of the 'Wall' where I endeavoured to finish the film. Only on ascent did any real semblance of normality return. Booze and diving definitely do not mix. Having concluded the hour's decompression I was almost up to eating something, but still dubious of my ability to follow through the day's main objective — the final push at Conch.

Numerous plans had been discussed at the previous night's party for tackling Conch. The trouble was that we were deceived by the cans of American beer, which tasted weak and watery — but were not! By the end of the evening we had eliminated the ridiculous proposals and were up to plan E — a solo exploration.

I was to dive in exactly as I had on the previous trip wearing three cylinders and using a stage unit. My hand-held bottle would be breathed to about 110 metres where it would be dropped. At this point I would transfer to a fresh stage unit carried in by George. This would be breathed until one third of the air had been used, in all probability to about 310 metres from base. It seemed relatively straightforward and to make the dive easier Bomber spent the following morning rigging up an inflatable life jacket to the second stage unit, thereby making it easier to handle deep into the cave.

All went well until we arrived at the beach. Here we discovered that I'd forgotten to put in a back pack for my third, body-mounted bottle. As Bomber was still ill, and had no intention of diving, he hadn't brought any gear. This was a bit of a crisis. There was no way that we could go back to Forfar to collect a back pack as we would miss the 5.30 deadline to dive.

Plan F was quickly formulated. Whether it was F for fiasco or F for fantastic remained to be seen. This involved George dropping out altogether and me using his twin back pack as a stage unit. Would such a bulky item be manageable? It had to be worth a try. Bomber quickly set to and rigged up the inflatable life jacket to George's pack. During this spell an interesting conversation developed with the local children. One boy was most disturbed when he found out that Bomber and Pam had been married for about four years but had not produced any children; he failed to understand the situation.

'What wrong wid you? You lazy mahn,' he said addressing Bomber in a serious tone of voice. 'My fader work hard; I got 11 brudders an' sisters.'

Poor old Bomber really got some abuse.

In an hour or so everything was assembled and the final queasy feelings of the hangover dissipated. As the final touches were made I could imagine Cousteau observing the scene from the deck of his boat Calypso.

'Eh Falco, who are zose bumbling fools? What is zat contraption?'

'Zey are English!'

Yes the stage unit was a real 'Heath Robinson' contraption with straps and hoses everywhere. We were doing things the hard way alright and necessity was certainly the mother of invention. But however amateurish we might have appeared we had still achieved the longest penetration on the island with our last dive here and Cousteau, for all his financial backing, had undertaken no original exploration whatsoever; he had merely followed Benjamin's lines!

Departure time was 5.45 pm. The 'supertanker' sledge, with line reel and fourth light attached weighed well over 60 pounds and a fair amount of air had to be injected to the jacket before neutral buoyancy enabled it to be handled with any reasonable degree of comfort. Then, with a good sucking current I clumsily started off. Progress was relatively easy. But had I mistimed the change of current? There were plenty of nagging doubts.

The first cylinder on the sledge took me to over 200 metres before the safety margin was reached. Before the margin came on the second I located an area of roof breakdown, at 370 metres, and securely moored the tanker on to the line. Slowly deflating the life jacket the whole thing settled; there was no way it was going to drift off anywhere. Finally the various air lines were tidied, to ensure that the mouthpieces would remain free of silt. There was now little reason to doubt a successful outcome and I had no worries about getting out.

I cruised quietly on with the current. How I envied the Florida divers. They had conditions like this right on their doorstep; soon I would be back in the cold, dank caves of South Wales. Every minute had to be savoured. The 'third' margin loomed up on my first cylinder. It was time to swap onto a side-mounted set. I spat out the gag and pushed in a replacement. A quick blow and the water was exhaled from the flooded mouthpiece. I breathed in — but nothing happened. The throat convulsed a couple of times and I realised that I hadn't turned the bottle on, either that or I had a valve failure. Rather than fumble my way through all

201

the straps to the pillar valve and check it out it was much more prudent to change back on to the first set. In the cold, tense environment of British sumps I would have had about 20 seconds to rectify such a situation before things became critical; here, feeling warm and at ease that time could be doubled. All things considered this was incomparably easier than the conditions under which we operated at home. The pillar valve was turned on — problem solved — and in minutes the end of the line was in sight.

The longest distance that I had ever explored a sump, without an air surface, was 338 metres back in Britain. Here I was almost twice that from base, at an infinitely greater depth — over 23 metres — yet feeling nowhere near my physical or mental limit. This was exploration at its most enjoyable.

At 700 metres from the entrance my reel expired, quite conveniently at an awkward looking squeeze in an area of massive boulder collapse. With ample air left in the three cylinders I surveyed back to the previous end then began hunting for specimens for George. The characteristic life form deep in to the system appeared to be a species of eel. This was my task — to catch one. As a boy brought up deep in the countryside all we ever seemed to do was steal birds' eggs, shoot anything that moved and run like hell when the farmer turned up. A particular forte was tickling shallow water river fish. Eels were always a challenge; it didn't matter how big they were, given a sturdy kitchen fork and a piece of rag they were done for.

'No problem George,' I'd said 'give me a couple of poly bags.'

I must have spent ages; swiping here, swiping there; it was just as crazy as George Benjamin filming sharks in a sump. Clouds of mud were rising all over the place; the eels were certainly better acquainted with the place than me! When I eventually got one into the bag it wasn't due to any skill on my part; he must have been either stunned or an Educationally Sub-Normal juvenile.

When eventually I'd securely wrapped my 14-cm long prize I emerged from the mud cloud just in time to witness something quite amazing. About 555 metres from the entrance a 15-cm diameter crab was scuttling-cum-swimming directly in front of me, clutching tightly a squirming pink and white coral shrimp. This was certainly a ruthless environment where each had to survive as best he could. I felt quite guilty about removing the small eel which would in no way benefit me; it was almost a crime. The coral shrimp was another matter. Its death was demanded by nature. Quietly pondering these matters I noticed that the ingoing current had now died away completely. Any further worries were banished. In a few minutes I would be assisted by the outgoing current and my adventure would draw smoothly to a conclusion.

By the time I regained my air dump my 50-watt light was dying rapidly; I switched to the 10-watt unit. Applying my thumb to the button on the life jacket air feed system a long whistling gave shape to the wrinkled yellow bag. Slowly, gracefully the 'supertanker' inflated and rose off the floor. All five of my cylinders were now partially depleted and this produced a lop-sided effect necessitating occasional buoyancy adjustment. Then it was a slow, easy-going haul back to the entrance and decompression.

The dive had taken 1 hour and 45 minutes, as a result of which I now had to complete another 66 minutes of decompression. Anywhere else but in the oceanic blue holes of the Bahamas this would be an irksome task; in Britain or cold water sites it was a simple case of suffering. Here however the water was virtually at body temperature, and I could even go on a tour of the entrances, all the while, of course, making sure that I remained at the precise depth required for a safe decompression.

There were so many different things to absorb, for example a laser-like shaft of sunlight piercing some shadowy cleft, a shoal of silvery specks flitting to and fro, a myriad array of endless colour; fish, crustaceans, molluscs, sponges, plants; it was an experience like nothing else on earth.

Time passed. Gradually the daylight failed; a strange sensation, as the entrance felt to be more eerie than the depths of the cave itself. I was alone, vulnerable. Who knows what strange creature might emerge? Perhaps it was the thought that nocturnal prowling sharks might arrive? I only ever carried a 5-cm long blade on my diving knife and I couldn't see any hungry predator being deterred by something quite so pathetic. Sliding back to the furthest recess of an alcove my position was semi-protected and from the narrow opening I watched the varied blue hole inhabitants completing their day's activities.

The euphoria rose to a climax as the final minutes were completed. No sooner had my head bobbed to the surface and my two remaining lights dimly revealed the mangrove near the shore than Bomber's voice rang out.

'Hurry up, we're being eaten alive by mosquitoes.' Back to reality.

What a sight met the eyes as I reached the beach. Like some wild disco dance George and Bomber were frantically leaping about, whirling towels and shirts around them, while Simcha seemed to be whipping Mel with some palm leaves — it was a scene of complete pandemonium.

'It's terrible!' screamed Pam, and suddenly, as though with one mind, they set on me. I was trying to tell them about the dive but they were too busy stripping the equipment off me to listen. A bottle fell on my toe.

'Take it easy.' But nothing of the sort.

'Give us your arm.' The instruments were torn off.

'Turn around.'

'Take the weight of that other bottle.'

A minute or so later everything had been stripped off and thrown in a horrible mangled heap on the back of the wagon and Mel was revving away at the accelerator pedal. I was still dripping as we sped off into the night.

'Well' I thought, 'so much for the longest cave dive on Andros!'

But the show wasn't over. Above us the skies were crystal clear yet all around lightning flashed. Apart from the lack of thunder it could well have been a bomb raid. Near to hand luminous fireflies sped past like sparks driven from a bonfire. With the wind on our faces we hurtled south each absorbed in his or her own thoughts; a stimulating experience capping what was unquestionably the most enjoyable diving that I had ever done. What a superb day.

A few more visits were subsequently made to Conch Blue Hole and the surveyed length of passages rose above 925 metres. But the best visibility in any of the 13 different holes that we visited was that experienced at Rat Cay Blue Hole, about one third of the way up the coast from Stafford Creek to Conch Sound. Here over 615 metres of passages were explored and surveyed — all at the relatively shallow depth of 16-18 metres. Even though there were no stal formations, photographically this site was better than Conch. But for a pictorial record the crowning dive had to be that at Stalactite Blue Hole. We made several dives at inland holes but nearly all were prohibitively deep or uninteresting. Stalactite Blue Hole is deep — over 60 metres — but it is also a photographic wonderland. It lies about 15 miles from the coast and had previously been explored and documented by Benjamin. Ours therefore was a tourist visit, but to a location were it anywhere else but on Andros Island that would be deluged by eager sight-seers and photographers. At the surface the site is just like all the rest of the blue holes, a huge circular pool of placid blue water. However, down at 22 metres depth the walls bell out and into the void exposed beneath the cavernous ceiling hang massive pendulous stals. Some are over 10 metres in length and terminate strangely at the sulphur layer. If there were 'seven wonders' in the diving world Stalactite Blue Hole would certainly feature on the list.

Our expedition to the Andros Blue Holes lasted just over one month and during that period we explored over 1,540 metres of previously unknown cave passages. Working in an area in which we had little or no experience, and severe financial constraints, we were all more than pleased to come away with the longest penetration currently established on the island.

Andros might not have been a holiday paradise but arguably it presents some of the finest diving to be found anywhere in the world. Floating along corridors in the warm tropical water, passing through grottos of dripstone, long encrusted by creatures of the sea, the blue holes present an extreme but fascinating challenge — a mysterious frontier at the very limit of technology.

9

A World Record at Conch Blue Hole

It was August 1982 and we were back on Andros. From the 1981 trip we realised that we were equal to the challenge presented by the blue holes and that a major exploration was ours for the taking. Conch Blue Hole was the objective. The site was irresistible and with a larger team of experienced divers to support and 'sherpa' equipment deep in to the system we were confident of attaining a much longer penetration than that of 1981.

On our return to Britain after the 1981 trip Rob Parker, Julian Walker and Tony Boycott had quickly been recruited ... not that it took a great deal of persuasion ... and expeditionary wheels had been set in motion once again. This done, I had the surprise of my life when Rob phoned with the announcement:

'It's a world record.'

Not only had my 700-metre penetration been the longest on Andros it was also the longest in any submarine cave.

From a personal viewpoint there was something distasteful about records and this was no exception. In comparison with some of the incredible diving feats that have been achieved at 'inland' sites, a 700-metre penetration did not sound very significant. The excitement, or motivation, came from the challenge. Conch possessed vast potential; its lure was magnetic.

On the flight out my thoughts turned for the thousandth time to the obstacle that had stopped us in 1981. Would the squeeze be passable? Would we be able to get through?

Memory is always deceptive. How often had I been lured back to tackle some unpassed obstacle only to discover why I had abandoned the initial exploration. Time erased the difficulties and blanked out the hard bits. But perhaps this was a good thing. If you seriously considered how much discomfort you'd gone through the first time you'd never go back twice.

In Conch at least there was no physical discomfort. But my worry was that having travelled thousands of miles to get there perhaps all we would find was that the water was filtering through an impassable obstruction, and there was a complete boulder choke. And if the squeeze was passable would it be feasible to undertake lengthy penetrations beyond? So much hinged upon the outcome of the first push.

There were other apprehensions on this trip as well and the first week was to prove a strange period for us all. Our team, for example, was split between two locations: the scientific element were based in virtual isolation down at the Forfar Field Study Centre while the rest of us occupied a holiday villa up at Nichols Town. The extent to which our 'luxury' villa lived up to the brochure was very much akin to our first experience of Forfar. It had obviously been designed as a compact residence for a maximum of four people — not for eight or nine heavily equipped cave divers!

Completing the picture was another group of five people who, by contrast with our squalor, lived in regal splendour in a similar sized villa next door — the film crew! Duncan Gibbins the Director, Chris Goodger the cameraman, Chris Rente the sound technician and two underwater cameramen, Peter Scoones and Pete McPherson had come out to film the venture.

A film of a world record dive was an exciting proposition but would there be a clash of interests? Considering the fact that the idea had been sprung upon us at the last minute, that no account had been taken of the team's opinions on the matter, and that financially nothing positive had been agreed there was cause for concern. But our leader, Rob, took little heed of such anxieties. The film crew would adopt the 'fly on the wall' tactics and not interfere with our plans. Conflict seemed inevitable.

It was several days after our arrival at Nichols Town before the first operation was mounted. As lead divers Rob Palmer and I dived together, supported by Rob Parker and Julian, to about 350 metres. In the event all my worries concerning the nature of the obstacle at 700 metres were quickly dispelled. The dreaded 'squeeze' was an irregular gap virtually two metres wide by nearly one metre high, leading directly to a large ascending chamber. I had taken the precaution of removing my back pack at 692 metres so as to be completely streamlined when I reached the end of the line. The situation that now confronted us was an unbelievable piece of luck. I took the lead and in an almost complete black out Rob had followed through ... without having to remove his back pack. This was most significant. If we had been forced to remove back-mounted bottles to pass the obstacle our range of penetration would inevitably have been severely reduced.

The first push terminated at 849 metres in what appeared to be a rapidly lowering oxbow or dead end. On the exit the way on was found at 829 metres; the route lying through another slightly constricted opening and leading to a spacious tunnel below.

After this operation our strategy underwent review. In the preparatory stage we had decided to field a pair of lead divers on each push but in practise there was a severe problem with supplying sufficient air for everyone. If this system was maintained our resources would soon be stretched. It seemed best therefore to revert to the system whereby only one of us took the lead at a time. Logistically it was easier. It was also more to my liking; I felt more confident on my own. Another factor was that Rob was under a lot of strain and I felt dubious about his panic threshold.

By now certain things had become apparent. This was proving to be the least harmonious expedition that I had been on; the heat, the overcrowding, the inherent stress of the diving and especially the demands of the film had all served to exacerbate personal relationships. Above water, tensions were running high; below, fortunately, we held together as a team.

Rob Parker and Julian accompanied me for the second push, transporting bottles to 492 metres. At this point cylinders were exchanged and I breathed my second stage unit up to 692 metres. Caution prevailed at the squeeze but once through I was on my way. From the 'tie on' mark at 829 metres the route descended sharply to 28 metres, a depth it was to maintain along a passage generally 10 metres or so in width. At 920 metres however there was a sudden transformation in character. Just beyond, the eliptical half-tube terminated, to be replaced by a jagged rift about 2 metres wide by 10 metres high. Of itself this was no problem were it not that wearing the heavy back-mounted bottle I was negatively buoyant and committed to bumping along for much of the time at floor level. The depth had already reached a constant

29 metres and ahead in the rift it must have been at 34 metres. Rather than descend I opted to continue at 29 metres, along some fortuitous ledges, all the while hoping that I would not be forced down and that the ledges didn't pinch out.

923 metres, or 3,000 feet, may have felt something of an achievement but the 107 metres that I had travelled in to new ground now began to feel like a long way. The excitement was still there, just, but now it was the challenge, reinforced by grim determination that urged me on — the drive that could not contemplate turning back until some other element came in to play; either the air safety margin, psychological pressure, daunting passage proportions or problems with the equipment.

About 20 metres in to the rift the passage narrowed at a restriction, the ledge ended and to continue a descent was necessary. Belaying the line at the widest point I wriggled forward and diagonally down, reaching the floor at 30 metres. The pressure was on. A tall, awkward section lay ahead.

The third margin arrived at 969 metres. I still had about two layers of line wrapped around the spindle of the reel but of an instant the inner warning lights began to flash. Enough was enough. The rift continued at the same 30-metre depth but at that moment the enthusiasm, the drive and adventurism melted. The only thought was exit.

As I left I completed the survey. Once through the squeeze at 700 metres the pressure was relieved and the rest was plain sailing. Despite having to carry two hand-held stage units from the 492 metre mark spirits were high. The occasional 'clang' accompanied the slow exit but I was enjoying every minute.

Peter Scoones recorded the arrival at the first decompression point but thereafter I was left largely to my own devices: 12 minutes at 9 metres, 41 minutes at 6 metres and 78 minutes at 3 metres. Ascending finally towards the surface, decompression complete, I knew exactly what to expect. Peering across the sea bed in the direction of the shore a fish eye view revealed a line of legs standing there neatly in a row. With the patience of ravenous herons the vultures were waiting to pounce. The film crew followed us everywhere and we had quickly become used to spontaneous interviews.

As we entered our second week at Nichols Town it became evident to us all that having a film crew around was hardly conducive to a relaxed easy-going expedition. Time was continually being lost waiting for the crew to get their gear together and posing in all manner of situations.

Duncan, the hippy-type director was an eminently likeable chap as were the rest of the crew. Unfortunately his visions of portraying the venture to the general public were influenced rather too much for my liking by his artistic temperament. I can see him now outlining in fairy tale jargon a lead-in shot which he considered to be an essential sequence in the film. With lips pursed together, head inclined back and tilted to one shoulder, arms outstretched in best theatrical tradition he proceeded to let us in on his vision.

He wanted a troop of fully equipped divers slogging through the jungle making as though they were heading for an inland diving site. The idea would not have been so bad if the group were actually heading for a pool where they could cool off when they got there, but no. Duncan had his spot sorted all right — miles from the nearest blue hole. I was horror struck. The reality was obvious. The temperature would be in the 90s, everyone would be sweating like pigs and the suffering could last for hours. I could see the scene now:

'Fantastic chaps, — fantastic; just one more take. Julian, would you collapse just by here please?'

I made sure I was doing something else on that day. I was here to go cave diving; so was Rob Parker, Julian and Tony. We were not here for self-glorification. Rob had assured us that the crew would adopt the 'fly on the wall' approach to filming and not interfere with our plans or diving. Now it was abundantly clear to us all that we were being manipulated, used, and none too tactfully. The initial scepticism had been borne out. Feelings of frustration were not helped by the normal run of the mill setbacks such as punctures or our vehicle breaking down. The day after the push to 969 metres the fan belt on the truck broke and a complete day was lost. For the next few days diving was only possible by hiring a taxi or using the local rubbish collection truck. And as we had come to appreciate, urgency was not something altogether common on Andros. To get a taxi at noon it was best to order it the day before and to check again at about 10.00 am. This coupled with the fact that one of the two compressors was out of action served to heighten the uneasiness.

Rob's push was to take place a few days later on 13th August. The logistics were as follows:

Departure
Time   Diver
4.45 pm   1 Rob Parker to 492 metres
                 carrying 1 x 80 for Rob Palmer
                                1 x 80 for M.Farr
              2 M.Farr to 692 metres
                 carrying 1 x 80 for Rob Palmer
5.00 pm   3 Tony Boycott to 492 metres
                 carrying 1 x 80, exit bottle for Rob Palmer
              4 Rob Palmer, breathing stage unit to 492 metres
6.10 pm   5 Julian Walker to bring out empties.

Cylinder wise, the plan involved the use of 20 out of our total supply of 21 bottles and this did not include any for the crew. Clearly we required more bottles and the following morning Julian and Chris Moore were to travel down to Small Hope Bay Lodge, the commercial dive centre about 50 miles due south, to borrow as many as its proprietor Dick Birch was prepared to loan. En route they were to collect some twin back packs from the Forfar Centre. Twin back packs used in conjunction with the normal twin side mounts would greatly increase our range of penetration.

But the next day we had a major disagreement. Until this was settled the main objective, the push, was in jeopardy. Owing to the tides it was to be a late start and quite apart from his personal preparation Rob was now under considerable pressure. Fortunately everything was resolved but not before Rob felt it prudent to call off the day's activity.

It was to be the 17th August before Rob got the chance to mount his push. With the addition of the twin back packs, from Forfar, the dive plan was simplified. Whereas by the previous plan Rob Parker had been involved carrying in a cylinder for me — a sherpa carrying a bottle for an advance sherpa — now this was unnecessary. By wearing the twin back pack and a twin side-mount set I could reach 692 metres carrying a hand held bottle without assistance from anyone else. The plan took the following form:

Time	*Diver*
8.30 am	1 M.Farr to 692 metres carrying 1 x 80 for Rob Palmer
	2 Rob Parker to 492 metres carrying 1 x 80 for R.Palmer (to get to 692 metres)
8.45 am	3 Tony Boycott to 492 metres carrying 1 x 80, exit bottle for R.Palmer, and retrieving R.Palmer's empty.
	4 Rob Palmer, breathing hand held 80 to 692 metres.
9.45 am	5 Julian Walker to 492 to help remove empties

The morning started drearily. Rob Palmer arrived from the crew's quarters at 6.30 am on the dot. I was glad this wasn't my push as I hated such early starts. My biorhythms were well established; they objected strongly to alterations. Rob got a brew on and haggard individuals slowly began to appear.

At 7 o'clock the crew set off for the beach. Twenty minutes later the rest of us were ready to set off when there was a burst of aggro. Rob was tense, his voice feeble and weak; I seriously doubted his effectiveness on the dive ahead. Shortly we were on our way. For me it was just a question of getting my stuff together and making sure I was ready to leave on schedule. Perfectly confident in my ability to cope with my role in the dive plan I also opted to take in a photographic system to obtain a few shots of hydroids on top of a stal about 300 metres inside the cave. I got my gear together and 10 minutes ahead of time set off.

The stal chamber was reached uneventfully and quickly a half a dozen or so pictures were shot of the preselected scene. From the moment I had first chanced upon this location the image had implanted itself indelibly on my memory. A large boulder occupied the centre of the passage which was adorned with several stalagmites. On top of just one, was set a miniature colony of hydroids. In close up it could have been a scene taken from a Christmas card; a beautiful little tree, covered in snow, set atop of a rocky mound. Framed against the black of the cavern the hydroid waved to and fro in the current — sifting essential nutrients from the passing water — eking out a meagre existence. Marine life had thinned appreciably by this distance in to the tunnel and this setting was very unusual indeed. Tragically, like many other spectacles of the natural world the stal was to pay the price for our exploratory achievement and on a subsequent dive I found it to be broken off.

Having deposited the camera for collection on the exit I pushed on deeper in to the cave. I was still alone when I arrived at 350 metres where it was time to make the routine swap to the second back-mounted set. I stopped, relaxed, and got the spare mouthpiece in my hand. On this occasion I'd made a point of asking Julian to check that all my bottles were turned on ... it was becoming a joke that I had been setting off with one or more cylinders turned off.

I took in a good breath, pulled out the used mouthpiece and popped in the second gag. Next on the routine was a sharp blow to remove the water flooding the air chamber. Then I sucked in. Nothing happened. Instantly 'valve failure', went through my head followed by 'abort the dive' and 'how on earth could this happen?' The explanation could wait. Quickly I picked up and purged the one I'd just pulled out, then stuck it back in my mouth. The lungs were empty; this swap had to be perfect first time. Salty water made straight for the throat, which instantly started to convulse. No question of another swap now; I held the gag in and coughed away. It was hardly a model operation and as composure was regained a sense of disgust flooded my thoughts. What a mess from start to finish!

To contemplate having to abort, of letting Rob Palmer down horrified me — the sense of failure, of being the weakest link in the team effort would be too awful. It would be better letting myself down. I began to look for the cause of the problem. Mouthpieces and pressure gauges seemed to hang everywhere but quickly a black and blue colour-coded pressure gauge was located, the partner to the rogue mouthpiece. Instantly the answer was forthcoming: 'Zero Air' registered on the gauge, — the bottle wasn't turned on! It was so stupid. There was no question of blaming anyone but myself. With a healthy 'hiss' the hoses were full once more and with the bottle switched on the changeover was conducted as normal. A crisis was over. Then it was on to 692 metres where the essential stage unit was tied off.

Decompression on this occasion was memorable for the superb innovation introduced by Peter Scoones, musical accompaniment!

By means of a waterproof 'bone conductor' and a cable link to the shore we were able to plug in to the dulcet tones of Fleetwood Mac. This was a tremendous psychological boost, effectively offsetting both cold and boredom. Why hadn't we thought of underwater music before? The current was too strong for literary appreciation. Rob had tried a newspaper on his first Conch dive and the odd scraps still wafted around even two weeks later. No matter how curious I felt about one of the large colourful pieces of paper suspended in the water I was never tempted to unravel the mystery. There was always the possibility that it originated from one or other of the tidally flushing Bahamian toilets sited a little way along the beach. In what seemed to be no time at all I joined the shore party.

Time passed and eventually a large group of us waded out to assist at the moment of Rob's surfacing.

'Here he comes,' said somebody.

'Malfunction,' says cameraman Chris.

'Quick, here he is,' says Duncan, a definite note of urgency creeping into his voice.

'Complete camera malfunction,' says Chris, shaking his head with a look of resignation.

The next we knew there was Rob in front of us and not a foot of film had been shot. The dejection seemed to rub off on the new arrival; there was no real spark of triumph, more a sense of deflation. Then came the news.

Arriving at 600 metres he realised that he'd lost his line reel, which had been loosely attached to his waist harness. This was a real blow. But rather than turn back and search for it, which would have been difficult in the poor visibility, he opted to carry on and collect my reel from the cul de sac where it had been abandoned on the 7th August. This was not an enviable or easy task but having retrieved it he continued uneventfully to the end of my line at 969 metres. The next section was awkward but in less than 30 metres the rift had been left behind. Beyond, the passage regained comfortable proportions. Rob took the reel on to 1,000 metres, the kilometre mark, before the line ran out. The passage ahead was again wide open.

I was now more keen than ever to press on and to do this it was resolved to make a preliminary dive to install cylinders deep inside the cave. This operation was scheduled for the very next day.

Morning came and with it the news that the battery on our truck was flat. With no transport and no chance of finding an alternative source in time to catch the 9.30 am slack water, the dive had to be postponed for a day. We filled bottles and sat around. Later, the scientific crew stationed at Forfar turned up with a truck and a successful photographic trip was made to Stalactite Blue Hole.

The plan for the 'installation dive' was simple: Rob Parker and I were each to wear four cylinders and between us transport three stage units together with a 300-metre reel, to 692 metres. Tony was also involved installing a 72 cu.ft stage unit at about 340 metres, to serve as a 'bail out' bottle just in case anything critical should happen to anyone on the main dive.

Rob and I needed to be away at 9.30 am if we were to make the best of the last hour of the suck cycle. Inevitably it was a rush getting away from the villa and having started as a rush that was how it continued. At the beach Rob Palmer and Julian kitted us up while Chris Moore expressed his doubts about the current.

'It's blowing.'

'Surely it must still be sucking,' I replied.

'Well it's slack water,' or something.

For a scientist who was engaged in monitoring the flow and who had been on site since 7.00 am that morning I wasn't too impressed by this assessment. We would have to find out for ourselves.

Twenty minutes behind schedule we dropped in to the entrance; anxieties pushed aside, we were off. No sooner were we in than it was evident that the flow was still sucking, and hard. Perhaps we had timed it better than we had anticipated. I led while Rob followed directly behind. Once in to the low section, 60 metres from the entrance, the current really whisked us away. I hadn't fully appreciated its strength until at 100 metres I swept broadside in to a rock pillar. For a second or two I endeavoured to straighten myself but then Rob arrived — crashing directly in to me. Could this be the first head on collision in cave diving? Wearing so much gear and with our hands full, apologies had to be made by facial expressions. Fortunately nothing was damaged and while Rob careered off down the tunnel I set to to sort myself out again.

On arrival at 692 metres we checked that the stage units were switched off and that each mouthpiece was still protected by a small polythene bag, tied on with a piece of string. In such a way it was hoped that no silt would invade the mouthpiece. Rob had located the 'lost' reel and now we had three full bottles further in than ever before. Looking to my gauges I had yet to reach the third margin on one of the side-mounted sets and the other was still full. Thinking to minimise the problems for the following day I now decided to take one bottle and the 300-metre reel through the squeeze and up to the 'shallow water' stal grotto beyond. I had ample air and this meant that I would only need to carry one hand-held bottle through the low section on the push.

I informed Rob of my intentions, we gave each other an 'O.K.' signal and then set off in our different directions. Even wearing four cylinders the squeeze posed no problems. It was a 'squeeze' only by comparison with the main passage size — a psychological squeeze which had assumed an imposing nature by virtue of the fact that it lay 700 metres of diving away from the entrance. Now it assumed a homely aspect and I popped nimbly through.

Bumping heavily up the slope it was another psychological relief to stop at -14 metres. This point was only half as deep as that prior to the squeeze and was as good as anywhere to drop the stage unit and the reel, at 735 metres. By the time these were secured to the line an inner sense was urging for exit. Rob was on his way out and I knew that I ought to be as well. I knew that by now I had exceeded the one-third margin on all the three cylinders used so far. But there was no need to worry, I told myself, the fourth bottle was still untouched. The obvious thing was to swap over; what could be more simple?

I located the fourth set, the Manta valve mounted on my left-hand side. That was strange! I normally followed precisely the same routine for breathing sets and the same routine for swapping over en route out. Normally this went back first, left second and right third. Here the routine had accidentally differed. The coincidence didn't really matter but I believed in routine, and routine was the best bet for not forgetting items in the preparatory stage.

But suddenly routine and confidence were shaken. I purged the mouthpiece to expel any sediment in the air chamber... nothing. Must be turned off at the cylinder, I thought... but no. The tap was on and the pressure gauge read 200 atmospheres;

the bottle was full. I pressed the purge button again but there was no silvery bubbling of air. A spate of cursing followed. This was unbelievable.

Illogically I popped the gag in to my mouth to see what effect sucking would have, but as I expected the answer was the same — nothing. Thought processes raced. Here I was 735 metres from the surface with one quarter of my original air supply rendered unusable by some fault in the valve. The three good bottles were below the one third margin and the visibility could be expected to be well down for the outward journey; it was a very delicate situation. On the other hand I did of course have three full stage units to choose from and there would be the extra 'bail out' bottle at about 340 metres. The current would also be of assistance in a short while.

There was no immediate worry. Rather than jeopardise the trip on the morrow I took the gamble that today could look after itself. I left all the stage units where they were and just concentrated on getting out.

Everything went smoothly back to the 600 metre mark; the squeeze was easy and the visibility was causing no difficulty. But at 600 metres my confidence received another blow. The current was still sucking! The strength of the flow was inconsequential to that previously but the fact that it was sucking spelt out a clear message: I could expect to get no help from the outflow for at least twenty minutes. Of itself this again was a minor problem but coming after those with the air, I knew that my breathing rate would inevitably increase due to tension. I thought of going back for a bottle — a thought countered immediately by the fact that I had less than 300 metres to go to reach the 'bail out' bottle. I felt a heightened sense of urgency.

Hardly had I moved forward into the huge trunk pasage than doubts began to pour in. I had made an inexcusable error before starting the trip, I had just admitted another failing on the part of my prediction of the changeover; what would be next.

A feeling of acute loneliness developed. Keep calm, keep calm, keep the breathing rate down; the thoughts were clear. But the anxiety was now very real. It seemed to take an eternity getting to 492 metres; I couldn't believe that I was moving so slowly. For the first time I realised that I was wholly committed to my decision made at 735 metres. The option of going back for air was gone; now it was forward or nothing. And somehow the unthinkable possibility had forced its way to the fore. What if I got to 400 metres or 300 metres and there was no 'bail out' bottle? Perhaps Tony had experienced some difficulty of his own and had had to abort! Everyone had experienced valve failures on this trip. What if Tony or Rob had had one today? The nerve racking questions coupled with cumulative anxiety suggested that more speed was required — that I pull on the line as my legs were beginning to ache. Never pull on the line is a maxim held by all cave divers and in this instance I was thankful that we had installed good heavy line capable of substantial abuse.

Suddenly, out amid the Sahara type area approximately 460 metres from the entrance a real crisis loomed. We had noticed previously that the line through this dune-like section was rather loose. It had come adrift from a boulder belay. Suddenly a loop wrapped itself around something high on my back pack; I was caught fast.

It was beginning to dawn on me that my luck might have run out, that I might die. Holding the anxieties at bay and trying to control the rate of breathing had left me exhausted. I backed back, turned around, fumbled a few times but to no avail. Of all the places to get caught this sort of double pack harness was probably the worst. I had to get back to 350 metres quickly; I reached for the knife on my leg. This was extremely drastic — the first time that I had ever had to use it in an emergency. Until this point I had considered that I was perfectly in control. A few seconds later I realised how critical everything had become and how anxiety was now affecting my coordination. I couldn't release the knife from the sheath. Even though the brain was relatively clear I was definitely losing control.

After a few more seconds I went for the emergency secondary knife, more easily accessible, attached to my waist harness. I reassured myself that I had firm hold of the correct, outgoing, line then made the cut. Instantly I started to pull forward and in a few more seconds I was moving, free again. By now my confidence had been shattered; I was physically and mentally exhausted. I moved on, breathing much faster than normal and conscious that without a fresh bottle exit could well be impossible. Wearing alloy cylinders I began to dread the positive buoyancy that would slowly develop as the air ran out. This was one hell of a situation to be in.

I had given up all hope of catching Rob who I presumed was well ahead. In a tricky situation I had always believed in being on your own; that on your own there was only one person to worry about, that you couldn't blame anyone else for the mess and your thoughts could be concentrated. Of a split second the ideas were to change. There was Rob in the distance, waiting to see what the trouble was! The crisis was over. Rob was cool, calm and collected and by diving together nothing could hinder a safe exit even if the 'bail out' bottle was not in place. Fortunately for me he had felt the line being pulled and had stopped. As I cruised up I felt the tensions drain away.

I held my gauges to Rob's face and no doubt exhibited more than a few traits of having had a close shave. Unruffled and fully in control of the situation he beckoned me on in front. I was feeling infinitely more controlled as we moved off, but absolutely spent. Every ounce of energy seemed to have drained away.

At about 350 metres any final doubts were dismissed; there, tied to the line as arranged, was an orange 72 cubic-foot bottle. I made a few exclamations to myself, picked it up and bumped on out. The current had just turned; everything was fine. Back at the entrance the sun's rays had never been more welcome. There was no doubt about it; it had been a close shave!

Decompression time was not wasted. It was a good opportunity to think over the whole incident and to check out the rogue valve. And very quickly I came to the conclusion that the so called 'failure' was entirely a case of human error — my error. In the safety of daylight and the open water, I identified the malfunction and at the same time the reason for the oversight was painfully obvious. I had reassembled the valve incorrectly following a previous dive. It had not been working when we went in! This was an unforgivable failure on my part.

Equally as incredible was the series of coincidences that had led me to 735 metres without discovering the fault. In the first instance I always made a point of checking valves on a cylinder after reassembling any part. Obviously I had missed this one. For three days the valve had travelled with me, in my kitbag, as a spare. Equally as amazing was the fact that I usually breathed valves underwater in a particular order. On this occasion another coincidence had disrupted the long established procedure and I had not discovered the fault until I had committed myself.

219

Back in Britain one was never pressurised into rushing the dive preparations. But here, each and every dive had to be made to a precisely worked schedule; time after time essential checks were either rushed or inadequate. The examples were blatant; gear was slung on just any how, bottles had not been turned on and there were countless other instances.

By the time we surfaced my confidence had been restored. Unfortunately even though all the stage units had been left intact my exit had jeopardised the push, planned for the next day. The line had been cut at 460 metres and before any further diving could take place it was essential to get the two ends reconnected. Julian, who had put himself out time and time again, now came to the rescue. He volunteered to go in at eleven o'clock that night to rectify the situation.

Everything hung in the balance until the outcome of the repair job was known. Julian's ability spoke for itself and the rest of us retired at a reasonable hour. I felt optimistic; most of the bottles had been filled and the valves had been checked out.

In the early hours a tired figure quietly returned and shuffled between the bodies crashed out around the lounge floor. I woke long enough to congratulate him and turned over; the dive was on.

Morning was heralded as usual by a deafening rattle emanating from outside the washroom window. First up started the compressor and Rob Palmer was shouldering his responsibilities well. As the bottles filled, each person set about his personal preparations. One could usually tell Rob Parker's whereabouts by finding the source of the music — on this occasion the verandah — where he was working on his diving slate.

'Back in business again,' he said, as he fixed a new elastic strap to his pencil.

'Had a tight moment yesterday; got cornered by my pencil . . . bloody thing got wrapped around the line and I had to cut myself free!'

We both laughed. Julian emerged shortly after, not surprisingly still looking weary after his solo trip.

'Had a terrible night! . . . been shifting bottles around the whole time, moving them, valving up and checking contents; very tiring work all this dreaming!'

In best tradition everything had worked out well and Julian

described his dive. He'd dropped another bottle at 300 metres then proceeded to 460 metres with a spare line reel. In the event the extra line was hardly necessary as on arrival the two ends lay fairly close together and he was able to take hold of them and just tie a knot.

Surprisingly I felt nowhere near so tense as I thought I might. With the main stage units already installed there was less that could go wrong on this push than on the previous occasions. Another incidental benefit of Julian's night dive had been a better knowledge of the tidal changeover. Now we could predict slack water with a lot more accuracy than our hit and miss attempts before hand. 'Slack' was forecast for 12.00 noon which meant that I had to be away at 11.00 am. And for this trip I intended to allow plenty of leeway in terms of final preparations.

We arrived at the beach at 10.10 am and for a change it was a pleasure to kit up at a comfortable rate. Everything was double checked and when it came to mounting the equipment everything was just as I wanted it. Rob Palmer and Tony were to dive first, 15 minutes ahead of me, so as to drop two stage units at 492 metres. As usual one was to take me on to 692 metres and the other was for use en route out. Rob and Julian were to come in later to help carry the used bottles out.

At 10.45 am Rob and Tony set off. Fifteen minutes later I was away. Even diving third the visibility was good and with a strong sucking flow I bumped along the floor absorbed solely in the practicalities of the dive. Yesterday was gone, I told myself. The events of the previous day had psychologically reinforced my determination; another failure could not be contemplated. Today would be a success.

At the strategic 492-metre marker it was obvious that we had a technical hitch. Where the hell were Rob and Tony? I hadn't seen them; they must have overshot. Initial reaction was annoyance but then there was one advantage: providing I caught up with them before my first stage unit ran out, and I still had a quarter of it left, then there would be more air at my disposal further in to the cave.

Without delay I carried on. At 520 metres there was still no indication of them. Where the hell were they? Then at 535 metres Rob cruised towards me with the required bottle and written on his slate he had:

'OVERSHOT! 1,700 ft.'

Directly behind him was Tony who overtook and disappeared. We 'O.K.'d, shook hands and with a final swirl of mud I was on my own.

With each successive metre beyond 535 metres I was amazed to see just how far Rob and Tony had travelled. And was I going to find that other bottle that was to get me out? The visibility that was already poor was being made worse by the sucking current. But despite the slow progress the breathing rate was perfectly controlled; what a contrast to yesterday.

At 600 metres I pulled myself noisily up in to the roof passage and there attached neatly to the line was my last elusive unit. The bottle was tested, breathed from and turned off. What a tremendous overkill from here on. At 692 metres I tried each of the other two bottles in turn. Both were breathing perfectly. I switched units and carried on.

The squeeze passed like any other piece of routine passage and shortly I reached the 735-metre mark where the grey bottle and the 300 metres reel glinted out of the gloom. As with the previous sets I ripped off the plastic bag covering the mouthpiece, switched on the tap and tried it out. This last set was nowhere near so smooth to breathe as the one I'd just dropped and I opted to take this one down to its third first.

Carrying the two hand-held bottles together with the reel was clumsy but from previous experience I knew that the rate of travel was not appreciably slowed. The poor breather got me to 829 metres. My sights were set on the 1,000-metre mark and there was no point scrutinising the route or looking for side passages. Even the canyon-like rift posed no difficulty. The mind had processed the previous information; now it too seemed as familiar as the hitherto 'dreaded' squeeze at 700 metres.

At 955 metres the last stage unit was dropped, the three body-mounted units were tested and I felt free. The rift was nowhere near so intimidating as hitherto. In a couple more minutes I was there, poised on the threshold — the end of the line. And there, hanging limp from the final belay was something that cheapened all that we had so far achieved, the distinctive colours of a miniature Union Jack. Seduced by the potential glory of the occasion, by a gimmicky suggestion made by Duncan, Rob had hung a flag at the furthest point and filmed it. What a joke the original idea had been — but here it was, another environment mercilessly conquered by the British; a cheap rag defiling the purity of the cave.

I turned away. The big reel creaked as the line unwound. Psychologically I was prepared to reach 1,230 metres, but I was just not prepared for acceptance of the sheer vastness that shortly appeared. The passage proportions were almost unbelievable. Here the visibility was over 15 metres and I felt compelled to switch on an Iodin to complement the main light. But it made no difference — there were no definite walls. This was a place so utterly different to any other part of Conch 1. The cave between 400 to 460 metres was huge but in that instance one could at least sense the walls somewhere off to left and right. This was altogether of another scale, a vast room bigger than anything I had previously experienced below water.

I arrived at a stalagmite. But instantly I was aware that it was unlike any other stal I had come across; it was virtually free of any marine encrustation and to touch, it felt like glass. It was just like any stal back home, a stal in a cave that might conceivably have been flooded but a few weeks before. Waving a hand by it I displaced a small puff of dust-like silt — a strange sensation, as though I had entered some time vault where nothing had changed for over 14,000 years.

Swimming on it soon became apparent that the place was totally devoid of life. There were no eels or small crabs which were present up to and beyond 600 metres; no sponges, anemones — nothing. I looked back and clouds rolled out across the floor and quietly dispersed. There were no apparent currents here. At 1,153 metres murky water was noted ahead and in an instant the message came through — somehow I'd achieved a loop! I tied off, surveyed and back tracked. The final 50 metres had been in association with a wall and I now decided to follow this in the other direction. There was plenty of air left.

Where the line veered sharply from the wall I tied on once more and followed the chamber round. Shortly evidence of marine life began to appear: things that looked like droopy phallic sponges, or sea squirts. There was only the odd couple hanging from undercuts in the wall, about 12 to 14 cm long, either white or grey in colour. On closer examination they seemed to have no substance at all; gossamer-like structures, the only life on the periphery of a barren desert. Exceptionally big holes characterised their body, working flat out to strain every bit of nutrient from the water. This suggested a possible current flow and indeed between the masive detached blocks lying on the cavern floor large openings were visible. These were at considerable depth and I had no intention of going down unless forced to.

Then something moving caught my eye. It was a 12-cm long brochelid, a lucifuga speleotes! We had encountered this rare specie of blind cave fish at several sites, both inland and oceanic, but this was the first time it had been sighted here at Conch. All on its own it wriggled or wove its way along about a metre or so above the floor, completely unperturbed either by me or the noisy rumbling of my exhausted air. It was almost a religious experience — meeting a survivor of a long gone age; a survivor eking out a lonely existence at the very edge of life itself.

Sixty metres from the junction there were more clouds. Was this another loop? By now I was confused and on my third bottle. It was time to survey and leave. Even though it had been a successful exploration I still felt a sense of frustration at not having established a definite way on and not have reached the magical 1,230 metre or 4,000 foot mark, which would easily have been within grasp had things been slightly different.

Passing the muddied Union Jack the current was fairly whipping along, which for the next 80 metres was not in my best interests. Frequently over this section visibility was down to .3 metre. It was a relief to collect the stage unit and regain spacious proportions. The second unit was picked up and in a swirl of mud I was through the squeeze, around the corner, to be confronted by a diver — Julian. Fantastic.

With our newly developed underwater communications system I pulled out my gag and shouted 'O.K.' As Julian had been there waiting apprehensively for 20 minutes his third was fast approaching. We set off taking all the bottles. Back at 492 metres we collected Rob Parker who had been on station for 38 minutes. He too had been about to turn back. Then, like a troop of bellringers clanging merrily homeward in the festive season, we set off on the final leg.

The entrance was reached after a dive of 2 hours and 46 minutes; another 201 minutes being required on decompression. What a chore this final decompression was to be. Details of the dive were scrutinised over and over and the euphoric feelings deliberately held in suspension. How easy it could be to accidentally float to the surface — and get bent. A moment's slip could mean a life of paralysis, a fate worse than death. It was a rude, outside thought but one that ruled every minute. I began to shiver and swam around like an imprisoned goldfish. But how colourful was this aquarium to which I was temporarily sentenced. It was fabulous.

As before there was so much to see and absorb; glorious arrays of tube fans, arrow crabs, pink and white banded coral shrimps. Each had its niche, its territory, its home — bounded by invisible borders. Beautiful little damsel fish for example defended their patch of seabed even against something as monstrous as a diver. Prying too close inevitably stimulated little acts of aggression. With a thud a hermit crab, perhaps three or four times the size of the fish, would be knocked over and driven away. With a diver the brave little fish would resort to a head-on confrontation with the face mask; recurrent butts relating the clear message 'please leave me alone'. What an experience! Why explore lifeless tunnels deep underground when wonders such as these exist?

The most enjoyable piece of teamwork that I had ever been involved with drew quietly to a conclusion. I surfaced, made my performance and gratefully downed a bottle of warm beer.

Despite the fact that we still had another 10 days at our disposal several factors effectively ruled out another push. The dive to 1,153 metres was our final limit. With the survey drawn up it was evident that I had circumnavigated the final breakdown chamber which measured over 46 metres by 37 metres. The place where the deep cavities had been viewed proved to be above the initial point of entry to the chamber. Discovering the way on could well be difficult and in all probability this will lie at depths in excess of 30 metres.

Even though the expedition was far from happy the end result was a satisfactory achievement. We were to learn later that the Italians in 1981 and the Spanish in 1982 had claimed world records for their submarine penetration in to a cave at Lanzarote in the Canary Islands — penetrating 518 metres and 853 metres. By comparison our dives of 700 metres and 1,158 metres were respectable international achievements.

A brief mention should be made of other explorations which we undertook in 1982. A 215-metre dive was made at a depth of 49 metres in a blue hole off Mastic Point to reach a boulder choke and a number of other sites visited the previous year were pushed to more of a conclusion. Rob and Julian also made a bold descent in Forfar Blue Hole passing the limit set in 1981, then a further series of tight squeezes to reach a large passage at a depth of 60 metres. All told another 1,230 metres of passages were explored during the course of the 1982 expedition, giving a grand total for the two years in excess of 3,077 metres.

On the scientific side a comprehensive programme was again undertaken but as time ran out it was abundantly clear that many, many more mysteries remain to be answered in the blue holes. By and large the many sites that extend below a depth of 45 metres have yet to be examined, especially in the south and inland.

Blue hole diving is challenging and enjoyable. The whole of the Bahamas has an abundance of sites that have never been examined at all — it has many years of exploration and the most superb cave diving in the world.

APPENDIX I

March 1968 Ogof Cynnes; discovery of cave and subsequent exploration of 1,230 metres.

July 1971 Ogof Ffynnon Ddu, first cave dive.

April 1972 Tullyhona Cave, Northern Ireland; discovery of 'Farr Country' — 1,230 metres.

July 1972 Dan yr Ogof, Mazeways 2 discovered after a lengthy period of exploration; subsequently one mile explored.

Sept. 1972 Prods Pot, Northern Ireland; Cascade Passage extended by 615 metres.
Arch Cave, Northern Ireland; discovery of Arch II, subsequently explored for over one mile.

Jan. 1973 Agen Allwedd; discovery of 615 metres in Turkey Sump Extensions.

July 1973 P8, Derbyshire; exploration of Sump 9.

Aug. 1973 Arch Cave — Noons Hole connection; the finest 'through trip' in the British Isles.

Feb. 1974 Boreham Cave, Yorkshire; major extension discovered but owing to floods only partially explored — 300 metres.

May 1974 Agen Allwedd; discovery of Maytime, 500 metres of passages beyond downstream Sump 3.
Hepste River Caves, Ystradfellte; discovery of Eastern Passage — 275 metres.

June 1974 Agen Allwedd tragedy.

Oct. 1974 Pollaraftra, Northern Ireland; 260 metres discovered beyond terminal sump.

July 1975 Uamh an Claonite, Scotland; discovery of 450 metres — subsequently the longest cave in Scotland.

Aug. 1975   Otter Hole, Chepstow; Sump 3 passed to discover 169 metres; extended for over 277 metres in August 1980.

Oct. 1975   Caving in North America and Mexico — three and a half months.

Feb. 1976   Wookey Hole, Somerset; discovery of Chamber 25.

Apr. 1976   Prods Pot, Northern Ireland; Terminal Downstream Sumps passed to discover over one mile.

July 1976   Allt Nan Uamh Stream Cave, Scotland; discovery of 450 metres.
Carrickbeg Rising, Northern Ireland; exploration of 'Farr Out' Series — 450 metres.

228

Apr. 1977	Participation in televised documentary set in Iran.
June 1977	Wookey Hole, Somerset; 45 metres depth reached beyond Chamber 25, a British depth record.
Aug. 1977	Expedition to Iran — three months.
June 1978	Dan yr Ogof; Mazeways 3 discovered, subsequently explored for 430 metres.
Aug. 1978	Roaring Well, Tipperary, Eire; 846 metres explored.
	Aille River Cave, Mayo, Eire; 308 metres explored.
Oct. 1978	Reyfad Pot, Northern Ireland; discovery of Pooka Passage — 450 metres subsequently explored a further 492 metres in April and August 1979.
March 1981	Peak Cavern, Derbyshire; Far Sump passed to discover 700 metres.
June 1981	Agen Allwedd; assault on Terminal Downstream Sump — Sump 4 explored for 215 metres.
Aug. 1981	Andros Island, Bahamas; one month cave diving expedition; 1,500 metres explored.
March 1982	Peak Cavern: following two solo climbing trips beyond Far Sump discovery of the largest chamber in the Peak-Speedwell system.
Aug. 1982	'Blue Holes II'; a world record set at Conch Blue Hole, Bahamas.
Sept./Oct.	British cave diving depth record of 60 metres established beyond Chamber 25 in Wookey Hole.
Aug. 1983	Fergus River Cave, County Clare, Eire; discovery of 400 metres of passages beyond the terminal sumps.
	Crag Cave, County Kerry, Eire; over a mile of exceptionally well decorated passages discovered after an 8-metre dive. A sump by-pass was opened the following day.
Jan. 1984	Agen Allwedd; discovery of 1984 Series — subsequently explored for over 500 metres.